THE DIAGNOSIS AND TREATMENT
OF MINIMAL BRAIN DYSFUNCTION
IN CHILDREN

THE DIAGNOSIS AND TREATMENT OF MINIMAL BRAIN DYSFUNCTION IN CHILDREN

A Clinical Approach

Edited by

Ruth Ochroch, Ph.D.

New York University
New York, New York

HUMAN SCIENCES PRESS
72 Fifth Avenue   3 Henrietta Street
NEW YORK, NY 10011 ● LONDON, WC2E 8LU

Printed in the United States of America
123456789   987654321

Library of Congress Cataloging in Publication Data
Main entry under title:

The Diagnosis and treatment of minimal brain dysfunction in children.

Papers based on the discussions at the 1975–1977 annual conferences of the American Orthopsychiatric Association.

Bibliography
Includes index.
1. Minimal brain dysfunction in children—Addresses, essays, lectures. I. Ochroch, Ruth. II. American Orthopsychiatric Association.
RJ496.B7D5   618.92'8589   LC 80-15858
ISBN 0-87705-503-3

This book is dedicated to my husband and children.

It is also dedicated to the many children and their families who allowed me to know of their suffering and who afforded me the opportunity to try to learn how to help.

CONTENTS

7

FOREWORD

When my wife and I were first told by their teachers that our two young children were experiencing difficulties in learning to read and write, we knew very little about the process of learning. We thought that youngsters, properly taught and practiced, mastered those basic skills at around six years of age and then moved on to more challenging intellectual pursuits. To hear that our children faced serious problems at the beginning of this continuum was disturbing, even frightening news. The terms used with us—dyslexia and learning disabilities—seemed unfairly heavy labels for two bright, normal appearing and acting children. Aware of the complex demands of contemporary existence on even the best prepared, to be counselled that our children were *learning disabled* was naturally not a welcomed message, despite vague assurances that *something* could and would be done to help them.

In the ensuing years we have learned more about the process of learning, including the fact that millions of individuals, young and old, have difficulties similar to those of our children.

We have learned that much can be done to help and that learning can be exciting and rewarding for those who, whatever the etiology, are classified as learning disabled.

One thing we have also learned—and re-learned—often at considerable expense in time, energy, dollars, and emotional stress, is that parents of learning disabled children often must be aggressive in seeking, even demanding, special assistance for their children. If that aggressive posture is to be effective and is to produce results, i.e., a happier, learning child, parents have to be well-informed about the intricacies of these problems.

This book will be a valuable aid to parents, teachers and others in that regard. As the title indicates, the approach is clinical, ranging from diagnostic skills to intervention methodologies. It is non-ideologic, presenting various points of view which greatly enhances its value. It covers these subjects comprehensively and calmly, the latter being a singularly desirable characteristic in the literature on this subject, since so much emotional overlay, especially among the professionals, is often present in the learning disability situation. Thus this book should help to further the badly needed communications among the various disciplines and the parents in order to provide effective help for the child.

Washington, D.C. Thomas E. Bryant, M.D., J.D.
April, 1980 Chairman, Public Committee on
Mental Health
Chairman, President's Commission
on Mental Health, 1977–78

PREFACE

The idea for this book arose from three yearly Institutes on Children with Minimal Brain Dysfunction, which I chaired and which were presented at the 1975, 1976, and 1977 Annual Conferences of the American Orthopsychiatric Association. These institutes served to fill a need for the "faculty" as well as the audience to cut across the professional boundaries, to learn how the other professionals evaluated and worked with these children, and to explain their own areas of competence. These exchanges seemed to enlarge the common pool of knowledge as well as to stimulate important questions. The exchange of information and experience also stimulated a respect for the contribution of each discipline and underlined the attitude that only through an interdisciplinary approach could children with so diverse a symptom picture be appropriately evaluated and helped.

There have been numerous publications in the last few years on this subject. Some have been addressed primarily to one discipline by members of that discipline. Others have dealt with only one aspect of the spectrum of disturbance that the child with minimal brain dysfunction exhibits. The necessity for an interdisciplinary team approach has not been previously presented. This volume is offered in the hope that the broad clinical approach advocated here will add to a deeper understanding of the syndrome and more effective overall help to the suffering child and family.

ACKNOWLEDGMENTS

I wish to express my appreciation to the American Orthopsychiatric Association, especially to Dr. Marian F. Langer, Executive Director, and to the Program and Continuing Education Committees for the opportunity to have organized and presented the Institutes on Children with Minimal Brain Dysfunction at the 1975, 1976, and 1977 Annual Conferences. I also wish to express my thanks to Ernest Herman, Managing Editor of the *American Journal of Orthopsychiatry,* for his encouragement and help.

The following articles are based on presentations or discussions held at the institutes:

"Psychotherapy of the Child with True Brain Damage" by Adolph E. Christ

"The MBD Child: The Art of Definitive History-taking for Diagnostic Clarification" by Jean Collard

"Orthomolecular Treatment of Children with Learning Disabilities" by Allan Cott

"The Rationale for Optometric Intervention in Learning Disabilities" by Harold N. Friedman

"A Developmental Model for Treatment of Hyperactive Children" by Gunnar Nirk, Pamela Rubovits, and Haven Miles

"The 'Case' for the Case Manager" by Ruth Ochroch

"Family Interaction and Treatment of the Hyperactive/MBD Child by Mollie S. Schildkrout

"Group Treatment of the Hyperactive/MBD Child" by Beverly Zbuska

"Specific Learning Disabilities: Communication and Language Process Disturbances" by Sydney Zentall

The paper by Adolph E. Christ, "Psychotherapy of the Child with True Brain Damage," is reprinted with permission of the American Orthopsychiatric Association, Inc. from the *American Journal of Orthopsychiatry,* Volume 48, 1977. The paper by Allan Cott, "Orthomolecular Treatment of Children with Learning Disabilities,' is an abstracted revision of his paper "Treatment of Learning Disabilities," and is printed with permission of the *Journal of Orthomolecular Psychiatry,* Volume 3, Number 4, 1974. The paper by Archie A. Silver, "Special Problems in Therapy with Children with Central Nervous System Dysfunction," is an abstracted revision of his paper "Anxiety Defense in Children with Central Nervous System Dysfunction," and is printed with permission of the *Audio Digest Publication,* Volume 6, Number 10, 1977.

CONTRIBUTORS

MARILYN B. BENOIT, M.D., Assistant Clinical Professor, Department of Psychiatry, Georgetown University *School of Medicine* Washington, D.C.

IRVING N. BERLIN, M.D., Professor of Psychiatry and Pediatrics; Director, Division of Child and Adolescent Psychiatry and the Children's Psychiatric Center, University of New Mexico School of Medicine, Department of Psychiatry, Albuquerque, New Mexico

JANET A. CAMP, M.PHIL., Research Assistant Professor, Department of Psychiatry and Behavioral Sciences, School of Medicine, and Research Scientist III, Long Island Research Institute, State University of New York at Stony Brook.

ADOLPH E. CHRIST, M.D., Director, Division of Child and Adolescent Psychiatry, Downstate Medical Center, Kings County Hospital, Brooklyn, New York.

JEAN COLLARD, M.S.W., Associate Director of Social Service, Neurological Institute, Columbia Presbyterian Medical Center, New York, New York.

ALLAN COTT, President, Academy of Orthomolecular Psychiatry and Consulting Psychiatrist, Allan Cott School for the Learning Disabled Child, affiliated with the University of Alabama at Birmingham.

HAROLD N. FRIEDMAN, O.D., Associate Professor, College of Optometry, State University of New York, New York.

LEAH LEVINGER, PH.D., Consultant, Child Psychiatry Department, Montefiore Hospital, Bronx, New York; Faculty, Bank Street College of Education, New York, New York.

BETTY S. LEVINSON, PH.D., Director and Clinical Psychologist, TRI-Services Center for Children with Learning Disabilities, Inc., Rockville, Maryland.

HAVEN MILES, M.S.W., Coordinator, Pre-School Unit, Services for Children, Families, and Youth, Providence Mental Health Center, Providence, Rhode Island.

GUNNAR NIRK, M.D. Clinical Director, Services for Children, Family, and Youth, Providence Mental Health Center; Clinical Assistant Professor of Psychiatry, Brown University Program in Medicine, Providence, Rhode Island.

CLAIRE D. NISSENBAUM, M.A., Associate Director for Program Development, TRI-Services Center for Children with Learning Disabilities, Inc., Rockville, Maryland.

RUTH OCHROCH, PH.D., Adjunct Associate Professor of Psychology, Graduate School of Arts and Sciences, New York University; formerly Consultant Supervisor, Special Project, Seizure Clinic, Neurological Institute, Columbia Presbyterian Medical Center, New York, New York.

FLORETTE ORLEANS, Dance Therapist Registered, American Dance Therapy Association; Therapeutic Activities Department, Mt. Sinai Hospital, New York, New York.

MARC N. OZER, M.D., Associate Professor of Child Health and Development, School of Medicine, George Washington University, Washington, D.C.

PAMELA RUBOVITS, PH.D., Consulting Psychologist, Services for Children, Families, and Youth, Providence Mental Health Center; Assistant Professor of Psychiatry, Rhode Island College, Providence, Rhode Island.

MOLLIE S. SCHILDKROUT, M.D., Associate Clinical Professor of Psychiatry, State University of New York at Stony Brook.

CLAIRE SCHMAIS, PH.D., Dance Therapist Registered, American Dance Therapy Association; Director, Dance Therapy Program, Hunter College, New York, New York.

ARCHIE A. SILVER, M.D., Professor of Psychiatry and Chief, Division of Child and Adolescent Psychiatry, College of Medicine, University of South Florida, Tampa, Florida.

IRIS SPANO, Assistant to the President, New York Branch of the Orton Society, New York, New York; Member, Advisory Committee, Foundation for Children with Learning Disabilities, New York, New York.

KYTJA VOELLER, M.D., Associate Professor of Pediatrics and Neurosciences, Medical College of Ohio, Toledo, Ohio.

BERTRAND G. WINSBERG, M.D., Director, Division of Child Mental Health, Health Sciences Center, Long Island Research Institute, State University of New York at Stony Brook.

BEVERLY ZBUSKA, L.C.S.W., Consultant, Ocean Park Community Center, Santa Monica, California; formerly Supervisor,

Child and Adolescent Groups, Bronx State Psychiatric Hospital, Bronx, New York.

SYDNEY ZENTALL, PH.D., Associate Professor, Department of Special Education, Eastern Kentucky University, Richmond, Kentucky.

Part I

INTRODUCTION

Chapter 1

A REVIEW OF THE MINIMAL BRAIN DYSFUNCTION SYNDROME

Ruth Ochroch

There has been a "word explosion" since the early 1960s (Black, 1974) of different definitions, descriptions, and nomenclatures emanating from the child mental health and child education professions about a sizeable group of children whose behaviors and symptoms have been puzzling and whose responses to interventions have been difficult to gauge. These children have been estimated to constitute 10–20 percent of the school-age population, and four boys to one girl are found in this group (Kline, 1978; Wender, 1971). Such children have been classified on the basis of assumed underlying neurocortical deficits as suffering with minimal brain dysfunction, with cerebral dysfunction, with a chronic brain or organic syndrome, with neurological deficits, with perceptual deficits, with general developmental lags, and so forth. They have also been classified on the basis of overt symptom formations as suffering with hyperactivity or hyperkinesis, with an attention deficit disorder with or without hyperactivity, with dyslexia or dyscalculia, with learning disabilities, and so forth.

A reading of the contributors to this volume as well as a review of the literature since the 1960s indicate that many of these terms are used interchangeably to describe the same type or group of children (Cantwell, 1975; Gold, 1979; Golden & Anderson, 1979; Werry, 1968; Werry, Minde, Guzman, Weiss, Dogan, & Hoy, 1972). Although there had been earlier descriptions of children with mild and atypical organic brain disorders (Bender, 1956; Straus & Lehtinen, 1947; Straus & Kephart, 1955), Clements in 1966 defined the syndrome for minimal brain dysfunction (MBD). It refers to children of near to above average general intelligence with certain learning or behavioral disabilities, ranging from mild to severe, which are associated with deviations of function of the central nervous system. These deviations may manifest themselves by various combinations of impairments in perception, conceptualization, language, memory, and control of attention, impulse, or motor function (Clements, 1966, p. 9–10).

Clements took the position that certain categories of deviant behavior, developmental dyscrasias, learning disabilities, and visual-motor perceptual irregularities must be accepted as valid indices of disturbed brain functioning. Numerous writers have supported this position, and as many have ignored it and focused on hyperactivity and learning disabilities. Cruickshank (1979) reaffirmed the neuropsychological approach and emphasized that perceptual processing deficits (neurological dysfunctions) underlie learning disabilities. He warned that the failure to recognize this endangered the management of the child, the appropriate training for the professions, and the gains for the child.

Reports since Clements's work (1966) elaborated on his basic categories and now detail additional difficulties of generalized physical and emotional maturity, poor or inaccurate body image, disturbance in kinesthetic integration, hypo- as well as hyperactivity, dysgraphia or agraphia, dyscalculia, and speech difficulties (Chalfant & Scheffelin, 1969; Henderson, 1974; Pollack, 1976; Rourke & Strang, 1978; Shaffer, 1979).

It is important here to differentiate between the child who may be hyperactive but who has adequate to good gross and fine motor coordination, is adequate to bright intellectually, and does adequately at school and socially, or the child who has a specific, isolated deficit (visual, auditory, motor, speech) but is adequate to bright intellectually and does adequately at school and socially, and the child who exhibits difficulties across the range of symptoms associated with the MBD syndrome. The psychological consequences are less devastating and the prognosis brighter for the first two than for the third.

Studies of the children with the broad range of MBD symptoms, defined above, indicate the presence of a number of additional disturbances in metabolism, including allergies (Adler, 1978; Cott, 1973; Feingold, 1976; Mayron, 1978; Wunderlich, 1979), in physical growth (Gold, 1978; Knobloch & Pasamanick, 1974), in psychological maturation (Bender, 1956; Gross & Wilson, 1964; Ireton, Thwing, & Currier, 1975; Silver, 1958; Weiss, Minde, Werry, Douglas, & Nemeth, 1972), and in social development (Bruininks, 1978; Bryan, 1978). These findings suggest that the cerebral dysfunctions may reflect some systemic disturbance affecting general body as well as central nervous system function. This is further supported by the reported recent advances in brain chemistry and physiology (Brody, 1974; Jaynes, 1976; Sagan, 1977). The child, then, can be beset by difficulties in general body functioning as well as by the visual perceptual, auditory, and language processing deficits that make for learning disabilities.

Hypotheses concerning etiology focus on genetic predisposition (Rossi, 1970; Rugel & Mitchell, 1977; Silver, 1971), poor nutrition, exposure to toxic substances and illness during gestation (Knobloch & Pasamanick, 1974; Mayron, 1978; Perino & Ernhard, 1974), perinatal stress (Colligan, 1974), and illnesses of early childhood (Knobloch & Pasamanick, 1974). Children of the impoverished have greater exposure to debilitating circumstances and a higher vulnerability (Alley, Solomons, & Opitz, 1971; Kearley & McLeod, 1976; Knobloch & Pasamanick, 1974; Perino & Ernhardt, 1974; Sapirstein, Bopp, & Rak, 1978).

Studies of children with MBD also indicate that they are more vulnerable to emotional disturbances (Graham & Rutter, 1969; Laufer, 1962; Rutter, 1978; Silver, 1958; Shaffer, 1979; Tarnopol, 1970, Weiss et al., 1972). This vulnerability reflects the differences in personality development which are the outcome of the psychophysiological interruptions in the normal maturational patterns and the family dynamics. Many of these children seem to have a basic predisposition to anxiety with an exaggerated "startle" response and seem to overreact to both physiological and psychological stress with very severe anxiety attacks, which have been labeled "catastrophic reactions." The personality development of these children reflects their anxieties about their neurophysiological difficulties and their efforts to deal with both the anxiety and the deficits plus of course the usual developmental demands. Their personalities must also reflect their emotional and psychological environment, which embodies the parents' bewilderment, disappointment, and love for and pain and anxiety about the child. Many of these children, irrespective of their level of activity, develop patterns of impulsive behavior with remarkable ability to avoid situations that impinge on their deficits and which bring on anxiety reactions. Others develop extremely rigid and compulsive patterns of behavior in an effort to make some sense or order out of the buzzing confusions that surround them. Thus, their rigidity may be a reflection of organic perseveration rather than a behavioral manifestation of psychologically based compulsivity. Further, the compulsivity or impulsivity may not stem from psychodynamic conflicts alone but from efforts to cope with deficient integration of sensory input and motor coordination. Therefore, these children will exhibit differences in ego development reflective of differences in body ego and the realistic limitations to coping that these children face.

The assumption of an underlying neurological disturbance with a range of symptom formations, as opposed to isolated symptom clusters, necessitates that diagnosis as well as intervention be done by a team. The team members must all have a broad knowledge of child development and of the syndrome, and a general understanding of and respect for each discipline's area of competence and where the disciplines overlap.

The diagnostic team should optimally consist of:

1. A case manager who will take responsibility for guiding the child and family through the diagnostic process, treatment planning, and referrals, and organize team conferences. The case manager could be a member of any of the disciplines and could serve in this capacity as well as in his/her discipline, for example, a pediatric neurologist.
2. A social caseworker to take the history and to see the child and family together, gather data, etc.
3. A pediatric neurologist.
4. A child psychiatrist.
5. A clinical psychologist who can do psychodiagnostic as well as specific learning disability testing; or learning disability specialist to test for specific learning disabilities.

Once the diagnosis has been established and the order of priorities for the interventions has tentatively been worked out, the family will need a great deal of help in understanding the meaning of the diagnosis, in accepting it, and learning to apply it to their child and themselves. They may find it overwhelming and crushing. The process of defining what kinds of help are needed and referring the child and family for such help also has to be worked out in great detail. Each step has to be explained and reinforced and paced according to the family's ability to deal with it.

The different types of services have been detailed by a number of the contributing authors and can include medication, special diet, optometric retraining, movement therapy, and work with a learning disability specialist. The question of whether to keep a child with learning and behavioral difficulties in a regular school with ancillary help, in a mainstreamed class with special services, or to place the child in a private special school (with or without funding) is a difficult one to answer.

The child's and family's need for psychological help has been repeatedly emphasized because of the child's and parents' increased vulnerability to emotional stress and because of the personality difficulties that reflect the child's poor self-image and sense of defeat. Berlin (1974), among many authors, stresses the need for very early identification and interventions. He emphasizes that, whether or not medication (or other intervention) works, it is urgent to help the child and family in distress, because the very early defective socialization patterns are difficult to change and can affect the child's entire life. In working with the younger child, it becomes necessary to develop ways of evaluating to what extent certain behaviors reflect psychodynamically triggered symptoms and to what extent they reflect adaptive and maladaptive coping patterns aimed at reducing the effects of the deficits. The therapist must consider these factors so as not to make the child inadvertently feel guilty for behaviors which he or she cannot realistically change and so as not to mislead the family about potential for change. And these differences in evaluation should of necessity bring about modifications in approach.

Follow-up studies indicate that, even though some specific neurological deficits may have disappeared and even though the hyperactivity may have decreased, because of medication (Eaton Sells, & Lucas, 1977; Ullman, Barkley, & Brown, 1978) or diminished in adolescence in keeping with hormonal-changes; the adolescent or adult is left with immature ego development, a sense of incompetence, poor work or study habits, and poor social skills (Bellak, 1979; Barkley, 1978; Blouin, Bornstein, & Trites, 1978; Frauenheim, 1978; Kline & Kline, 1975; Kline, 1978; Weiss et al., 1972; Weiss et al., 1978).

The recent literature offers behavior treatment, biofeedback, modeling, psychotherapy, and other modalities (Feighner & Feighner, 1974; Gargiulo & Kuna, 1979; Nagle & Thwaite, 1979; Millman, 1974). The authors make the points that early intervention is crucial and that the child needs help in changing behavior and learning patterns in the classroom, and the child and family need help in shifting their ways of relating and reacting. In view of the discouraging results reported above, it seems evident that programs for early identification should be strengthened and that multifaceted early interventions and support systems should be made available to the child and parent. In order to do this, training of teachers, psychologists and other professions will have to be greatly expanded. Otherwise, the effects of the childhood minimal brain dysfunction will remain a lifelong disability.

REFERENCES

Adler, S. Behavior management: A nutritional approach to the behaviorally disordered and learning disabled child. *Journal of Learning Disabilities,* 1978, *11*(10), 651–656.

Alley, G. R., Solomons, G., & Opitz, E. Minimal cerebral dysfunction as it relates to social class. *Journal of Learning Disabilities,* 1971, *4*(5), 246–250.

Barkley, R. Recent developments in research on hyperactive children. *Journal of Pediatric Psychology,* 1978, *3*(4), 158–163.

Bellak, L. Psychiatric aspects of minimal brain dysfunction in adults: their ego function assessment. In L. Bellak, (Ed.). *Psychiatric Aspects of Minimal Brain Dysfunction in Adults.* New York: Grune & Stratton, 1979, 73–102.

Bender, L. *Psychopathology of children with organic brain disorders.* Springfield, Ill.: Charles C. Thomas, 1956.

Berlin, I. N. Minimal brain dysfunction: Management of family distress. *Journal of the American Medical Association,* 1974, *229*(11), 1454–1456.

Black, W. F. The word explosion in learning disabilities: A notation of literature trends 1962–72. *Journal of Learning Disabilities,* 1974, 7(5), 323–325.

Blouin, A., Bornstein, R. A. & Trites, R. L. Teenage alcohol use among hyperactive children: A five year follow-up study. *Journal of Pediatric Psychology,* 1978, *3*(4), 188–194.

Brody, J. Famed biomedical group says research is periled by government funding for specific diseases. *New York Times,* 10 October 1974, p. 41

Bruininks, V. L. Peer status and personality characteristics of learning disabled and nondisabled students. *Journal of Learning Disabilities,* 1978, 11(8), 484–489.

Bryan, T. H. Social relationships and verbal interactions of learning disabled children. *Journal of Learning Disabilities,* 1978, *11*(2), 107–115.

Cantwell, D. P. & Satterfield, J. H. The prevalence of academic underachievement in hyperactive children. *Journal of Pediatric Psychology,* 1978, *3* (4), 168–171.

Chalfant, J., & Scheffelin, M. A. *Central processing dysfunctions in children: A review of research* (NINDS Monograph No. 9). Washington, D.C.: U.S. Government Printing Office, 1969.

Clements, S. D. *Minimal brain dysfunction in children—Terminology and identification* (NINDS Monograph No. 3, U.S. Public Health Service Publication No. 1414). Washington D.C.: U.S. Government Printing Office, 1966.

Colligan, R. C. Psychometric deficits related to perinatal stress. *Journal of Learning Disabilities,* 1974, *7*(3), 155–161.

Cott, A. Treatment of learning disabilities. *Journal of Orthomolecular Psychiatry,* 1973, *3,* 343–355.

Cruickshank, W. M. Learning disabilities: Perceptual or other? *Association for Children with Learning Disabilities Newsbriefs,* 1979, (125), 7–10.

Eaton, M., Sells, C., & Lucas, B. Psychoactive medication and learning disabilities. *Journal of Learning Disabilities,* 1977, *10*(7), 403–410.

Feighner, A. C. & Feighner, J. P. Multi-modality treatment of the hyperkinetic child. *American Journal of Psychiatry,* 1974, *5,* 85–90.

Feingold, B. F. Hyperkinesis and learning disabilities linked to ingestion of artificial food colors and flavors. *Journal of Learning Disabilities,* 1976, *9*(11), 476–483.

Frauenheim, J. G. Academic achievement characteristics of adult males who were diagnosed as dyslexic in childhood. *Journal of Learning Disabilities,* 1978, *11*(8), 476–483.

Gargiulo, R. M., & Kuna, D. Arousal level and hyperkinesis: Implications for biofeedback. *Journal of Learning Disabilities,* 1979, *12*(3), 137–138.

Gold, P. Suspected neurological impairment and cognitive abilities: A longitudinal study of selected skills and predictive accuracy. *Journal of Clinical Child Psychology,* 1979, *8*(1), 35–38.

Gold, R. F. Constitutional growth delay and learning problems. *Journal of Learning Disabilities,* 1978, *11*(7), 427–429.

Golden, C., & Anderson, S. *Learning disabilities and brain dysfunction.* Springfield, Ill.: Charles C. Thomas, 1979.

Goldstein, K. *The Organism.* New York: American Book Company, 1939.

Graham, P. & Rutter, M. Organic brain dysfunction and child psychiatric orders. In S. Chess & A. Thomas (Eds.). *Annual progress in child psychiatry and child development.* New York: Brunner/Mazel, 1969.

Gross, M. D. & Wilson, W. C. Behavior disorders of children with cerebral dysrhythmia. *Archives of General Psychiatry,* 1964, *2* 610–619.

Henderson, P. *Disability in childhood and youth.* New York: Oxford University Press, 1974.

Ireton, H., Thwing, E., & Currier, S. K. Minnesota child development inventory: Identification of children with developmental disorders. *Pediatric Psychology,* 1974, *3*(4), 15–19.

Jaynes, J. *The origins of consciousness in the breakdown of the bicameral mind.* Boston: Houghton Mifflin Company, 1976.

Kearly, M. & McLeod, J. Learning disability and socioeconomic status. *Journal of Learning Disabilities,* 1976, *9* 596–599.

Kline, C. L. Developmental dyslexia in adolescents: The emotional carnage. *Bulletin of the Orton Society,* 1978, *28,* 160–174.

Kline, C. L., & Kline, C. L. Follow-up study of 216 dyslexic children. *Bulletin of the Orton Society,* 1975, *25,* 125–144.

Knobloch, H., & Pasamanick, B. (Eds). *Gesell and Amatruda's developmental diagnosis: The evaluation and management of normal and abnormal neuropsychologic development in infancy and early childhood, (3rd Ed.).* New York: Harper & Row, 1974.

Mayron, L. Ecological factors in learning disabilities. *Journal of Learning Disabilities,* 1978, *11*(8), 495–502.

Millman, H. L. Psychoneurological learning and behavior problems: The importance of treatment considerations. *Journal of Clinical Child Psychology,* 1974, *3*(1), 26–30.

Nagle, R. J. & Thwaite, B. C. Modeling effects on impulsivity with learning disabled children. *Journal of Learning Disabilities,* 1979, *12*(3), 331–336.

Perino, J., & Ernhard, C. B. The relation of subclinical lead level to cognitive and perceptual performance in black preschoolers. *Journal of Learning Disabilities,* 1974, *7*(10), 616–620.

Pollack, C. Neuropsychological aspects of reading and writing. *Bulletin of the Orton Society,* 1976, *26,* 19–33.

Rossi, A. O. Genetics of higher level disorders. *Journal of Learning Disabilities,* 1970, *3*(8), 387–390.

Rourke, B. P., & Strang, J. D. Neuropsychological significance of variations in patterns of academic performance: Motor, psychomotor and tactile-perceptual abilities. *Journal of Pediatric Psychology,* 1978, *3*(2), 62–66.

Rugel, R. P., & Mitchell, A. Characteristics of familial and nonfamilial readers. *Journal of Learning Disabilities,* 1977, *10*(5), 308–313.

Rutter, M. Brain damage syndromes in childhood: Concepts and findings. In S. Chess & A. Thomas (Eds.). *Annual progress in child psychiatry and child development 1978.* New York: Brunner/Mazel, 1978.

Sagan, C. *The Dragons of Eden.* New York: Random House, 1977.

Sapirstein, G. N., Bopp, M. J., & Bak, J. J. Social status of learning disabled children. *Journal of Learning Disabilities,* 1978, *11*(2), 98–102.

Shaffer, M. Primal terror: A perspective of vestibular dysfunction. *Journal of Learning Disabilities,* 1979, *12*(2), 89–92.

Silver, A. A. Behavioral syndromes associated with brain damage in children. *Pediatric Clinics of North America,* August 1948, pp. 687–698.

Silver, L. B. Familial patterns in children with neurologically-based learning disabilities. *Journal of Learning Disabilities,* 1971, *4*(4), 349–358.

Strauss, A. A., & Lehtinen, L. D. *Psychopathology and education of the brain-injured child.* New York: Grune and Stratton, 1947

Strauss, A. A., Lehtinen, L. D., & Kephart, N. *Psychopathology and education of the brain injured child* (Vol. 2). New York: Grune & Stratton, 1955.

Tarnopol, L. Delinquency and minimal brain dysfunction. *Journal of Learning Disabilities,* 1979, *3*(4), 200–208.

Ullman, D. G., Barkley, R. A., & Brown, H. W. The behavioral symptoms of hyperkinetic children who successfully responded to stimulant drug treatment. *American Journal of Orthopsychiatry,* 1978, *48*(3), 425–437.

Weiss, G., Minde, K., Werry, J. S., Douglas, V., & Nemeth, E. Studies on the hyperactive child: Five year follow-up. In S. Chess & A. Thomas (Eds.), *Annual progress in child psychiatry and child development.* New York: Brunner/Mazel, 1972.

Weiss, G., Hechtman, L., & Pearlman, T. Hyperactives as young adults: School, employer and self-ratings obtained during 10-year follow-up evaluations. *American Journal of Orthopsychiatry,* 1978, *48*(3), 438–445.

Wender, P. H. *Minimal brain dysfunction in children.* New York: John Wiley & Sons, 1971.

Werry, J. S. Studies on the hyperactive child: An empirical analysis of the minimal brain dysfunction syndrome. *Archives of General Psychiatry,* 1968, *19,* 9–16.

Werry, J. S., Minde, K., Guzman, A., Weiss, G., Dogan, K., & Hoy, E. Studies on the hyperactive child-VII: Neurological status compared with neurotic and normal children. *American Journal of Orthopsychiatry,* 1974, *43*(3), 441–451.

Wunderlich, R. C. Allergy, brains and children coping: Evidence from treatment. *Perceptions Newsletter,* 1979, *1*(6), 1–2.

BIBLIOGRAPHY

Black, W. F. Cognitive, academic and behavioral findings in children with suspected and documented neurological dysfunction. *Journal of Learning Disabilities,* 1974, *9*(3), 182–187.

Cantwell, D. P. *The hyperactive child: Diagnosis, management, current research.* New York: Spectrum Publications, 1975.

Cruickshank, W. M. *The brain-injured child in home, school, and community.* Syracuse: Syracuse University Press, 1966.

Eaves, L. C., Kendall, D. C., & Crichton, J. U. The early identification of learning disabilities: A follow-up report. *Journal of Learning Disabilities,* 1974, *7*(10), 632–638.

Eisenberg, L. Psychiatric implications of brain damage in children. In S. I. Harrison & J. F. McDermott (Eds.). *Childhood Psychopathology.* New York: International Universities Press, 1972.

Gallagher, J., Kunstadter, R. H., Cole, C. H., & Clements, S. D. *Minimal brain dysfunction in children: Educational, medical and health related services* (Public Health Service Publication No. 2014). Washington, D.C.: U.S. Government Printing Office, 1969.

Goldstein, K. *The Organism.* New York: American Book Company, 1939.

Group for the Advancement of Psychiatry. *Psychopathological disorders in childhood* (Vol. 6). New York: 1966.

Gorssman, R. P. Learning disability and the problem of scientific definitions. *Journal of Learning Disabilities,* 1978, *11*(3), 120–123.

Gunderson, B. V. Diagnosis of learning disabilities: the team approach. *Journal of Learning Disabilities,* 1971, *4*(2), 107–113.

Myklebust, H. (Ed.). *Progress in learning disabilities* (Vol. 1). New York: Grune and Stratton, 1968.

Rapp, D. J. Does diet affect hyperactivity? *Journal of Learning Disabilities,* 1978, *11*(6), 383–389.

Rie, H. E. Hyperactivity in children. *American Journal of Diseases of Children,* 1975, *130,* 783–789.

Safer, D., & Allen, R. P. *Hyperactive children: Diagnosis and management.* Baltimore: University Park Press, 1976.

Sapir, S. G., & Nitzburg, A. C. *Children with learning problems—Readings in a developmental-interaction approach.* New York: Brunner/Mazel, 1973.

Special report on the learning disabled adolescent. *Learning Disability Quarterly,* 1978, *1*(4).

Spring, C., & Sandoval, J. Food additives and hyperkinesis: A critical evaluation of the evidence. *Journal of Learning Disabilities,* 1976, *9,* 560–569.

Stone, N. S., & Levin, H. S. Neuropsychological testing of the developmentally delayed young children: Problems and progress. *Journal of Learning Disabilities,* 1979, *2*(4), 271–274.

Task Force on Nomenclature and Statistics. *Psychiatric association diagnostic and statistical manual of mental disorder* (3rd ed. DSM III-Draft). Washington, D.C.: American Psychiatric Association, 1978.

Thompson, H. L. Malnutrition as a possible contributing factor to learning disabilities. *Journal of Learning Disabilities,* 1971, *4*(6), 312–314.

Vygotsky, L. S. *Thought and language.* Cambridge: Massachusetts Institute of Technology Press, 1962.

Part II

DIAGNOSTIC PROCESSES

Chapter 2

DIAGNOSTIC ASSESSMENT OF CHILDREN WITH DEVELOPMENTAL PROBLEMS
A Therapeutic Process

Mark N. Ozer

This chapter will reconsider the character of the diagnostic assessment of the child with learning and/or behavioral problems. The diagnostic assessment is considered as a data collection procedure leading to a plan for treatment. The ultimate products of the data collection include not only a specific plan for the future but also a specific degree of commitment to the implementation of the plans by those participating. It is therefore crucial to view the process by which the plan has been generated. There must be concern for both the *type* of data collected and the *source* of such data.

I have found it helpful to consider "diagnosis" in terms of its meaning as derived from the original Greek. The concept of "thinking through" from its Greek roots infers an investigatory process by which one comes to know the nature of a condition, situation, or problem. The final statement or conclusion about the nature of some phenomenon is then a second stage. Such a conclusion as to the category of the problem then presumably provides the basis for an appropriate treatment plan. If one focuses on the process of thinking through rather than merely on the final statement or conclusion, the effects of the diagnostic assessment may become both more immediate and more therapeutic to those involved.

THE TYPE OF DATA SOUGHT

The impact of the investigatory process may be clarified by considering as the first variable the type of data sought. The questions asked by the diagnostician control the data available for use in the final statement or conclusions, which may then be used in the formulation of the treatment plan.

In the assessment of medical problems, the basic question relates to the nature of an illness. The basic question then is:

1.   What is the problem? What is it that is bothering you?

By a further series of questions, the character of the problem is elaborated. If the problem is described as pain, then the site of the pain, its frequency, and its character are explored. The diagnostician then seeks to make conclusions as to whether physical disease is present and, if so, about its organ site and probable cause.

Neurology, as a branch of medicine, seeks to make these same conclusions about disease in the nervous system. A history of the illness is taken; motor and sensory, as well as mental, functions of the nervous system are tested to find patterns of loss associated with disease in the brain, spinal cord, and muscles (Bender, p. 4–7, 1967). The first conclusion, as to whether physical disease is present, is then made, depending upon the particular pattern of loss of function. The characteristics of such patterns also help to indicate where in the nervous system the problem may exist—the second conclusion—so that it may possibly be removed. For example, weakness on motor testing and sensory loss on the left side of the body is a pattern of loss that may be associated with disease on the right side of the brain. The cause of such difficulties—the third conclusion to be made—can also be established on the basis of history and patterns of loss. In looking at disease in this way, the disorder of function is presumed to be due to some cause foreign to the individual, such as a blood clot or tumor (Reise, 1950). The cause is removed, and the patient may then recover the functions lost. This approach is particularly useful for the formulation of treatment plans for the surgical removal of physical lesions of the nervous system. One may call this entire approach the neurological disease diagnostic model.

This model of seeking to define the character of an illness was the context in which the diagnostic approach to developmental problems in children arose. Historically, cerebral palsy was the first of the developmental "diseases" described. There were frequently actual physical changes in the brain or spinal cord that one could see on examination of the patient after death or by some other means. Such physical changes were not different in kind from those that occur with other diseases of the nervous system. It is not surprising that the same sort of data were sought. However, one is not dealing with the same sort of problem.

The cause of the cerebral palsy that we see in the patient had its effect some time in the past, and the child is developing so as to compensate for such an injury. The data relating to cause thus seem less important than in the case of neurological disease of recent origin. Whether there was a lack of oxygen at birth or some other injury or infection in the past does not affect what may need to be done now in helping that child function more effectively. The data pertaining to site in the nervous system also seem less relevant to any treatment plan, since one is not going to remove some part of the brain, as one might in the treatment of a tumor (Crothers & Paine, 1959).

The diagnostic statements that may be generated in respect to neurological disease are not really useful in the treatment of developmental problems. Their lack of relevance seems particularly obvious when the concept of cerebral palsy was applied at first to what was felt to be lesser degrees of brain damage, than to the concept of brain dysfunction when no obvious physical findings could be seen (Paine, Werry, & Quay, 1968). It has been suggested that a plan for treatment in the area of developmental problems in children requires different data from those sought in the area of neurological disease (Ozer, 1968). In order to have different data, it is necessary to ask questions beyond those relating to the character of the problem or to the illness model.

The child with various handicaps (or the adult after the acute stage of neurological disease) must be viewed as an integrated functioning organism rather than merely in terms of loss of function. The actual patterns of function may be seen as the result of more or less effective attempts to compensate for what may have occurred in terms of insult to the nervous system. For example, the language patterns found in the patient with injury to the left side of the brain are not merely the result of such injury. What we may choose to call "aphasia" is the result of those parts of the brain that remain functional, albeit in the context of recent or extensive injury. Similarly, in the child focus must be on data as to areas of function even in those areas that have been considered problematical.

An additional question to be asked in the diagnostic assessment is addressed to areas of "wellness" rather than illness alone. After definition of the problem area, the question then is:

2.   When have things gone well in your area of concern?

In seeking the islands of wellness, quite a different model of the organism is being elaborated. For example, in review of children in whom the problem has been defined as "distractibility," data are sought of those times when they are attentive and perhaps displaying even partial degrees of such attentiveness. The search for these additional data requires a mode of thinking that views a problem as relativistic rather than absolute, of what is rather than of what is not. Such data are directly relevant to the development of eventual treatment plans for change in the future.

Still an additional question may be asked in order to develop treatment plans for the future:

3.   In the areas (or times) when things have gone well, what helped? What worked?

In testing children with behavioral and/or learning problems, one may sample the actual learning of some relevant task (Bijou & Peterson, 1971). In the context of some problem area, one is defining not only areas of wellness but some conditions under which such development may be enhanced. For example, if the problem area had been defined as reading, one could then sample, on a short-term basis, some reading task. In the context of success on some portion of that task, one may explore those strategies that may be effective (Ozer, 1977). The data derived from such an exploration could then be directly applied to the formulation of a treatment plan. The diagnostic assessment has thus begun to sample the individual in terms not only of the areas of accomplishment but of the process by which change can come about. The means by which change occurred in the diagnostic assessment could then become the means by which a treatment plan might be accomplished (Ozer & Richardson, 1974).

The last question to be addressed in the formulation of a treatment plan for the child with developmental problems is the one that leads to the definition of the actual goals of such a plan:

4.   What are the goals for the future?

The treatment plan itself might then include the stated goals (i.e., the ends), the means derived from the exploration of what had been effective in the experience of those involved, and some time-line for evaluation of the plans made. At the time of evaluation, the planning process would then be recycled (Ozer, 1979).

Like the data collected in the investigation of neurological disease, the data collected in the diagnostic process for developmental problems are relevant to the development of a treatment plan. The data collected in the diagnostic assessment of the child with developmental problems, however, goes beyond those required in the assessment of neurological disease. Explored also are the areas and degrees of development that have occurred and the means by which such development may have come about. Such additional data help define a new model for the diagnostic process. I choose to call this model a "child development" one as contrasted to that applied to neurological disease.

The Source of the Data

The direct formulation of a treatment plan for developmental problems has required the thinking through of additional data. The degree to which the plan is actually implemented is the second aspect to be considered. The diagnostic process,. the making of the plan, is reconsidered in terms of the degree of participation of the patient in the data collection. One must reconsider the source of the data as well as the type of data collected. We are asking different questions. The implementation of the plans made requires the diagnostician to ask these questions of those responsible for the actual treatment.

In the diagnostic model exploring illness, the basic question about the character of the problem is addressed to the patient. The diagnostician truly does not know what is disturbing the other person. The effectiveness of the diagnostic process is enhanced to the degree that the patient is a conscious participant in the data collection. The diagnostician helps the patient specify the character of the complaint so that appropriate judgment may be made of the site and cause of the complaint. The ancient medical dictum remains true: "Listen to the patient, he is telling you the diagnosis."

The conversion of the diagnostic procedure into a planning process for the treatment of developmental problems requires the conscious involvement of the treatment agents. Even more clearly than in the treatment of illness, the growth and development of the child is in the hands of the clients rather than the professional who serves as the diagnostician. It is those who are most familiar with the child—the teachers, the parents, and the child—who are the primary participants in the process of development. It is they who must be the primary participants in the formulation of the treatment plans. The role of the professional serving as a diagnostician is that of a "consultant" to those primary participants.

The diagnostician samples the child's performance for a relatively short time and in a limited range of activities. The traditional source of data via a testing procedure must be extended in time and in terms of range of situations. It is the active participation of the clients in the data collection that permits such an extension into the life of the child. It is necessary to address the questions to be used in the formulation of the treatment plan to those who have more extensive experience with the child. Just as in the case of the exploration of illness, the diagnostician alone cannot know what is truly disturbing to the child and to those who are to varying degrees responsible for the child's development. Even more important in the diagnostic assessment for the treatment of developmental problems is the need to enlist the primary participants in addressing the additional questions described in the earlier portion of this chapter. The diagnostician alone cannot be responsible for describing the situations in which the child has been successful, the conditions under which such successes may have come about, and the goals that are meaningful to those involved.

The diagnostician now serving as a consultant in planning

helps the primary participants by formulating the questions. It is the primary participants who must eventually take the responsibility for formulating the answers. It is particularly crucial for commitment to plans for the future that the primary participants begin to address the questions relating to the areas of "wellness" and to the means by which such achievements may have occurred. It is hearing oneself speak of one's own successful experiences and one's own sense of bringing about such successes that provides hope for the future and a sense that one may set goals for oneself.

Diagnosis has been reconsidered as a planning process. Treatment may therefore be reconsidered as an ongoing planning cycle in which plans are made and revised in light of experience. To enable the clients to participate in the planning process is the goal of the treatment program. It is the process of increasing one's awareness of one's own needs and successes and of one's own ways of bringing about success in relation to one's own goals that makes the diagnostic process both more immediate and more therapeutic.

REFERENCES

Bender, M. B. *The approach to diagnosis in modern neurology.* New York: Grune and Stratton, 1967, 4–7.

Bijou, S. W., & Peterson, R. F. Psychological assessment in children: A functional analysis. In P. McReynolds (Ed.), *Advances in psychological assessment* (Vol. 2). Palo Alto: Science and Behavior Books, 1971.

Crothers, B., & Paine, R. S. *The natural history of cerebral palsy.* Cambridge, Mass.: Harvard University Press, 1959.

Ozer, M. N. The neurological evaluation of school age children, *Journal of Learning Disabilities,* 1968, *1,* 84–86.

Ozer, M. N. Assessment of children with learning problems: A child development approach. In W. Otto, N. A. Peters, & C. W. Peters (Eds.), *Reading problems: A multidisciplinary perspective.* Reading, Mass.: Addison-Wesley Books, 1977.

Ozer, M. N. A cybernetic approach to assessment: A problem solving planning system. In M. N. Ozer (Ed.), *A cybernetic approach to the assessment of children: Toward a more humane use of human beings.* Boulder: Westview Press, 1979.

Ozer, M. N, & Richardson, H. B. Diagnostic evaluation of children with learning problems: A process approach. *Journal of Learning Disabilities,* 1974, *8,* 88–92.

Paine, R. S., Werry, J. S., & Quay, H. C. A study of minimal cerebral dysfunction. *Developmental Medical Child Neurology,* 1968, *10,* 505–510.

Reise, W. Principles of neurology: In light of history and their present use. *Nervous and Mental Disease Monographs,* 1950, 3–13.

Chapter 3

THE MBD CHILD
The Art of Definitive History-taking for Diagnostic Clarification

Jean Collard

History-taking to establish the presence of minimal brain dys-function (**MBD**) is a challenging process because, among the multiple possibilities for deviation, the specific pattern of the behavior and/or learning difficulty of the individual child and the interplay of factors in the family and child's situation must be understood for precise diagnosis and treatment planning. The wide-ranging and diverse symptoms of the syndrome all relate to specific difficulties in one or more ways in the child's ability to master the varied day-to-day activities and responsi-bilities required of children at various stages of their develop-ment. Thus an important aspect of the history involves documentation of exactly how the child's functioning deviates from what the child is normally expected to know and to be able to accomplish physically, cognitively, socially, and emotionally in relation to family, school, peers, and social environment.

Since many of the symptoms associated with minimal brain dysfunction occur in all children in some degree and at some stage of their development, investigation of maturational lags must be included along with data about current functioning. Classroom teachers, for example, can usually identify at least one student who is having difficulty in some area of functioning, but may not be aware, without knowing the child over time, whether the behavior is an age-related aspect of normal development or a symptom of more serious ongoing brain dysfunction. Variations in symptom formation and uncertainty as to the exact nature and cause of the syndrome complicate history-taking and can result in inadequate diagnoses and unsuccessful treatment programs.

For many years prior to the 1960s, professional literature abounded with descriptions of perplexing problems of children which did not fall into any known classification of childhood disorders and were resistant to available treatment methods. However, seminal work was beginning to appear, both from research on brain processes and from clinical work with brain-injured and stroke patients, that suggested the relationship of conditions such as the aphasias to specific aspects of brain function (Magoun, 1958; Straus & Lehtinen, 1951). Indication that disorders of behavior or intellectual function in children could also be related to deviations of central nervous system functioning induced an attempt to classify such disabilities (Clements, 1966). The list of medical and educational symptoms so compiled identified disorders of speech, motor function, thought, memory, attention, impulsivity, and hyperactivity, as well as difficulties in social relationships and specific learning disabilities. Publication of commission reports clarified nomenclature and focused attention on the relation of such deficits and how the brain "learns" (Clements, 1966). Subsequent advances in neurological brain research and clinical endeavors in neuropsychology and rehabilitation medicine are now documenting the specific relationships between brain processing and such disabilities. The reciprocal result of this relationship and its reverberations in interaction between child and environment are at the basic core of data which the history must address.

THE PROCESS

The collaborative process on which effective history-taking is based focuses on the needs of the child and of the adults concerned with the child's development, in order to clarify what is causing the difficulties. The professional's knowledge of what must be learned about the child and family's present situation and previous experience is essential in order to offer help in ameliorating the problem. This collaborative undertaking assumes the ability of the interviewer to offer an unpressured, open approach which introduces the expectation of a two-way exchange in working together to discover what is wrong and what can be done about it. It also involves a special quality of assessment which necessitates specific kinds of questions and requests for recollection from child and family that the history-taker will need to stimulate and which may at times be arduous and stressful for parent and child. Thus, the parents' participation is needed to ensure their awareness and understanding of the complexities which are endemic to this syndrome. Patience and sensitivity in recognizing the parents' concern as to whether the professional will understand the meaning of the child to them or their part in his development is also important to a full understanding of the history. The difficulty some parents have in accepting that anything is wrong with the child may result in the projection of the difficulty, particularly when behavioral problems provoke retaliation from other children. A major concern sometimes voiced or vigorously defended against is the parents' feeling of guilt and concern about "What have I done wrong?" The parent who experiences the child's problem as overwhelming and beyond control may also influence similar feelings of hopelessness and despair in the child. The opportunity to explore their child's abilities as well as deficits, and their perception of them, with a professional can give insight which is experienced as therapeutic by parent and child.

For the social worker or other professional who expects to explore and understand the complex MBD syndrome, a great deal of knowledge is required to pursue this understanding of the individual child in family and situation and to know the kinds of areas which are essential to cover. The knowledge base involves several fields, medicine and the behavioral and social sciences. And the multidisciplinary collaboration of varied professionals is required for diagnosis and treatment. The history-taker usually has general familiarity with the role of the neurologist; psychiatrist; psychologist; physical and speech therapists; learning specialists with special training in areas such as reading, arithmetic, writing, and language; the teacher; and the social worker. The history-taker must know also the kinds of information that are useful for each specialty either in assessment or in therapy.

The purpose for which the history is being taken must be clear. The overall type of information which is needed for a full history is included in the outline below. The child may, however, already have been seen by the neurologist or school psychologist or guidance counselor, and certain information may already be available. If the social worker is taking the history, as is usual in most clinics and hospitals, the worker's eclectic background in working with other disciplines and relating to human difficulties, wherever they may surface, should enable assessment of what is needed and what still remains to be done. Specific information may be required about family problems which can affect the child's adjustment in school. The parents' misperceptions of their child's problem, and how to deal with it, must be clarified. Often, a family brings the child to a hospital center after numerous treatment attempts and with vanishing hopes for a final definitive diagnosis. In such a situation, very careful assessment of previous clinical material, a rigorous search for what may have been missed, and a clear understanding of the parents' role with the child may be what is needed.

The guiding principle in all **MBD** history-taking is that the information about symptoms be precise as to facts and specific as to area of problem and that it clarify the functional problem, that is, what the child can and cannot do. History-taking seeks answers to questions raised by the data of what further needs to be understood, in order to provide focus for the clinical examination and other tests. In the experience of the author, the work of other professionals supports and amplifies the material of a sound and effective history, and together they form the basis for a clear and valid treatment program. The essential information to cover in the history is the following:

I. Referral information
    a. The symptom picture—the problems identified by the parent or other person making the referral and the difficulties these present for both.
    b. Specific concerns of the parent about the present referral and previous efforts to cope with the problem.
    c. Background data regarding the referral problems: how long have the various problems persisted, under what circumstances did they arise, and what steps were previously taken to clarify or deal with the difficulty? Specifically, who were the significant others who have been involved with the child's problem?
2. Profile of the MBD Child
    a. Physical and intellectual achievement patterns, skills, and motivation.
    b. Ability to relate socially, peer relationships.
    c. Emotional control (attention, distractibility) and affective tone.
    d. Deficits noted—how handled or treated.
    e. Habits, likes and dislikes, special talents.
    f. School adjustment, progression of difficulties, special classes, special schools, psychological testing.

g. Recreational pursuits, ability to play, camp experience, group experiences—usual or planned to overcome special difficulties.

h. State of health—energy levels, sleep patterns.

3. Etiological Factors

a. Genetic—known genetic conditions and similar problems to child's among other family members.

b. Prenatal and perinatal difficulties of the mother and child, such as illnesses and trauma during pregnancy, placental problems, abnormal delivery, and such early postnatal difficulties as low birth weight, anoxia, and failure to thrive.

c. Maturational lags—failure to achieve specific aspects of various developmental levels at normal periods. Specific deficits or deviations noted at specific age levels.

d. Illnesses and trauma, particularly those known to affect central nervous system functioning.

4. Family Profile

a. Family constellation and relationship of family members to the child. Their understanding of the child's problems and their attitudes toward the child and vice versa.

b. Family structure and functioning—familial, socioeconomic, and cultural—as these interact with the child's problem.

c. Family stresses and coping methods which may be affecting the child.

5. Psychosocial and Cultural Factors—the factors in raising the child which could affect psychosocial functioning.

a. Loss of a parental or other close relationship due to death, divorce, moving, and the like.

b. Major family stress at significant periods in child's life.

c. Pervasive, long-lasting difficulties related to fam-

ily disorganization, poverty, social dislocation, and other familial or social problems.
6.   Assessment of clinical and diagnostic implications of the material.

THE SYMPTOM PICTURE

Referral for professional attention comes most frequently from parents, schools, and other professionals as a result of a series of crises related to the seemingly unmanageable behavior of the child or to a concern about learning failures. Recent information, not only in professional journals but also through such public sources as newspapers and television, about the relationship between brain functioning and the "different" child's behavior, is also currently focusing public attention on the symptoms of this syndrome. The resulting pseudosophistication about MBD can create problems for the history-taker, since while relieving parents' guilt about their responsibility for their children's problems, the popular approach tends to seek "the answer" in a single source rather than in the complexities of interaction determining the unique and varied problems of the child. In reviewing the varied behavioral and intellectual deviations which make up the symptom picture of the MBD syndrome, this paper follows the latter approach, seeking "the answer" in the complexities of interaction.

The troublesome behavioral symptoms of hyperactive behavior, which center around problems of motor activity and inability to modulate behavior, include restless and at times seemingly ceaseless activity, impulsivity, and the inability to sit still or concentrate attention in one area for any length of time. The pattern of constant activity is often described as having a "driven" quality and is in more severe situations, particularly with older children, accompanied by reckless and even delinquent behavior. The age at which such behavior becomes problematic can vary with the tolerance of the parents and the surrounding environment. School, with its demands for greater control, precipitates a substantial percentage of the referrals for professional assistance.

Children with a high level of activity, a low threshold for frustration, difficulties in impulse control, and frequent distractability are disturbing in the classroom and disorganizing for other children and for group functioning. Socially immature and unpredictable behavior also interferes with meaningful interaction with other children and results not unrealistically in complaints by the child of not being liked or of being picked on by other children. The hyperactive behavior invites continual crises, which can be as baffling and emotionally wearing for teachers as it is for parents. Even when this behavior is understood as the coping attempts of a driven child, it can result in reactions and secondary elaborations which make it difficult to contain such children in normal home and classroom situations. As problems compound, it is difficult to trace the factors that precipitate an explosive situation in the interaction between child and environment.

The main focus of the problem may also be at home, where the parents' expectation of "normality" in adherence to family routines is constantly thwarted. Restlessness, fidgetiness with nicknacks or utensils at the dinner table, jerky movements resulting in "careless" breakage and sloppy homework, along with irritability at controls can result in labeling the behavior as willful and wayward by parents (and school) and indeed in such self-perceptions by the child.

The converse pattern of hypoactivity, which some children demonstrate, is characterized by slow, repetitive, and persistent patterns of behavior. These children dislike and resist change, and their disturbed behavior may center around perseverative activity, rigidity, or withdrawal and avoidance of involvement with others. Such patterns may follow a period of hyperactivity. Some clinicians believe that this is a compensatory pattern in the older school-age child. Interestingly, both the hyperactive and hypoactive children appear to do better in familiar and structured situations, and difficulties mount when they are faced with demands they feel unable to meet. Although symptoms of hyper- or hypoactivity may reflect psychodynamically triggered anxiety, it is now known that dysfunction in the sensory integrating centers such as the reticular activating system in the brain stem and thalamus (which has arousal and inhibitory functions) can have relevance for hyperactive behavior and learning disabilities (Ayres, 1972). It is also important to note that it is not uncommon for children described as predominantly hyperactive to have learning problems, and the converse is also true.

Disabilities in learning include a complex group of verbal and performance problems related to difficulties the child experiences in receiving, processing, and responding to information both from the outside environment and from his own body. The ability to speak, to comprehend and express language, to perform perceptual-motor skills, to remember, and to think cognitively all precede the ability to read, write, or master arithmetic. The peaks and valleys in such skills which are typical of the MBD child are particularly confusing until understood in terms of the differing functions of the two cerebral hemispheres. Thus a child may have high average test results with superior performance ability but delayed language development and inability to find the exact word in object naming. Delayed lateralization of the hemispheres may result in retardation in learning, with specific deficits in the left hemisphere involving difficulty or delay in verbal skills or sequential processing, so necessary in reading. Problems of space and form perception and the ability to do arithmetic usually concern difficulties in the right hemisphere. Most children by the age of five years achieve lateral cerebral dominance and are right-handed. Mixed or confused dominance appears to be correlated with neurological immaturity. Recent research confirms well-integrated function of the two hemispheres as a factor in higher academic skills (Ayres, 1972; Masland, 1976). Uneven performance and hyperactive behavior can result in the child being labeled as "a problem" unless it is understood that the child suffers from a functional brain disorder. Even when the behavior is markedly disruptive, with clowning, demands for attention, and disturbance of others, it is frequently defensive and diversionary to draw attention away from the underlying learning problems. Frequent failure, feelings of incompetence in relation to other children, and the resultant lack of motivation are predictable results when the basis of the child's difficulties is not understood.

Some symptoms are mild and nonspecific. Parents and other persons around the child often assume these will disappear as the child matures, and indeed, they may be age-specific and related to slow maturation of the central nervous system. An alert history-taker will watch for aspects of gross motor functioning, such as clumsiness and awkwardness, and aspects of fine motor coordination, balancing difficulties (skipping or hopping), convergent and divergent eye muscle imbalance, poor speech patterns, and tightness of muscle groups such as deep tendon reflexes. These and other "soft signs" may have been so mild that they were of minor concern, and yet they are vital clues to central nervous system maturation.

It is equally important that the history-taker understand the meaning of the disability for the child and for the parents. Although the problem may previously have been only dimly sensed or derogatorily labeled, the child and parents have been attempting to deal with the disability in some way. Some children may have the courage and determination to fight to prove their self-worth. For others, the disability can signify feelings of helplessness, hopelessness, and despair. Children who are able to be open and frank in discussing their understanding and feelings about their problems may have the interest and concern to reach out for help. Frequently, however, the child's perception of the problem is expressed defensively or through behavior revealing distress, anger, and anxiety. Distress may be displayed by complaining, whining, or clinging. Some children are disobedient, demanding, angry to the point of tantrums; still others are dawdlers, negative, and uncommunicative. The underlying feeling of the child is often that something is wrong or bad about him, a reflection not only of his own self-image but also of the attitudes of others toward him and the problem he presents.

For parents, the pressures of helping and supporting the child who is "different" can strain coping capacities. Few parents, even though they are able to present an objective picture of the child, have a sufficiently exact understanding of the areas of difficulty. Clinical practice provides convincing data regarding the hopes, confusions, and doubts with which parents approach the need for professional help.

THE DEVELOPING CHILD

The causes which have been related to symptoms of minimal brain dysfunction include genetic factors of inheritance, undetected structural abnormalities of the brain, biochemical or metabolic imbalance, illnesses, injuries, and infections, particularly during the prenatal and perinatal periods. Deviations in brain functioning may be related to the above but are also influenced by interactions of the child with the physical and social environment. Maturational lags and psychological and sociofamilial factors also have been involved. Socioeconomic conditions, with associated poverty, inadequate nourishment, lack of medical care, and physical and emotional stress have been found to have significance. Hersov (1976) mentions studies of teenage pregnancies between the ages of thirteen and sixteen years as carrying risk of prematurity and congenital anomalies when associated with unmarried state, poor socioeconomic conditions and inadequate antenatal care.

Early indications of infant distress—respiratory difficulties, weak sucking response, overexcitability, incessant crying, over- or underactive motor reflexes, vomiting, and disturbed sleeping patterns—are not infrequently found in the histories of the MBD child, particularly those with low birth weight and less than normal gestation periods, and these children are more vulnerable to psychological stress (Chess 1969, Kinsbourne 1974, Knobloch & Passamanick 1974, Shaffer 1976). Histories, particularly of young mothers, indicate that interference of their own concerns, fears, and anxieties, often unrelated to the baby, affects the development of feelings of closeness with and understanding of the baby. Marital tensions, the attitude of the father toward the baby, environmental pressures, and the presence or absence of an encouraging support system during this early peroid are among the complexity of factors which determine maternal reactions and the ability to cope. Parents living under conditions of great stress, with limited sociocultural and financial supports, have greater difficulty in coping with worrisome symptoms, with tragic results for the child.

The symptomatic behavior described earlier have a course and a history which relate in one way or another to the maturational development of the child. With normal physical development and maturation of the central nervous system, the child is increasingly able to master age-appropriate skills. The ability to undertake new and more complex activities is based on the accomplishments of the preceding stages. With retardation in neurological maturity or in specific areas of central nervous system damage, the related functional abilities are attained more slowly. The normal child moves through the stages from complete dependency to the generally stable and self-confident independence in functioning of the five year old. Development in the intervening years includes many possibilities and pitfalls which can have a considerable influence on the child he becomes. The significance of these years in the development of the MBD child is understood in relation to: (1) the age-appropriate tasks the child needs to master; (2) characteristic behavior through which the young child attempts to achieve competence at various developmental levels; and (3) deviations in development which complicate mastery for the MBD child. All children vary somewhat in the time at which they achieve developmental milestones. Many normal children present problems of behavioral lag in one or more of the areas that also identify the MBD child. While marked delay in achieving maturational steps can cause great concern, lesser difficulties, such as those involving some aspect of speech or fine motor control, or the way the child relates or socializes and adapts to new situations, are often overlooked in early stages of development. They do have significance for our area of interest.

The new-born infant has a limited global repertoire of behavior with which to cope with his new extrauterine environment. His basic needs are for feeding, sleeping, and tactile warmth, enhanced by close holding. The neurologically immature child may seem less stable, with more difficulty swallowing, poorer head control, exaggerated startle response, and/or vomiting, crying, and respiratory distress; these symptoms merit attention in the history as cues of possible current or future dysfunction. The ability to roll over, grasp, transfer, sit, crawl, and eventually pull himself to a standing position and walk with support may be delayed in the neurologically weak child. Weak vocal or facial muscles may retard the ability for vocalization. Aspects more closely related to environmental interaction, such as sleeping and eating patterns and social responsiveness, are early indicators of the child's individual temperament and parental approaches (Chess, 1969). The parents' pleasure in the child's growing achievements at this stage and their understanding and encouragement of growth needs are particularly important to the toddler who is having problems in attempting new steps or in stabilizing skills not yet mastered.

The period from eighteen months to three years make up one of the most important periods of the child's life. Neurologically, the myelination of his nervous system is progressing rapidly. Sensory-motor integration is a complex process which continues over a number of years, but the constant movement seen in the child of this age apparently has an enhancing effect on the integratory functions of the still-plastic brain (Ayres). Thus, the child increasingly consolidates basic skills of locomotion, speech, manipulation of objects (directed toward mastery of such activities as eating, dressing, handling toys), toilet training, and socialization. Growing physical strength and control make previously unavailable opportunities possible. The ability to communicate no longer is dependent solely on body language as speech, though still concrete, becomes increasingly fluent. The two to three year old is interested in words and loves to be read to but his comprehension of what is heard can be primitive. The fact that the child of this age learns by doing makes it important that others are available to help the child understand and correct misapprehensions and to offer protection when judgment for this is still lacking.

Most mothers seem to have sympathy for the frustrations of this period, but to know how to handle the myriad of contradictions can be perplexing and anxiety producing. For the MBD child, particularly, the need for a reasonable and structured environment and for help in modulating behavior or stimulating interest is great. Parents who have a confident and realistic understanding of the child's difficulty know what help is needed, and can encourage efforts to persevere. They can make the difference between feelings of security and worth and of distress and even chaos.

In many respects the MBD child at this stage may not seem very different from the normal child. Behavior at this age can be reflective of the more immature infant and tends to be disinhibited (with direct sensory-motor discharge sometimes referred to as primary process behavior), without elements of the cognitive processes characteristic of the child at the next developmental stage. However, the physical and emotional immaturities of the MBD child can give rise to uneven and out-of-bounds behavior which is confusing to parents. Misperceptions of space and distance may result in clumsy motor ability. Speech patterns may be retarded. The child may be overly distractible and overactive or self-absorbed and socially unresponsive, and he may deal with frustrations by head-banging or rocking. When such patterns persist, the child becomes "stuck" in socially maladaptive behavior, has difficulty in integrating new abilities into smooth and self-confident performance, and retreats or regresses. The history-taker will want to explore the possible determinants and circumstances of the behavior.

In contrast to the two-year-old child, the three to five year olds are increasingly competent in daily routines and motor abilities. The growth in maturity of the central nervous system makes possible the perfecting and stabilization of the mental, motor, and adaptive development of the abilities acquired earlier. There can still be considerable instability and emotional lability, with stuttering, hand tremors, and nail biting. The child's emotions are more conflicted; there is sensitivity to reactions of others and less assurance of acceptance. Nightmares and temper tantrums may still be troublesome but generally behavior is more realistically oriented and the child is more easily helped in modulating behavior. Changes involving integration of the reticular activating system with cortical networks may temporarily disturb emotional balance and ability to inhibit "out of bounds" behavior, even while attention span and ability to concentrate are increasing (Ayres, 1972).

MBD children may have real difficulty during this stage; they may be less able than normal children to inhibit unacceptable impulses, be socially immature, or unable to use thinking to replace action or to delay the meeting of needs. Normal abilities in daily living expected of the child aged three to five may be delayed because of neurological immaturity. The MBD child, under stress, may even regress in coping skills because of the additional demands put upon him. Symptoms may appear in difficulties in eating skills and table manners, in faulty sphincter control of bowel and bladder, and in peaking of overexcited behavior.

The MBD child may also be unaware of the feelings or wishes or others. In other words, at the age when emotional lability is a factor in normal development the MBD child is particularly vulnerable. Parents often find the resulting behavior difficult and incomprehensible. Attitudes toward the child's behavior and awareness of causative factors should be carefully explored.

Parents who understand the child's need for help with modulating activities, for a less overstimulating environment, for help in focusing on purposeful activity, and for support and reinforcement of less primitive and disorganized functioning may be able to help ward off later difficulties. Nursery school and kindergarten with well-trained professionals can be exceedingly helpful at this stage in identifying developmental lags and specific areas of sensory-motor dysfunction. Also, the opportunity for interaction with other children and the help available in mastering difficult steps can be growth producing for the child and often for the parents as well.

Latency is the period when the diagnosis of MBD is frequently made. This phase of development is of significance because the child is out in the world, in school and interaction with others. The history-taker may discover in the material relating to earlier developmental periods many landmarks when the condition could have been recognized and interventions and some form of treatment undertaken. It is perhaps not irrelevant that, at the stage when intelligence or cognitive thinking is becoming ascendant over imagination and emotion (Winnicott, 1965), the child who is the focus of attention is the one who is unable to make this transition and uses primitive defenses to express his concerns and unhappiness. Thus, it is in the history and current reality that the clear dimensions of the MBD problem for the child and family can be defined. Understandable also is the derision of the MBD child expressed by "normal" children, who are themselves struggling to achieve the new competence demanded by parents and other adults.

Although many of the motor problems of the child disappear by the latency period, the adolescent may again exhibit symptoms of clumsiness and awkward uncertainty. Faced with pressures of out-of-bounds behavior, emotionality, and impulse, the expected and normal adolescent crises and conflicts of aggressive independence versus dependence, and of defiance versus self-doubt are particularly disturbing to the MBD child. Deficiencies of impulse control and previous problems limit his readiness to cooperate with instinctual drives, physical changes, and social expectations. During this difficult time for the adolescent and for the parents, the need is for the parent to be a role model and to be "there," to provide structure but not demands which cannot be met. It is also a time when a decision needs to be made about readiness for treatment, based on history and correct understanding of the problems with which both the adolescent and his parents are struggling.

Conclusion

Current research is refining the diagnosis of MBD and suggests various treatment measures. Further knowledge of brain functioning and central nervous system development highlights their relationship to social behavior and the mastery of developmental tasks. Many treatment possibilities can be anticipated from such endeavours.

The point need not be labored that it is a difficult task to secure sufficient and relevant data for understanding the potential, as well as the problem, of the individual child. Current realities of budget limitations and staff pressures tend to jeopardize the quality of history-taking. It is appealing to equate efficiency with brief and minimal explorations and understandings of the complexity of the whole situation. These complexities, however, require careful and extensive review, and this review must be examined and reexamined during the entire course of treatment, in order to make full use of the significant findings.

History-taking insures understanding of child, family, and situation, but it has a further potential. Findings should throw light upon that delicate area between transitory difficulties that are merely phase specific and the more critical ones caused by severe disorder. Furthermore, the understanding of significant data about many MBD children throws light on the needs of normal children and has implications for institutional change to meet such needs.

REFERENCES

Ayres, A. J. *Sensory integration and learning disorders.* Los Angeles: Western Psychological Services, 1972.

Chess, S. *An introduction to child psychiatry.* New York: Grune and Stratton, 1969.

Clements, S. D. *Minimal brain dysfunction in children.* NINDS Monograph No. 3, U.S. Public Health Service Publication No. 1415, Government Printing Office, 1966.

Hersov, L. Adoption. In M. Rutter & L. Hersov (Eds.), *Child psychiatry: Modern approaches.* Oxford, England: Blackwell Scientific Publications, 1976.

Kinsbourne, M. Disorders of mental development. In J. L. Menkes, (Ed.), *Textbook of child neurology.* Philadelphia: Lea and Febiger, 1974.

Knobloch, H. & Pasamanick, B. *Gesell and Amatruda's developmental diagnosis 3rd Ed.* New York: Harper and Row, 1974.

Magoun, J. *The waking brain.* Springfield, Illinois, Charles C. Thomas, 1963.

Masland, R. L. The advantages of being dyslexic. *Bulletin of the Orton Society,* 1976, *26,* 10-18.

Shaffer, D. Brain injury. In M. Rutter and L. Herson (Eds.) *Child psychiatry: Modern approaches.* Oxford, England: Blackwell Scientific Publications, 1976.

Strauss, A., & Lehtinen, L. *Psychopathology and education of the brain-injured child.* New York: Grune and Stratton, 1947.

Winnicott, D. W. *Maturational processes and the facilitating environment: Studies in the theory of emotional development.* New York: International University Press, 1965.

BIBLIOGRAPHY

Adelman, H. S. Diagnostic classification and learning problems. *American Journal of Orthopsychiatry,* 1978, *48,* (4), 717–726.

Ayres, A. J. *The development of sensory integration: Theory and practice.* American Occupational Association, Dubuque, Iowa: Kendall-Hunt Publishing Co., 1974.

Cantwell, D. P. Hyperkinetic syndrome. In M. Rutter & L. Herson, (Eds.), *Child psychiatry: Modern approaches.* Oxford, England: Blackwell Scientific Publishers, 1976.

Dekabian, A. *Neurology of infancy.* Baltimore: Williams and Wilkins Co., 1959.

Dubey, D. Organic factors in hyperkinesis: A critical evaluation. *American Journal of Orthopsychiatry,* 1976, *46,* (2), 353–366.

Escalona, S., & Gorman, H. Emotional development in the first year of life. In M. Senn, Ed., *Problems of Infancy and Childhood.* New York: Josiah Macy Foundation, 1952, *6,* 11–91.

Gitterman, N. P. Group services for learning disabled children and their parents. *Social Casework,* 1979, *60* (April), 217–226.

Hart, E. D. *The child with disabling illness; Principles of rehabilitation.* New York: W. R. Saunders Co., 1974.

Ilg, F. L., & Ames, L. B. *Child behavior.* New York: Harper and Row, 1955.

Kreston, M., Arnold, C., & Wynder, E. Health economics and preventive care. *Science,* 1977, *195,* 457–462.

Lambert, N., Sandoval, J., & Sassone, D., Prevalence of hyperactivity in elementary school children as a function of system definers. *American Journal of Orthopsychiatry,* 1978, *48,* (3), 446–476.

Mahler, M. S., Pine, F., & Bergman, A. *The Psychological Birth of the Human Infant.* New York: Basic Books Inc., 1975.

Nelson, K., & Ellenburg, J. Predictors of epilepsy in children. *New England Journal of Medicine,* 1976, *295,* (19), 1029–1033.

Newman, C. J., Dembe, C., & Krug, O. He can but he won't: A psychodynamic study of gifted underachievers. In *The Psychoanalytic Study of the Child,* (Vol. 28). New Haven: Yale University Press, 1973.

Small, L. *Neuropsychodiagnosis in psychotherapy.* New York: Brunner/Mazel, 1973.

Sugarman, B. A. Atypical children: Perspectives on parent-professional interaction. *Social Casework,* 1979, *60,* (2), 104–110.

Weiss, G., Hechtman, L. & Perlman, T. Hyperactives as young adults: school, employer, and self-ratings obtained during ten-year follow-up evaluation. *American Journal of Orthopsychiatry,* 1978, *48,* (3), 438–445.

Wender, P. H. *The hyperactive child.* New York: Crown, 1973a.

Wender, P. H., & Wender, E. *The hyperactive child and the learning disabled child.* New York: Crown, 1973.

Chapter 4

A PROPOSED EXTENDED BEHAVIORAL, COGNITIVE, AND SENSORIMOTOR PEDIATRIC NEUROLOGICAL EXAMINATION

Kytja Voeller

Since the late 1950s, there has been much interest in the evaluation and treatment of the learning disabled (LD) child. The neurological examination figures prominently as an assessment tool. In fact, some school systems require a neurological examination for admission into LD classrooms. Some writers have felt that subtle abnormalities on the neurological examination, "soft signs," were even more meaningful and helpful than the neurological examination, and a considerable literature has been generated regarding what constituted soft signs and their usefulness in the assessment of LD children. (Werry, Minde, Guzman, Weiss, Dogan & Hoy, 1972; Peters, Romine, & Dykman, 1975). Investigators working primarily in research have focused on such methodological issues as inter-observer reliability ratings and examinations which effectively distinguish the child with LD from his normal peers. (Werry, Minde, Guzman, Weiss, Dogan & Hoy, 1972; Rutter, Graham & Yule, 1970). Recently, the value of the neurological examination and the soft-sign examination has been questioned. (Ingram, 1973;

Schmitt, 1975). Some writers have even suggested that the neurological assessment is irrelevant and the evaluation should be left in the hands of educators and school psychologists (Hart, Rennick, Klinge, Schwartz, 1974).

First, the issue of how useful the standard neurological examination (SNE) really is in the assessment of the LD child will be addressed. Some of the literature relating to the SNE and the soft sign examination will then be briefly reviewed. Finally, the examination which the author has found useful in evaluating the LD child will be outlined and illustrated by two clinical vignettes. It is the author's view that LD children fall into three general etiological categories: inherited learning deficits (e.g., familial dyslexia); chromosomal anomalies (e.g., Turner's syndrome and some mosaics); and, the numerically most significant group, children with pre-, peri-, or postnatal encephalopathy (e.g., resulting from severe maternal toxemia or a prolonged, difficult delivery with hypoxia or postnatal head trauma, respectively).

THE STANDARD NEUROLOGICAL EXAMINATION

The standard neurological examination, summarized in Chart 4.1, as it is commonly performed on the adult and older child, evolved out of the careful clinical observations and pathological correlations of nineteenth-century neurologists. It has proved to be an exceedingly useful tool for the localization of lesions involving the nervous system and focuses mainly on the motor and sensory systems. To answer the question regarding the usefulness of this examination in the LD population, we reviewed the records of 90 children (50 boys and 40 girls with IQs above 80) randomly chosen from a group of children referred to the author for a pediatric neurological examination for learning problems. The findings of the SNE are shown in Chart 4.2.

The information with regard to the SNE for this

Chart 4.1   Standard Neurological Evaluation

1. Level of consciousness

2. Cranial nerves:
   - I   Olfaction
   - II   Visual acuity, visual fields, fundascopic examination
   - III, IV, VI   Extraocular muscle function; pupillary reflexes
   - V   Facial nerve (also taste, lacrimation, stapedial muscle function)
   - VIII   Hearing; vestibular system
   - IX, X   Glossopharyngeal nerve, vagal nerve; motor function of palate, larynx; visceral functions; sensation of tongue and pharynx, taste on posterior third of tongue
   - XI   Spinal accessory-motor function of sternocleidomastoid and trapezius
   - XII   Motor function, tongue

3. Gross motor:
   Hand preference
   Station, gait
   Cerebellar function
   Tone, muscle mass, strength
   Deep tendon reflexes; superficial reflexes
   Pathological reflexes (Babinski)

4. Sensation:
   Light touch, pin prick
   Vibratory position
   Cortical sensory functions
   Double simultaneous stimulation

group of LD children can be summarized as follows: (1) It is apparent that a relatively small percentage of children have abnormalities defined by classical "hard" neurological signs: (2) Out of a potential total of five categories of abnormality, the mean number of abnormalities was 2.45 for girls and 2.72 for boys: (3) On any one item of the examination, most children were either normal or had only mild abnormalities; only a small percentage were clearly abnormal. However, (4) few, if any, LD children had *no* abnormalities. (5) Brisk reflexes in the lower

Chart 4.2 Findings of Standard Neurological Examination in a Group of 90 Children of Normal Intelligence Referred for Evaluation of Learning Disability

Finding	Percent	Finding	Percent
Cranial Nerves		Cerebellar signs (hypotonia, pendular reflexes, dyssynergia, dysdiadochokinesia, intention tremor)	
No abnormality	62		
Strabismus or other abnormalities of extraocular muscles	4	None	20
Duane's retraction syndrome	1	Mild	43
Ptosis	1	Moderate	29
Assymetry of nasolabial fold	28	Severe	8
Consistent classical lateralizing signs (defined as combining flattening of nasolabial fold, asymmetrical deep tendon reflexes, weakness, external rotation of leg on one side, consistent with mild hemiparesis)		Abnormalities on sensory testing	
		No abnormalities	63
		Position sense (lower extremity only)	4
		Vibratory sensation	None
None	61	Double simultaneous stimulation	
Right	13	Face extinguishes hand	21
Left	11	Face extinguishes ipsilateral hand	6
		Face extinguishes contralateral hand	1
Abnormalities of deep tendon reflexes		Random displacements	3
Normal reflexes	25	Unilateral extinction	2
Asymmetrically brisk (not included above, they were isolated)	4	Other (e.g., unusually long latency of response)	1
Uniformly brisk	33		
Brisk in lower extremities only	53		
Hypoactive reflexes	1		
Extensor plantar responses			
Unilateral	4		
Bilateral	1		

extremities was the only abnormality found in a substantial percentage of these children.

It should be apparent that for the group of children designated as learning disabled, the SNE has a high rate of "false negatives" and is not a reliable indicator of the presence of the condition. It is true that children with severe motor impairment (who indeed constitute a subset of the larger set of LD children) may have clearly defined abnormalities on the SNE. However, even if this examination does correctly identify them as "abnormal," it does not contribute much to the analysis of their learning problems. The abnormalities on the SNE are secondary to cortical spinal tract abnormalities and will predict difficulties in gross, fine, and/or graphomotor performance but will not explain why the children have difficulty reading.

SOFT SIGN AND OTHER EXAMINATIONS OF SUBTLE NEUROLOGIC DEFICITS

As interest in the LD child developed, the examinations began in the early 1960s to shift toward evaluations of signs of subtle (soft) neurological dysfunction. A number of descriptive studies (Clements, 1966; Kennard, 1961; Paine & Oppe, 1966; Touwen, Prechtl, & Heinz, 1970) focused on sensorimotor neurologic signs. Attempts at controlled comparisons of LD youngsters and normal youngsters have resulted in inconsistent findings. Several authors, in evaluating their results, observed that there is a decrease in the number of special neurologic signs in children with learning disabilities as they grow older (Peters, Romine, & Dykman, 1975) and that the incidence of these neurologic signs were minimal in the groups they examined (Werry, Minde, Guzman, Weiss, Dogan, & Hoy, 1972). Other authors found that the soft neurological signs they examined for did not distinguish between learning disabled and normal children (Adams, Kocsis, & Estes, 1974; Copple & Isom, 1968; Hart, Rennick, Klinge, & Schwartz, 1974). Hart et al. (1974)

concluded that the neurological examination was so weakly related to academic criteria that they could not support the common practice of having the physician be the only profes- sional to certify a child for placement in classes for the percep- tually handicapped.

The NIMH Physical and Neurological Examination for Soft Signs (PANESS) was developed as a method for rigorously defining soft signs in children involved in psychopharmacologi- cal research. Unfortunately, the battery did not discriminate between neurologically impaired children (hyperactives) and normal controls (Camp, Bialer, Sverd, & Winsberg, 1978; Werry & Aman, 1976).

Partly as a response to these methodological difficulties, the concept of minimal brain dysfunction has not always been happily accepted by neurologists and pediatricians (Gomez, 1967; Ingram, 1973; Schmitt, 1975). It is logical to ask why it is so difficult, in a group of children with unequivocal behav- ioral and learning deficits, to arrive at definable neurological deficits, whether they be "hard" or "soft." Why does the SNE or the soft sign examination not adequately differentiate LD children from normal peers? Why do these examinations not help in defining the nature of the learning deficit?

First, the SNE is set up to localize lesions; and the LD child may have "lesions," but these are subtle and different from the usually circumscribed lesions inflicted on the mature brain by trauma, tumor, or stroke. Lesions which occur early in the development of the brain differ in their diffuseness from lesions of the adult brain. The effects of hypothyroidism, for instance, which results in a decrease in the numbers of synaptic profiles that are formed, represents an entirely different patho- logical process from any which can affect the mature brain (Cragg, 1970). A lesion in one area of the immature brain can result in remote changes in structure, because one developing neural system can take over a territory which it would not inhabit because of damage to a system which would normally invade that area in the process of normal growth (Lynch,

Mosko, Parks & Cotman, 1973). Experimental studies in infant monkeys indicate that subcortical lesions result in profound behavioral effects, whereas cortical lesions inflicted at the same developmental stage have virtually no behavioral sequelae (Goldman & Rosvold, 1972).

Disturbances in morphogenesis of the nervous system are typically manifested in children. Agenesis of the corpus callosum, for instance, is often associated with a characteristic neuropsychological profile with related learning deficits (Reynolds & Jeeves, 1977). A case report by Galaburda & Kemper (1979) describes the cytoarchitectonic abnormalities in the brain of a 20 year old with developmental dyslexia. The patient's normal intelligence and profound difficulties learning to read had been established prior to his accidental death. The neuropathological findings revealed a wide left cerebral hemisphere, polymicrogyria in the left planum temporale as well as milder forms of cortical dysplasia in other areas. It is of interest that other male relatives were also dyslexic.

Another methodological issue has to do with the reproducibility of findings on the neurological examination. Segments of the SNE generally do not have very good replicability. In fact, the specific findings on a given patient may fluctuate widely from day to day, or even from the evening, when the patient is fatigued, to the next morning, when the patient is rested.

There is a large literature on observer errors in medicine (e.g., Oldham, 1968) and on the development of quantitative observations on the neurological examination (Potvin & Tourtellotte, 1975; Potvin, Tourtellotte, Henderson & Snyder, 1975). In clinical practice the SNE is best used to arrive at global judgments, which then provide a basis for decisions regarding the location of the lesion. There is likely to be a high degree of congruence between the decisions of different neurologists regarding the location of the lesion, although agreement on individual segments of the examinations may be poor.

Most of the soft sign examinations are derived from the SNE and suffer from the same methodological problems. What is worse, however, is that the soft sign examinations have generally been set up on a higgledy-piggledy basis, with little rationale for the choice of specific items. Thus, the ability of the SNE to localize lesions is lost (although the population of children one is examining often has lesions of a different type than are encountered in an adult population), and one is left with poorly replicable signs which may or may not distinguish the LD child from normal controls. Soft signs, like abnormalities on the SNE, will not explain why a child cannot read.

Another methodological problem relates to the fact that both hard and soft abnormalities are found in higher concentration in younger children and in retarded children than in older children or those of normal intelligence. Thus, unless the parameters of age and IQ are carefully defined, statistical differences will be blurred by too broad an age range and range of IQ (e.g., the 11-year-old retarded neurologically impaired child who may have as many soft signs as his five-year-old normal counterpart). Furthermore, even neurologically impaired children will lose abnormalities as they grow older, so that soft signs which satisfactorily discriminate between six year olds may not be present in 10 year olds. There are other implicit (and probably incorrect) assumptions underlying soft sign examinations—namely, that all LD children will have sensorimotor deficits and will have them throughout childhood. Although it is not unlikely that the majority of LD children will have some degree of motor dysfunction, some of them will be motorically normal and will have cognitive deficits that may not be picked up by the SNE. Therefore, an adequate test should also deal with a broad spectrum of cognitive processes.

A final reason why the soft sign examination lacks usefulness is that it does not take into consideration the individual child's coping strategies. The author has seen children with the same pattern of deficits who differ significantly in their awareness of their problems and their willingness to make compensations. Children who acutely sense their deficits and are overwhelmed by them may make no attempt whatsoever to cope and therefore perform at an even lower levels than their abilities would indicate. Children who deny their deficits or make no effort to monitor what they are doing will also perform poorly but for different reasons. Children who are aware of their deficits and have experienced enough success to have their coping style reinforced may perform at higher levels than their abilities would indicate. Also, the child's individual coping techniques should be observed. Problems with coping are indicated by the use of denial, projection, and self-deprecatory remarks, as well as by tears and depression. In the author's experience, these coping strategems may vary considerably with the specific tests being performed.

Not all workers in the field have been wedded to the concept of soft signs, and not all have equated the SNE with an adequate examination. Again, beginning in the early 1960s, investigators were linking learning deficits to cortical functions, to cortical association areas, and to the neurodevelopmental aspects of a child's maturation (Birch & Lefford, 1967; Boshes & Myklebust, 1964; Kinsbourne 1973a, 1973b; Myklebust, 1967; Rutter, Graham, & Yule, 1970). Several of these investigators have developed and objectified their own tests of neurological characteristics and of higher cortical functions that tend to differentiate the neurologically impaired from the normal child (see especially Birch & Lefford, 1967; Rutter et al., 1970).

The Halstead-Rietan battery (Reitan & Heineman, 1968) in many ways provides a solution to some of the methodological problems discussed above. The responses are quantifiable and replicable, and survey a range of neuropsychological facets. However, the equipment is expensive and not portable, and the test is time consuming, making its usefulness in routine clinical evaluations difficult. However, this type of battery clearly taps cortical function.

FEATURES OF A USEFUL EXAMINATION

We will now consider the features that are to be found in an examination of LD children which will provide the maximum clinical and research information.

1. The examination should be sufficiently easily learned so that it can be used by different examiners with good inter-observer reliability ratings. Endpoints should be clear, and quantitative observations should be used rather than qualitative judgments.

2. Normative data should exist so that it would be possible to compare a given child to peers of the same age and sex. Quantifiable data permit one to define the child's status in terms of standard deviation from the norm.

3. The examination should cover a wide behavioral and cognitive spectrum and should not be simply limited to sensorimotor items. It is clear that language processing deficits and subtle parietal lobe deficits may be of greater importance to a child's learning abilities than the sensorimotor deficits. Thus, the examination should include items related to receptive and expressive language, visual-spatial ability, praxis, and other parietal lobe abilities.

4. Academic performance should be assessed—reading (which may require an in-depth analysis), spelling, and arithmetic.

5. The examination should not be so lengthy or involve so much cumbersome equipment that it has to be administered in one place. It should be sufficiently portable so that field studies in schools could be conducted on specific populations of LD children and normal controls.

6. It should be sufficiently flexible so that if an area of deficit is noted, this can be explored in greater depth.

Thus, the examination described in the following section screens a wide spectrum of cognitive and neurological behaviors. If an area of deficit is noted, further evaluation of that specific area can be carried out in greater depth.

7. There should be opportunity to observe an individual child's style of handling deficits. Children's self-concepts and the success of their coping mechanisms are of tremendous importance in determining the final outcome. Obviously, these observations cannot be easily quantified and may not lend themselves to replicable research studies, but they are of great importance for the individual child.

8. The examination should also generate valid research data which are sufficiently replicable and quantifiable to be subjected to rigorous statistical analysis.

DESCRIPTION OF THE EXAMINATION

The following is presented not as a finished product but rather as an examination which the author has found useful. It consists of observations of the child, the SNE, and the extended neurological examination (ENE)[1] as outlined in Chart 4.3 and is subject to constant revision. It will be clear that the examination does not contain "new" tests but uses tests already developed for the assessment of children and adults. Most tests are standardized, but if not, we attempt to develop norms.

Physical Examination

The first segment of the examination consists of a physical examination in which special attention is paid to neurocutane-

[1]M. Denckla coined the term "extended examination" to denote an examination assessing more than the SNE.

Chart 4.3   Extended Neurological Examination

Hand-foot-eye preference	Academic
Praxis	Oldfield Naming
Fine motor battery	Receptive Language
Use of pencil	Peabody Picture Vocabulary
Human figure drawing	Auditory Reception (ITPA)
Right-left orientation	Auditory Association (ITPA)
Finger naming	Boston Aphasia Phrase Repetition
Language processing	Digit Span
Fluency, articulation,	Visual-spatial
grammar, running speech	Raven's Progressive Matrices
Picture description	Block Design
Color naming	
Graphomotor	
Bender Gestalt	
Beery	

ous lesions, "dysmorphic features," and asymmetries of the face, cranium, and extremities. Any other physical anomalies or defects are noted.

Behavioral Responses

Observations made throughout the test battery of the child's behavioral responses to different segments of the examination are recorded. It is here that one gains insight into the child's coping mechanisms and self-concept. Does the child work through most of the examination in a happy fashion only to withdraw when academic work is presented? Is the child a verbal, pleasantly related child who suddenly becomes hostile when asked to throw a ball? The child's level of hyperactivity and capacity to sustain attention are also noted.

Standard Neurological Examination

This is the SNE which follows the outline in Chart 4.1. The one addition is ball throwing, which is quantified to the extent of type of throws, and percentage of missed throws.

Extended Neurological Examination

HAND PREFERENCE. The assessment of hand preference consists of 10 pantomines ("Show me how you brush your hair, brush your teeth . . ."). Hand preference and how well the child is able to incorporate the utensil into the learned act are recorded. Children who gesture vaguely in the region of the mouth when asked to brush their teeth receive lower scores than children who squeeze out the toothpaste and meticulously brush the uppers and lowers. A praxis scoring system is currently being developed, and norms are still being defined (Voeller, unpublished). Kaplan (cited in Goodglass & Kaplan, 1972, p. 52) has observed that praxis develops around age eight.

FOOT AND EYE PREFERENCE. These preferences are recorded. It should be stated that the author does not imbue the concept of "mixed dominance" with any great pathological significance. However, if a child manifests unequivocal hand preference before one year of age, particularly if the hand preference is atypical for the family and if there are some focal neurological signs on the side of the nonpreferred hand, it is likely that the child has sustained unilateral cerebral injury.

FINE MOTOR BATTERY. This segment consists of three tests; two of finger dexterity, described and normed by M. Denckla (1973); the other, the Purdue Pegboard—adapted for children by Costa, Scarola & Rapin, 1964. Its usefulness in testing neurologically impaired children was established by Rapin, Tourck & Costa, 1966. It is clear that on the repetitive and sequential tests developed by Denckla, there is a distinct improvement between 8 and 10 years of age in both normal and neurologically impaired children. At 10 years of age, the Purdue Pegboard still discriminates between many neurologically impaired and control children, whereas fewer older neurologically impaired children perform poorly on the Denckla tests (Voeller & Denckla, in preparation). Inter-observer reliability ratings have been developed (Denckla, 1973), and the test is useful not only in the evaluation of the individual child but in terms of generating information for statistical analysis of groups of children. The use of the pencil is observed at this point in the test. The hand used, the manner in which the child holds the pencil, and the degree of effort involved in drawing, copying geometric forms, and writing words should be noted.

BODY IMAGE. The child is asked to draw a picture of a person, which is scored by Goodenough criteria (Goodenough, 1926). Additionally, the child's way of handling this task is noted, and the placement on the page is observed (Koppitz, 1968). It is the author's impression that some children with subtle hemiparesis will tend to draw one set of extremities smaller or larger than the other. Right-left discrimination on self and other is recorded (Ayres, 1972), and if the child appears to have deficits in praxis and body schema, the Imitation of Postures subtest from the Ayres series is used. The child is also asked to name the fingers. In the event that it becomes clear that the child has dyscalculia or significant right-left disorientation, the Kinsbourne finger identification test is administered (Kinsbourne & Warrington, 1962).

LANGUAGE PROCESSING. The child is asked to describe the picture in the *Mental Examiner's Handbook* (Wells & Ruesch, 1945, p. 185). We are currently in the process of developing norms for school-aged children in terms of how many details are noted, fluency, and length of phrase. Results obtained so far indicate that some children are quite capable of generating long, grammatically correct sentences but may be unable to relate the parts of the picture to the whole and resort to pointing out individual areas: "There are bushes . . . the father's mad . . . the boy is behind the wall." Other children will resort to terse, monosyllabic answers which suggest a fluency problem. The quality of speech is also noted: is it dysarthric, agrammatical? Are there neologisms or paraphrasia?

The next segment consists of the Color-Naming test from the *Mental Examiner's Handbook* (p. 153) which has been normed on school-age children.[2] Some dyslexic children take longer and make more errors than their normal peers. The Oldfield Naming Test (Oldfield & Wingfield, 1964) has also been normed on school-age children by M. Denckla[3] and has been modified for use in the pre-school and primary grades by Voeller (unpublished). Naming deficits often correlate with reading disability and in the preschool population are potent predictors of dyslexia.

Receptive language is assessed using the Illinois Test of Psycholinguistic Ability (ITPA) Auditory Reception subtest as well as the Auditory Association subtest (which obviously has an expressive component). The Peabody Picture Vocabulary Test (Dunn, 1965) is also used to assess receptive language (with visual reinforcement). A child's version of the Token Test, (De Renzi & Vignolo, 1962) for children who appear to have significant receptive language problems, is being developed. The Phrase Repetition Subtest and the Responsive Naming Test from the Boston Aphasia Scale are administered (Goodglass and Kaplan, 1972). Norms are being currently developed for Phrase Repetition in the school-age population. Digit span (forward and backward) is administered at the rate of 1 digit per second. Singing is also assessed.

VISUAL-SPATIAL PROCESSING.   The Raven's Progressive Matrices (Raven, 1956) is used to assess the child's ability to deal with visual-spatial material. This test is particularly useful because it is untimed and does not require a motoric response. Although it taps functions similar to the Wechsler Intelligence Scale for Children (WISC) Block Design and Object Assembly (Wechsler, 1949), it is an additional assessment of visual-spatial ability. Children who are distractible (and thus penalized by working against a stopwatch) and those who are having diffi-

[2]Personal communication from M. Denckla.
[3]Personal communication from M. Denckla.

culty with fine motor skills (and therefore fumble the blocks and puzzles) will not do well on the WISC subtests, but may perform adequately on the Raven. The WISC Block Design and Object Assembly subtest scores are assessed in this context.

CONSTRUCTIONAL. This task consists of copying the Bender Gestalt designs and/or Beery DVMI figures (Beery, 1967). In certain cases, one would wish to examine a child's handling of the WISC Block Design. The Seguin Formboard or the Marble Board can be utilized during this segment of the examination if further information is required.

ACADEMIC. Inasmuch as the referring complaint relates to the child's handling of academic material, it is appropriate to observe how the child reads. Several standard assessments of reading are being used. Most recently, the Woodcock Reading Mastery Test (Woodcock, 1973) is being used, because it allows for an analysis of components of reading. The Wide Range Achievement Test (WRAT) (Jastak & Jastak, 1965) is also administered, because it provides a rapid assessment of academic skills. In the event that a child has clear dyscalculia, more specific tests, such as the Key Math Test, (Connolly, Nachtman & Pritchett, 1976) can be administered.

As mentioned earlier, throughout the entire test the quantitative assessment is coupled with a qualitative assessment of the child's approach to specific tasks. The child's self-image and approach to compensating for deficits are noted.

The test battery takes about two hours. With an older, extremely cooperative child who requires no in-depth assessments, the test can be completed in less time. In younger children, or those who are hyperactive or have behavior problems, a longer period is required. Sometimes several sessions are needed. If a given cognitive area needs careful assessment, additional tests would obviously be administered. The neuropsychological segments of the test can be administered by a nonphysician with a background in learning disability or psychological testing. The battery is easily taught, and there is good inter-observer reliability after training is completed.

As was mentioned above, the test battery is subject to constant revision and will be altered as it becomes apparent that certain segments do not discriminate between the neurologically impaired and the normal child, or are redundant. It is possible that more adequate tests will be developed and will be used to replace existing sections of the test.

CASE EXAMPLES OF SPECIFIC CHILDREN

The following examples of children with learning disabilities are drawn from the author's case files. They illustrate some of the patterns of neurological impairment encountered in LD children. Pseudonyms are used to preserve anonymity.

Case Vignette #1. Learning disability and behavior problems in the context of a normal neurological examination

Betty, an eight-year-old girl, posed major problems for the school system because of unrelated bizarre behavior, nonstop talking, and very poor reading comprehension. The school system felt that since she achieved a third-grade reading level on the WRAT, she did not meet the legal criteria for classification as a learning disabled child. The school recommended regular class placement and encouraged the parents to seek psychiatric help. The past medical history was negative. The patient was on Ritalin when initially seen for "hyperactivity."

During the course of the examination, she talked continuously, and most of her observations were at best semirelevant. "Are boys supposed to be a doctor? Are you the boss? Why do you have a telephone?" SNE was entirely normal. Major deficits were noted in language areas. She spoke fluently with no dysarthria. In describing the standard picture, difficulty in organizing her observations was apparent: "Daddy's mad . . . the boy is hiding from him . . . and the girl isn't hiding . . ." Here, she was asked to tell more about the story: "Angry, there is a broken window . . ." On both the *Color-Naming Test* and the *Oldfield Naming Test* her performance fell 2 standard deviations beyond the mean for an eight year old. On the Phrase Repetition Subtest of the *Boston Aphasia Scale,* she could repeat only 50 percent of the predictable or unpredictable phrases. Our preliminary normative data indicate that the average eight year old can name at least 14 of the 16 phrases presented. On the Responsive Naming Test of the Boston Aphasia Scale, Betty had obvious difficulties. Latencies of response were long, and she did not always comprehend. When asked, "What color is coal?" she replied, "What is coal? Cold?" "No," said the examiner, "coal." "Coal? What do you mean?" Other performance results were: Auditory Reception (ITPA), 6 years 3 months: Raven's Progressive Matrices, 67th percentile; the Beery, 7 years 2 months; WISC-Revised (R), verbal scale IQ 69, performance IQ 87, full-scale IQ 76. The only areas that she handled well on the WISC-R were block design, scaled score (SS) 10; object assembly, SS 11; and picture arrangement, SS 9.

It was felt that Betty had a significant receptive language deficit, with milder expressive language problems. Nonverbal abilities seemed intact, if not above average. It was felt she was not truly hyperactive but rather became very agitated when she could not comprehend. Stopping the Ritalin did not result in any increase in activity or distractibility. She was entered into a small, structured classroom, staffed by teachers oriented to handling both behavior and learning problems. It was insisted that she ask for auditory feedback if she did not understand what was being said to her. She was not permitted to utter more than two unrelated sentences at a time.

On follow-up a year later, Betty was noticeable less anxious. Irrelevant verbalizations had diminished. She was sufficiently aware of her deficits to ask for repetition. When asked to hop on one foot, she turned to the examiner and said: "I don't understand, what did you say?" Interestingly enough, when the WISC-R was repeated at 9 years 11 months, the verbal IQ was 84, the performance IQ was 100, and the full-scale IQ was 90.

It should be obvious to the reader that Betty would have been considered "normal" on the SNE and would have manifested few if any soft signs. Her anxiety and nonstop talking had been interpreted as hyperactivity. The usual assessments would not have picked up the significant comprehension deficit. With appropriate educational input and behavioral therapy, she was able to improve her level of function significantly.

Case Vignette #2. Minimal left-sided signs in association with bizarre behavior and significant learning disability

Bobby, a nine-year-old boy, was brought unwillingly by his parents because the school felt they could not manage him. The child had been previously diagnosed as a "childhood schizophrenic" and had psychotherapy, which the parents did not perceive as helpful. He was described as "very immature." In the classroom, he was remote and uninvolved, and ruminated incessantly about Dracula. He often seemed "to be in a world of his own," frequently got lost in the school, and had little awareness of behavior appropriate to the situation. His reading, while poor, was much better than his mathematical ability. He could not tell time which often led him to anticipate events many hours before they were destined to occur.

Obstetrical history was unremarkable. He was a "sluggish," mildly hypothermic newborn. He did not start to walk unsupported until 17 months (about 96th percentile, according to the standards of Neligan and Prudham, 1969), said individual words at one year, but sentences did not appear until age three. He manifested a clear-cut right-hand preference before he was one year of age, suggesting possible right-hemisphere damage.

Throughout the examination, he talked in a low-pitched, nasal monotone with a peculiar robotlike intonation. His utterances could be described as semiappropriate social chitchat: "Cause I want to tell my Mom and Dad to you for something." The SNE revealed minimal left-sided signs and a slight left reflex preponderance. He performed at age level on the language battery, except that, while he could recite the days of the week correctly by rote, he could not answer such questions as, "What day comes after Tuesday?" He did poorly on the Raven's Progressive Matrices, on the Beery DVMI, on the Word Recognition of the WRAT, and on the Woodcock. The Key Math Test revealed major deficits in all areas except word problems. His fine motor as well as graphomotor skills were very poor, and he had extreme difficulty on both the figure drawings and the Bender Gestalt. Earlier intelligence testing had consistently placed him in the dull-normal to borderline levels. A repeat WISC at age nine placed him at a retarded level with particularly poor performances on block design, information, and arithmetic. His best scores were on similarities and picture arrangement.

It appeared that this boy had right-hemisphere involvement with some mild left-sided motor signs. His directional confusion, problems with arithmetic, time-telling, and poor performance on visual-spatial tasks were consistent with a right parietal deficit. His peculiar social inappropriateness and difficulties "reading" social situations seemed consistent with this diagnosis (Tucker, Watson and Heilman 1977). Although the SNE did reveal a minimal left hemiparesis, this did not by itself explain the learning and behavioral problems.

SUMMARY

In this chapter, we have discussed the usefulness of the SNE and the soft sign examination in the assessment of the LD child. Although an LD child may manifest abnormalities on these examinations, the examinations generally do not elucidate the nature of the learning deficit. The "extended" examination is a neuropsychological battery based on many different existing tests which survey a variety of cognitive functions. When coupled with the standard neurological assessment and interpreted in the light of what is known about higher cortical function in the human, the resulting information provides a basis for ascertaining the nature and extent of a child's learning problems as well as suggesting a basis for the development of an appropriate remedial program.

The test battery follows a "psychometric test" format with quantitative scores and enables one to compare the performance of a given child to that of the child's peers in a variety of areas. It is not necessary to deal with the external behavior only—one can rigorously assess the underlying deficits. For instances, both children described in the preceding case vignettes, had an "out-to-lunch" quality, but the reasons were quite different: the girl was hampered by a receptive language deficit; the boy manifested the behavioral concomitants of right parietal dysfunction.

The quantitative character of the battery also helps untangle complex clinical situations in which motivation and self-concept play a critical role. It has been pointed out that two children with the same pattern of deficits can perform quite differently because of motivational factors. On the other hand, one could do a child a great disservice if motivational factors were not the essential problem. For instance, one may enounter a 12 or 13 year old who is performing poorly in school, despite normal intelligence. The author has evaluated some children in this category who turn out to be neurologically intact and who are competent performers on the neuropsychological battery. It is entirely possible that they might have manifested definable problems if examined four or five years before, but they now lack the necessary academic skills and the motivation to acquire them. Other children, however, continue to manifest clear neurological signs and deviate significantly from the norm in their performance on certain segments of the language battery. It is obvious that the management of these two types of children will be quite different. The first child will likely respond to a vigorous program of remediation, with confidence-building, success-reinforcing experiences. Under certain circumstances, psychotherapy may be indicated. For the second type of child, remediation and the other measures will go only so far. The child is likely to require a protected academic environment, remediation over a long period of time, and possibly a different set of occupational goals.

It is also possible to use the test battery to compare children to themselves at various points in their academic careers. We have followed a number of children with annual evaluations through their academic careers. Most LD children who are poor performers on the fine motor battery at age six will be within 1.5 SD from the mean by the age of 10 years. However, while some children show gradual improvement, they fall increasingly behind their peers. The patterns of language deficits may also change with age. Periodic reassessment of these children is therefore important, since they may change for better or for worse with age.

Because the test battery taps a whole spectrum of cognitive functions, it is possible to avoid drawing conclusions based on a single test performance. For instance, there are several reasons why a child might perform poorly on the naming test. It may be due to an expressive aphasic process, a genuine word-finding problem, or a misperception of the object in question. It is only by observing the *pattern* of the performance on the language tests as well as the performance on the visual-spatial tests that the nature of the problem becomes apparent.

The test battery also provides information which lends itself to the acquisition of quantifiable data that can be subjected to statistical analysis. Inter-observer realibility ratings can be obtained. In general, subjective assessments are rarely required, since the information is based on quantitative observations. It should be obvious that much still needs to be done in expanding the norms to younger and older age groups and refining some of the tests. However, the battery does appear to be useful in the assessment of the LD child.

Acknowledgments

The author wishes to thank the editor, Ruth Ochroch, for unfailing energy and assistance, John Van Dyne for help in reworking difficult passages, Lois Hodgson for careful reading of the manuscript, Laura Smith for meticulous help in the preparation of the manuscript, Martha Denckla for many stimulating discussions, and John Kemph for the time and impetus.

REFERENCES

Adams, R. M., Kocsis, J. J., & Estes, R. E. Soft neurological signs in learning-disabled children and controls. *American Journal of Diseases of Children,* 1974, *128,* 614–618.

Ayres, A. J. *The Southern California Sensory Integration Test.* Los Angeles: Western Psychological Services, 1972.

Beery, K. E. *Developmental Test of Visual-Motor Integration.* Chicago: Follett Publishing Co., 1967.

Birch, H. G., & Lefford, A. *Visual differentiation, intersensory integration, and voluntary motor control.* Chicago: University of Chicago Press for the Society for Research in Child Development, 1967.

Boshes, B., & Myklebust, H. R. A neurological and behavioral study of children with learning disorders. *Neurology,* 1964, *14,* 7–12.

Camp, J. A., Bialer, I., Sverd, J., & Winsberg, B. G. Clinical usefulness of the NIMH physical and neurological examination for soft signs. *American Journal of Psychiatry,* 1978, *135,* 362–364.

Clements, S. *Minimal brain dysfunction in children* (NINDS No. 3, Public Health Service Publication No. 1415). Washington, D.C.: U.S. Government Printing Office, 1966.

Connolly, A. M., Nachtman, W. & Pritchett, E. M. *Key math, diagnostic arithmetic test.* 1976. Circle Pines, Minnesota, American Guidance Service.

Copple, P. J., & Isom, J. B. Soft signs and scholastic success. *Neurology,* 1968, *18,* 304.

Costa, L. D., Scarola, L. M., & Rapin, I. Purdue Pegboard scores for normal grammar school children. *Perceptual and Motor Skills,* 1964, *18,* 748.

Cragg, B. G. Synapses and membranous bodies in experimental hypothyroidism. *Brain Research,* 1970, *18,* 297–307.

Denckla, M. B. Development of speed in repetitive and successive finger-movements in normal children. *Developmental Medicine and Child Neurology,* 1973, *15,* 635–645.

De Renzi, E., and Vignolo, L. A. The token test: a sensitive test to detect receptive disturbances in aphasics. *Brain,* 1962, 85:665–678.

Dunn, L. M. *Peabody Picture Vocabulary Test.* Circle Pines, Minn.: American Guidance Service, Inc., 1965.

Galaburda, A. M. & Kemper, T. L. Cytoarchitectonic abnormalities in developmental dyslexia: A case study. *Annals of Neurology* 1979, *6*:94–100.

Goldman, P. S. & Rosvold, H. E. The effects of selective caudate lesions in infant and juvenile rhesus monkeys. *Brain Research,* 1972, 43:53–66.

Gomez, M. Minimal cerebral dysfunction (maximal neurologic confustion). *Clinical Pediatrics,* 1967, *6,* 589–591.

Goodenough, F. L. *Measurement of intelligence by drawings.* New York: Harcourt, Brace and World, 1926.

Goodglass, H., & Kaplan, E. *The assessment of aphasia and related disorders.* Philadelphia: Lea and Febiger, 1972.

Hart, Z., Rennick, P. M., Klinge, V., & Schwartz, M. L. A pediatric neurologist's contribution to evaluations of school underachievers. *American Journal of Diseases of Children,* 1974, *128,* 319–323.

Ingram, T. T. S. Soft signs. *Developmental Medicine and Child Neurology,* 1973, *15,* 527–529.

Jastak, J. F., & Jastak, S. R. *The Wide Range Achievement Test, manual of instructions.* Wilmington, Delaware: Guidance Associates, 1965.

Kennard, M. A. Value of equivocal signs in neurologic diagnosis. *Neurology,* 1961, *11,* 753–764.

Kinsbourne, M. Criteria for diagnosis: Minimal brain dysfunction as neurodevelopmental lag. *Annals New York Academy of Sciences,* 1973a, *265,* 268–273.

Kinsbourne, M. Diagnosis and treatment: School problems. *Pediatrics,* 1973b, *52,* 697–710.

Kinsbourne, M., & Hiscock, M. Cerebral lateralization and cognitive development. In J. S. Chall (Ed.), *Education and the brain* (Pt. 2 of 77th Yearbook of the National Society for the Study of Education). Chicago: University of Chicago Press, 1978.

Kinsbourne, M., & Warrington, E. K. A study of finger agnosia. *Brain,* 1962, *85,* 47–66.

Koppitz, E. M. *Psychological evaluation of children's human figure drawings.* New York: Grune and Stratton, 1968.

Lynch, G. S., Mosko, S., Parks, T., & Cotman, C. W. Relocation and hyperdevelopment of the dentate gyrus commissural system after entorhinal lesions in immature rats. *Brain Research,* 1973, *50,* 174–178.

Myklebust, H. R. Learning disabilities: Definition and overview. In H. R. Myklebust (Ed.), *Progress in learning disabilities* (Vol. 1). New York: Grune and Stratton, 1967.

Neligan, G., & Prudham, D. Norms for four standard developmental milestones by sex, social class, and place in family. *Developmental Medicine and Child Neurology,* 1969, *11,* 411–420.

Oldfield, R. C., & Wingfield, A. Response latencies in naming objects. *Quarterly Journal of Experimental Psychology,* 1964, *17,* 273–281.

Oldham, P. D. Observer error in medicine. *Proceedings of the Royal Society of Medicine,* 1968, *71,* 447–449.

Paine, R. S. & Oppe, T. E. *Neurological examination of children.* Spastics Society Medical Education and Information Unit in association with William Heinemann Medical Books Ltd. Suffolk, England: Lavenham Press, Ltd., 1966.

Peters, J. S., Romine, J. S., & Dykman, R. A. A special neurological examination of children with learning disabilities. *Developmental Medicine and Child Neurology,* 1975, *17,* 63–78.

Potvin, A. R., Tourtellotte, W. W., Henderson, W. G., & Snyder, D. N. Quantitative examination of neurological function: reliability and learning effects. *Archives of Physical Medicine & Rehabilitation,* 1975, 56:438–44.

Rapin, I., Tourk, L. M., & Costa, L. D. Evaluation of the Purdue Pegboard as a screening test for brain damage. *Developmental Medicine and Child Neurology,* 1966, *8,* 45–54.

Raven, J. C. *Colored Progressive Matrices.* London: H. K. Lewis & Co. Ltd., 1956.

Reitan, R. M., & Heineman, C. E. Interactions of neurological deficits and emotional disturbances in children with learning disorders: Methods for differential assessment. In H. R. Myklebust (Ed.), *Learning disorders.* Seattle, Washington: Special Child Publications, 1968.

Reynolds, D. McQ., & Jeeves, M. A. Further studies of tactile perception and motor coordination in agenesis of the Corpus Callosum. *Cortex,* 1977, *13,* 275–272.

Rutter, M., Graham, P., & Yule, W. *A neuropsychiatric study in childhood* (Vol. 35/36). Lavenham, Suffolk, England: Spastics International Medical Publications with the Lavenham Press Ltd., 1970.

Schmitt, B. D. The minimal brain dysfunction myth. *American Journal of Diseases of Children.* 1975, 129:1313–1318.

Touwen, B., Prechtl, C. L., & Heinz, F. R. *The neurological examination of the child with minor neraous dysfunction.* Lavenham, Suffolk, England: Spastics International Medical Publications with the Lavenham Press Ltd., 1970.

Tucker, D. M., Watson, R. T., & Heilman, K. M. Discrimination and evocation of affectively intoned speech in patients with right parietal disease. *Neurology,* 1977, *27,* 947–950.

Voeller, K., & Denckla, M. *Fine motor performance in neurologically impaired boys.* In preparation.

Wechsler, D. *Wechsler Intelligence Scale for Children.* New York: Psychological Corp., 1949.

Wells, F. L., & Ruesch, J. *Mental examiners' handbook.* New York: Psychological Corp., 1945.

Werry, J. S., & Aman, M. G. The reliability and diagnostic validity of the Physical and Neurological Examination for Soft Signs (PANESS). *Journal of Autism and Childhood Schizophrenia,* 1976, *6,* 253–263.

Werry, J. S., Minde, K., Guzman, A., Weiss, G., Dogan, K., & Hoy, E. Studies on the hyperactive child: Neurological status compared with neurotic and normal children. *American Journal of Orthopsychiatry,* 1972, *42,* 441–450.

Woodcock, R. W. *The Woodcock Reading Mastery Test.* Circle Pines, Minn.: American Guidance Service, Inc., 1973.

Chapter 5

MINIMAL BRAIN DYSFUNCTION
The Psychiatric Examination
Marilyn B. Benoit

Minimal brain dysfunction is a nonspecific disease entity which has stimulated much investigation and controversy among practitioners and researchers in the pediatric, psychiatric, neurological, psychological, and sociological fields. The term, however vague, does provide a frame of reference for professionals discussing the minimal brain dysfunction syndrome, and most of us agree that the term refers to a syndrome which has been identified in 4–10 percent of school-age (ages 5–11 years) children of average intelligence in the United States. The syndrome has variable expression and can include any combination of the following symptom complex: hyperactive, non-goal-oriented behavior; short attention span with high distractibility; poor impulse control; low frustration tolerance; clumsiness; specific learning disabilities; visual-perceptual motor problems; and soft neurological signs with or without electroencephalographic changes. Such a symptom complex no doubt warrants a multidisciplinary "attack" on the problem of minimal brain dysfunction. In spite of the differences of opinion which have emerged, our focusing on this disease entity has served the purpose of unifying and integrating efforts from the various disciplines to improve the quality of life for the people whom we all serve: the children.

The children suspected of having minimal brain dysfunction who are referred to a child psychiatrist tend to be a preselected subgroup whose difficulties are manifested behaviorally. When one considers that as high as 75 percent of minimal brain dysfunction can present with hyperactivity as a chief complaint, the child psychiatrist becomes significantly important in the treatment of this disorder. Both clinic and private practice records reveal that most referrals are initiated because of poor social and academic performance at school secondary to behavioral problems. Generally, the parents also report significant problems at home. The following is from an actual case report:

> John (fictitious name) is a six-year-old boy referred for a psychiatric evaluation. The chief complaint from the teacher reads, "John is very aggressive, hits, kicks, screams, is unfriendly, can do the work, but won't stick to it, moves from one task to another. Has poor sense of self. He is unable to remain seated or concentrate on his work very long and is easily distracted." Mother's remark at the evaluation was, "I feel frustrated and burdened because John is and always has been so difficult."

This example was cited because it is so very typical. By the time the psychiatric referral is made, other professionals have often been involved and the index of suspicion of minimal brain dysfunction is quite high. The child's disruptive classroom behavior has received the attention of the school psychologist, and often psychological testing has already been done. In the case of John, psychological testing revealed poor dexterity on fine motor tasks; he was highly distracted by noises and activity around him; and he was hyperactive. Also, it is not infrequent that these children have had speech, eyesight, and hearing tests which have ruled out any pathology in their sensory modalities. At this point, one might question why the services of a child psychiatrist might be needed when other professionals can detect minimal brain dysfunction. One might suppose that it could be to prescribe medication, because there is a significant percentage of children (33–50 percent) who respond well to psychostimulant medication and make a good adjustment at home and at school. However, the pediatrician is well able to undertake that responsibility. The child psychiatrist is in the unique position of being able to evaluate the child behaviorally, emotionally, and medically. It is therefore imperative that the child psychiatrist functions, not merely to confirm a diagnosis of minimal brain dysfunction, but to question the diagnosis in spite of the high index of suspicion. It is incumbent upon child psychiatrists, because of their medical training and responsibility, to make use of that indispensible medical tool, the differential diagnosis. The evaluation must include the medical, social, and personal history in order to provide a longitudinal view of the biological, psychological, and social development and functioning of the child. It is this history, combined with the direct observation of the child in the playroom, which is the cornerstone of a careful evaluation. Because the details of various aspects of the history are discussed elsewhere in this book, the playroom evaluation is the only segment which is treated at length here.

Playroom Evaluation

The playroom evaluation allows the child psychiatrist an opportunity to assess the child's functioning on a one-to-one basis only. This is an important variable to consider, because the chief complaint most often describes the child's behavior in a group setting. It is not surprising, therefore, that not too infrequently, the child psychiatrist sees very little (and sometimes none) of the hyperactive, highly distractible aggressive behavior described by the referring person. Such a discrepancy does not necessarily mean that the child does not have minimal brain dysfunction. What it does mean is that group settings are overstimulating for the particular child, and we could use the observational data to make specific recommendations for a treatment plan. (With such children medication should be tried only if environmental manipulation—that is, a more individualized program—fails or is impossible.)

The evaluation begins the very moment that the examiner sees the child in the waiting room. One must take a mental note of what the child does while waiting. How does the child interact with the parent(s)? Is the child challenging and provocative? Is the child seated, playing quietly, or "getting into things?" What is the parent(s) behavior like? Is the parent anxious, nagging, intrusive, or withdrawn? How does the child separate? It is important to introduce oneself and clarify what the child understands to be the reason for the evaluation.

When the child is "introduced" to the playroom, he/she should be allowed some unstructured time (approximately 10–15 minutes) to explore and play if he chooses to. Most children do enjoy exploring the playroom. It is the driven, purposeless quality with which the hyperactive, minimal brain dysfunction child approaches the task that is different from the exploration of the normal child.

In addition to evaluating the quantity and quality of the child's motor activity, the examiner needs to simultaneously assess the child's speech. Is he constantly asking questions? Does he wait for an answer before proceeding to the next question? The experience of being "bombarded" with "chatter" is not an unusual one with the hyperactive child; it can be reminiscent of being with a hypomanic adult. This verbally proficient child often tends to have an air of independence and attempts to control the interview situation. Apart from the volubility of speech, one must evaluate the logicality and the coherence of the speech.

The content of thought is also scrutinized. Themes of sadness, fear, and aggression may be elicited through play and storytelling. Such techniques as story completion or a game of making up stories, discussion of favorite television shows, drawings, puppet play, dollhouse play, cowboys and Indians, police and robbers, and exciting scene productions can be very revealing. Direct questioning about school, friends, and family may be anxiety provoking and therefore requires some tact and sensitivity as regards both the timing and the phrasing of such questions. Through one's interaction with and observation of the child, it should be possible to make some global assessment of intellectual functioning. Clues suggestive of organicity can be gleaned from observation of the child's gait; coordination; fine motor control (observe while drawing or writing his name); orientation to person, time, and place, and quality of reality testing.

Such a thorough evaluation often requires as many as three sessions to complete. The advantage of having at least two sessions is that the anxiety is generally less after an initial session, and the second session affords the examiner an opportunity to screen out any significant anxiety component in the child's behavior. In the case of six-year-old John, mentioned previously, the notes on the playroom behavior stated: "Concentration span was short, with frequent changes in activities without much continuity. While he played independently, he was interested in keeping a running dialogue, during which he did most of the talking. John appeared to be a whirlwind motorically. He was in constant motion, constantly changing toys and activities, finishing some, but often abandoning one project for another. There were several games concerned with going to war in which airplanes, small and large, were crashing into each other." In addition, psychiatric examination revealed that this child was working on oedipal issues and experiencing anxiety from conflicts related to those issues. His neurological examination was within normal limits except for fine motor coordination. The diagnosis was "constitutional hyperactivity." John was also thought to show poor self-esteem secondary to negative interactions with his peers and the adults around him. If John's interpersonal experiences are representative of children with constitutional hyperactivity as a manifestation of minimal brain dysfunction, we must provide some intervention to inter-rupt the negative vicious cycle that occurs.

The tasks of school-age children are the learning of aca-demic and social skills. They acquire these skills in their in-teraction at school, at home, and during play. At school the child's impulsivity, aggressivity, and failure to attend to tasks all interfere with learning, and he gets the feedback that he is a failure. Because the negative behaviors get punitive responses from the teacher (e.g. being removed from the classroom), the child soon becomes socially ostracized at school. There is no respite at home either. The parents become overwhelmed and are frustrated and angry with the child after various tactics fail to control the child's behavior. Apart from describing hyperac-tive, impulsive behavior, many parents describe these children as being angry, hostile, oppositional, negativistic, clinging, de-manding, and socially inept. The consensus is that these are generally unhappy children who, through no fault of their own, are constantly at odds with themselves and the world around them. Some of these children reveal concerns about being "crazy"; they are well aware that they are different (negatively so) from their peers.

The internal flooding that takes place because of their central nervous system dysfunction can cause an inner sense of disorganization that may account for the sense of "craziness." The absence of an inner sense of orderliness can seriously hand-icap a child whose sense of identity evolves from an increasing ability to experience mastery over the self and the environment. Can it be that bossy minimal brain dysfunction children, through their attempts to control others, are really making desperate attempts to establish external controls because their internal control processing system fails? Clumsy children who cannot get their bodies to respond as they would like simply cannot enjoy a feeling of mastery over the self. When these children learn that the brain controls the body, they fear that there is some serious insult to their central nervous system. Their bodies are seen as defective, and a feeling of inadequacy follows.

The unfortunate psychodynamic phenomenon that occurs is that the adults who interact with these children also begin to feel inadequate in their roles. The teacher usually conveys a feeling of impotence in dealing with the minimal brain dysfunction child, and the parent, who has even less emotional distance, too often feels like a "bad parent." An adult who becomes engaged in the "bad parent–bad child" or "bad teacher–bad child" dyad becomes angry, frustrated, and eventually ineffective. This further compounds the child's difficulties. An ineffective adult leaves the minimal brain dysfunction child feeling unprotected; he is left to himself to contend with the disorganization he feels from overstimulation, both internally and externally.

Because these children feel that they cannot depend on the caretaking adults in their environment, some assume an attitude of pseudoindependence. Already feeling defective and inadequate, these children defend against dependency feelings to avoid further vulnerability. Another outcome one might see is represented by the child who succumbs to passive, dependent, withdrawn behavior because of overwhelming frustration and impotence. It is evident, therefore, that the minimal brain dysfunction child, whose dysfunction goes unrecognized and untreated, can develop significant emotional difficulties secondary to his/her affliction. With our heightened awareness of the minimal brain dysfunction syndrome and our ability to identify minimal brain dysfunction children, we need to institute aggressive treatment measures to prevent the deleterious effects on the child's emotional, social, and academic functioning.

TREATMENT RECOMMENDATION

The treatment of the minimal brain dysfunction child has to be very carefully designed. It requires the same multidisciplinary approach that was necessary for the diagnostic evaluation. Any treatment must take into consideration the special education needs of the child (if learning disabilities are present), the behavioral and emotional problems present, and the child guidance needs of both the parents and the teacher. Environmental manipulation may suffice, for some children. Therefore, treatment may involve special placement for others; the institution of specific management techniques in the child's usual settings may be all that is required.

Further intervention with pharmacotherapy may be needed for some children. These children are in the subgroup of minimal brain dysfunction children who are hyperactive under any condition—at home, at school, at play, in stores, and even in the one-to-one interview in the psychiatrist's office. For these children a trial of stimulant medication would be recommended, with adjunctive use of behavioral techniques in management and psychotherapy where indicated. Though the use of drugs in the treatment of minimal brain dysfunction remains controversial, the psychostimulants are still the treatment of choice (Piepho, Gourley & Hill, 1977). It is important to emphasize, however, that other diagnostic possibilities must be considered before instituting any drug treatment. The psychostimulant drugs would be quite inappropriate for the child who presents with behaviors suggestive of minimal brain dysfunction, but who is really an anxious child whose anxiety fuels his "hyperactivity." Psychotherapy is the treatment of choice for such a child. Also, the psychotic or borderline child who has some stigmata of minimal brain dysfunction (and indeed is a minimal brain dysfunction child) is more appropriately treated with a major tranquilizer. It is also important to evaluate for the presence of a seizure disorder, in which case an anticonvulsant would be the drug of choice.

It is evident, therefore, that there can be no one treatment approach to the problem of minimal brain dysfunction. This attests to the complex nature of the illness itself. In the case of John, stimulant medication was used. He was treated with magnesium pemoline, 37.5 milligrams each morning (except weekends and vacation), with striking improvement in his behavior at home and at school. Transient insomnia and anorexia were reported. Adjunctively, he was seen in individual play therapy once weekly for nine months, and mother was also seen for child guidance. The therapist maintained contact with the schoolteacher who was also being seen around classroom management issues by a school consultant from the clinic. Another young boy who was seen at the same clinic for similar behaviors and who had identified specific learning disabilities, proved to be borderline psychotic. This youngster was removed from the regular classroom, placed in a therapeutic special education school, and treated with thioridazine, 150 milligrams each day at bedtime. He was also seen in individual psychotherapy twice weekly, while the mother was seen for child guidance work.

In both cases cited, the multidisciplinary team approach was essential to the proper management of the case. One cannot overemphasize the importance of such involvement. As the various disciplines continue their research efforts, we inevitably will gather more data that will assist us in identifying more specific subgroups within the category now under the umbrella of minimal brain dysfunction. As our diagnostic acumen improves, with the use of more discriminating criteria, we can hope to use more type-specific treatment regimens requiring the services of one, some, or all of the disciplines involved.

REFERENCE

Piepho, R. W., Gourley, D. R. & Hill, J. W. Minimal brain dysfunction—Current therapeutic concepts, *Journal of American Pharmaceutical Association,* 1977, *17* (8), 500–504.

BIBLIOGRAPHY

Bax, M. Who is hyperactive? *Developmental Medicine and Child Neurology,* 1978, *20* 277–278.
Eisenberg, L. Hyperkinesis revisited, *Pediatrics,* 1978, *61* 2, 319–320.

Keith, K. D., & Erickson, C. G. Minimal brain dysfunction—A note on behavioral research, *Clin. Pediatr* (Phila.), March 1978, *3*, 215–217.

Miller, J. S. Hyperactive children: A ten year study, *Pediatrics,* 1978, *61* 2, 217–222.

Millichap, G. J. Learning disabilities and related disorders—Facts and current issues, Chicago: Year Book Medical Publishers, Inc., 1977.

O'Leary, S. G., & Pelham, W. E. Behavior therapy and withdrawal of stimulant medication in hyperactive children, *Pediatrics,* 1978, *61* 2, 211–217.

Sandberg, S. T., Rutter, M., & Taylor, E. Hyperkinetic disorder in psychiatric clinic attenders. *Developmental Medicine and Child Neurology,* 1978, *20*, 279–299.

Wolraich, M. L. Stimulant drug therapy in hyperactive children: Research and clinical implications, *Pediatrics,* 1977, *60* 4, 512–517.

Chapter 6

PSYCHODIAGNOSTIC EVALUATION OF CHILDREN WITH MINIMAL BRAIN DYSFUNCTION

Leah Levinger
Ruth Ochroch

The special contribution of the psychologist, as a member of the diagnostic team, is the comprehensive evaluation and integration of various aspects of the child so that he or she becomes a whole child rather than an appendage to his or her pathology. This requires the critical evaluation of the child's performance, of the test results and their digestion, so that the final integrated summation reflects the clinical thinking of the psychologist. The psychologist must have an understanding of the syndrome, knowledge of the tests and their limitations, familiarity with developmental patterns, and empathy and acuteness as a trained observer. All this is necessary to comprehend the meaning to the child of the difficulties in coping, the child's enjoyment in his competence in unimpaired areas, and the resulting unique personality of the child.

The authors, as two experienced diagnosticians and each a trainer of more than 20 yearly classes of Ph.D. clinical psychology students, assert that it is the professional responsibility of the psychologist-diagnostician to digest the data from all the measures used and transform the data into a thoughtful clinical evaluation. They are opposed to a test-by-test description, which leaves the evaluation and integration of the test findings to the reader of the test report. An evaluation based upon each test or subtest does not yield a picture of the child's skills, impairments, and/or feelings, or of how the child perceives, thinks, learns, moves, or lives. Depending on the child, a low score may represent gross confusion, indecisiveness, paralyzing discouragement, inability to comprehend the task, or a capacity to solve the task but in an idiosyncratic and laborious way. Further, the child's ability to perform a function cannot be definitively grasped without reference to a whole series of tasks, which need to be drawn from a variety of tests.

There are many indications, from the test data and the child's behavior during the test contact, which, if taken out of context, might make just as good sense in a diagnosis of another syndrome. There are overlaps between the child with minimal brain dysfunction (MBD) and various other diagnostic groups, particularly the borderline psychotic child and the child with developmental lags (Adelman 1978, Gross & Wilson, 1964; Knobloch & Pasamanick, 1974; Millman, 1974; Rutter, 1978; Tarnopol, 1970; Wender, 1971). It is the patterning of difficulties that really designates the MBD child. Also, as the psychologist grows in his acquaintance with this syndrome and is sensitized toward very delicate minute differences within the test material and the behavior, he will find that, while certain elements could superficially appear interchangeable with other syndromes, the patterns are really unique.

The psychologist-diagnostician is aware that children develop at different rates and so, in evaluating a child, should attempt to differentiate between "maturational lags" and functional deficits (Ireton, Thwing, & Currier, 1975; Usprich, 1976). A maturational lag is a developmental delay in the appearance of certain competencies at the expected age, but competencies that the child will hopefully develop at a later age. A deficit is a failure in functioning that is here to stay, even though the individual may learn to compensate for the deficiency. Deficits may occur as isolated phenomena, such as tone deafness or color-blindness, or they may cluster into syndromes.

The nomenclatures used as to whether a child has perceptual deficits, neurological deficits, is learning disabled, is neurologically impaired, or is suffering from minimal brain dysfunction will depend on the professional making the diagnosis, the part of the country in which the child lives, what diagnostic titles the school system requires in order to provide specific help for the child, and what services the state and federal government will fund (Black, 1974; Grossman, 1978).

AREAS AND INSTRUMENTS OF EVALUATION

In recent years, test batteries have been designated as "psychoeducational" or "neuropsychological." The implications are that the purpose of the testing is different and therefore, beyond a "core" battery, will contain different tests. Such differentiations fail to address themselves to the concept that an individual's functioning reflects a pervasive interrelationship between *soma* and *psyche*. Further, in that the MBD syndrome is reflected in a variety of behavioral, functional, and learning difficulties, it is necessary to evaluate each major operational area. The details of each deficit are always re-evaluated by the re-education (remediation, retraining) specialist in each area. This is underscored, because the purpose of the psychological testing is to help plan for re-education in the appropriate areas and in the proper sequence.

Most of our tests are based upon visual, visual-motor, auditory, perceptual, and language processing tasks, and the child's performance on these tests thus reflects various aspects of neuromotor and central nervous system functioning. The deficits that appear as learning difficulties occur in the central and peripheral nervous systems (Black, 1976; Cruickshank, 1966, 1979; Denckla, 1973; Fuller, 1978; Golden & Anderson,

1979; Pollack, 1976; Rourke & Strang, 1978; Silver, 1971; Usprich, 1976). In order to get a rounded picture of the child's functioning, the psychologist must evaluate the child's coordination, control of motility, perceptual motor functioning, graphomotor skills, auditory functioning, speech and language, cognitive functioning, and personality. Further, judgments about the chronicity versus the newness or acuity of a disturbance in functioning will depend upon the psychological knowledge of development and on the degree and kind of anxiety about the difficulty, or the adaptation to it, shown by the child.

The test battery will vary depending upon the age of the child, the tests that are fashionable at the particular time, the relevance of the test to the particular child, and frankly, the psychologist's training and preference for using one test over another. There actually is no standard battery and, in a few years, the battery detailed here may very well be partially obsolete as new instruments are developed. The important consideration for a battery of tests is that the instruments complement each other, that they cross-check various areas of functioning, and that they be done in a minimum of time. Also, it is important to select tests which will duplicate as closely as possible tasks with which the child has to deal in everyday living and in school and that challenge and reward as well as frustrate and depress the child.

Psychological test batteries for children usually include figure drawings;[1] the Bender Gestalt; an individually-administered intelligence test (e.g., the Wechsler Intelligence Scale for Children Revised, the Stanford-Binet L-M); the Rorschach; and the Children's Apperception Test, original (animal) and human versions. There are a host of special tests that check specific areas in which deficits may appear. These special tests include the Benton Visual Retention Test, the Frostig Developmental Test, the Illinois Test of Psycholinguistic Ability, the

[1]Full titles and sources of the psychological tests discussed are listed in the appendix to this chapter.

McCarthy Scales, the Raven Matrices, the Slingerland, the Wepman Auditory Discrimination Test, and as many more as already mentioned. A series of diagnostic as well as evaluative educational tests for reading, arithmetic, spelling, and writing may be used, if indicated. They are for screening purposes, since the specifics of any learning disability will be individually evaluated by the specialist to whom a child is referred. Every testing situation must include a conscious, systematic evaluation of the child's approach to tasks and his capacity to cope with them, to relate to the examiner, and to control bodily movements.

Gross and Fine Motor Coordination

The area in which most psychologists are probably least trained and therefore neglect is the evaluation of the child's overall coordination: gross motor coordination, kinesthetic integration, sense of directionality, fine motor coordination, and control of motility. Some of these skills can be derived from acute general observation, and some must be tested with specific tasks (Denckla, 1973; Knobloch & Pasamanick, 1974; Rourke & Strang, 1978; Shaffer, 1979; Stone, 1979).

Gross motor coordination involves the evaluation of whether a child's gait is patterned, whether there are tandem movements and alternating arm swings. It also includes an evaluation of posture, stance, and smoothness of coordination in walking, skipping, running, hopping, and crossing the midline. The next area, kinesthesia, is related to the child's capacity to maintain an internal sense of balance and to his perpendicularity and ability to extend this to a sense of perpendicular alignment of external objects. It also has to do with the child's capacity to orient himself in space and to orient other objects in space equally (Shaffer, 1979). Next is directionality, which deals with left versus right orientation, in which the body midline is the divide. The sense of directionality also reflects the establishment of handedness and of lateral dominance (Flax, 1966; Suchoff, 1974).

Fine motor coordination is reflected in the maturity and deftness of grasp in handling pencils and small items; the differentiated, controlled use of fingers, and freedom from the Palmer reflex. Integration of these skills with visual abilities determines the capacity to print, write, and draw—the graphomotor skills (Pollack, 1976).

The next area is control of motility, which deals with the presence of hyper- versus hypoactivity, relative consistency of motility, and the child's general pace of moving and working. It is important to differentiate between children who are naturally active but who can control motility when it is appropriate, and those children who cannot (Cantwell, 1975; Rie, 1975; Safer & Allen, 1976; Werry, 1968).

Perceptual-Motor Functioning

In the perceptual-motor areas, the first line of inquiry is that of vision. Two visual functions, acuity and occular-motor coordination, are usually neglected by psychologists. First, it is important to determine the child's acuity of vision—the capacity to see fine details and lines clearly. It is important to observe whether the child's eyes become reddened, whether the child will rub his or her eyes, and whether or not the child will complain about blurring, double vision, or other difficulties. It is useful to observe the placement of the child's eyes in the head in terms of whether they are equidistant from the bridge of the nose and are approximately at the same horizontal level. Occular-motor coordination relates to whether or not the child can wink each eye separately and can track using his eyes alone without accompanying head movements. It further involves evaluations of whether the child's eyes, while tracking, move smoothly or jerkily or overshoot their focus. Difficulties in these functions are frequently reflected in the child's reading word by word or by the child's frequent loss of place or skipping of words in a line. It is also important to note whether the child's eyes converge evenly and whether there is blurring or doubling of vision at close or far range. These are, of course, at best crude screenings, and any suspicion of difficulties in these areas should be referred to the appropriate specialist (Allen, 1977; Getman, 1974; Optometric Extension Program, 1968).

The next areas, and these are far more familiar to most psychologists, have to do with the higher levels of visual perception. The child's sense of spatial organization should be checked to determine whether it is organized or whether it tends toward the chaotic. This can be gauged by the order of placement of the Bender Gestalt figures and the placement and sequence of the figure drawings. Next is spatial judgments and orientation, which are reflected in the sense of the shape, points of contact between figures, perpendicularity, and direction in which a figure faces. This can be assessed by an evaluation of the Bender Gestalt, the figure drawings, and the sequence of work on several subtests of the WISC-R. The next area, short-term visual memory, can be checked for by recall tests on the Bender Gestalt, the speed with which a child will learn digit symbols, the Benton Visual Retention Test, and the visual memory tests on the Illinois Test of Psycholinguistic Ability (ITPA), the Frostig, the Slingerland, The McCarthy Scales, and so on.

Another important area has to do with the reliability of internalized visual images or long-term visual memory. This relates to the intactness of the body image and early and/or usual visual imprintings as referent points. This is reflected on the tests by the figure drawings, the quick recognition of what is missing on the various picture completion tests, and the capacity to visualize the familiar object from the amorphous blot material on the Rorschach (Buck, 1966; DiLeo, 1973; Gesell, Ilg, & Bullis, 1949; Harris, 1963; Machover, 1949; Suchoff, 1974; Weinstein, 1961).

The final area of perceptual motor evaluation has to do with visual integration and synthesis. This refers to the capacity to solve space-form problems by visualization rather than by trial and error. This is reflected, for example, in the capacity to handle all two-dimensional space-form tasks and to anticipate the size of drawings relative to the space allowed (Bender, 1938, 1956; Suchoff, 1974).

The next major area involves graphomotor skills, the capacity to draw, print, and/or write. Observations are based on the quality of line, control of sizes, capacity to make lines meet and close, and control of perpendicularity, all as a reflection of the capacity to reproduce what is in the mind's eye.

Auditory, Speech and Language Functioning

Another major area is the auditory, in which acuity as well as the higher auditory perceptual processes should be evaluated. Auditory acuity refers to the ability to hear sounds and to distinguish between like sounds. The higher auditory perceptual functions relate to the sequencing of incoming sounds and the synthesis of sound, meaning, organization, and memory. Organization and sequencing reflect the capacity to order sounds into familiar units, to grasp the meaning of what is said, and, if necessary, to fill in units of sound not clearly heard on the basis of the sense that the flow of sound is making. This also includes a sense of rhythm. Memory has to do with the recall of immediate auditory stimulation and the retrieval of stored auditory information. Also, the capacity to recognize a tune or to reproduce a tune is a reflection of memory (Henderson, 1974; Pick & Pick, 1970). Special tests have been developed to check on all of these areas. However, some reading readiness tests, such as the Gates MacGinitie, and the Gray Oral Reading Test, yield information on sound differentiations and discriminations in younger children and can be used within the normal battery. The organization of sound into meaningful units and its corollaries can be gotten from a number of items on the WISC-R, the Wechsler Pre-School and Primary Scale of Intelligence (WPPSI), and the ITPA. If a child appears to have difficulty in grasping what is being said, it is important to distinguish whether one is dealing with difficulties in acuity of hearing, in organization and memory, or pseudoimpairments because of anxiety.

Another significant area for investigation is that of speech and language. On an observational basis, one must evaluate the clarity of speech and language, which has to do with pronunciation and enunciation. It is important here to observe the way a child's mouth and facial muscles move or fail to move as the child is attempting to speak. Organization of speech and language has to do with the level of spoken language and the capacity to sequence words to express thoughts and to associate names with objects and sound (Davis, 1970; Henderson, 1974; McGrady, 1968; McNeill, 1970; Osgood & Miron, 1963; Rawson, 1978). This information can be derived again from a variety of subtests on the various Wechsler tests, from the ITPA, and from the Stanford-Binet L-M. The diagnostician should also differentiate between when the child is responding to structured questions and when the child has to organize language spontaneously in order to respond.

General Intellectual Functioning

Intellectual functioning can only be evaluated in keeping with awareness of all the areas discussed above. Intelligence is now far more difficult to evaluate then when psychologists used to have faith that an IQ was a meaningful number. It is extremely difficult to evaluate the actual level of intellectual functioning of MBD children, because of the patchwork quilt arrangement of capacities and deficits. With MBD children, it is axiomatic that one may not, cannot, rely upon any single measure. The subtests of the various intellectual measures are frequently more reliable than any numerical IQ. The various subtests of a Wechsler, the ITPA, and form level ratings of the Rorschach responses may have to be combined to give some sense of the child's capacities. In addition, the psychologist must be sensitive to the child's general vocabulary and expressive level and to the child's grasp and comprehension of the task.

Still another area of investigation is the child's cognitive style, which may range from loose, vague, or impulsive to tightly controlled. One must be especially sensitive to the child's organization of thought and sequencing, whether verbal or nonverbal (Bryan, 1977; Gold, 1979). The use of Rorschach locations and order, the extent to which form is used in an integrated rather than a haphazard dimension, the coherency of stories on the various thematic tests, the order in which the Bender Gestalt and figure drawings were executed—all yield valuable information. Also of importance is the content of the cognitive activities—sophistication and richness of images versus mechanical, perserverative, simplistic, concrete, or literal ones. Again, one has to evaluate the vocabulary used, the content of the responses, and the associations triggered by these projective tools.

Disturbances in cognitive functioning affect the child's ability to test reality, to have an intact sense of the nature of reality and of reality boundaries. Indications of chaotic or fragmented thought processes would also indicate disturbance. Also important is the extent to which affect disorganizes or helps integrate cognitive functioning. This information is derived from the Wechslers, particularly the Picture Completions and Picture Arrangements subtests, the figure drawings, the Rorschach and the thematic picture tests.

Special attention should be paid to the child's verbal capacity. This transcends language skills in that it has to do with the child's capacity to do controlled, ordered verbal reasoning of both an abstract and an applied nature. This information is derived from the Wechslers, the ITPA, or any test of analogies. Also important is the child's social understanding (Bryan, 1977). The Wechslers and the various storytelling tests reveal the child's understanding of social implications of either auditory or visual stimuli and his capacity to grasp the essential meanings of the social situations and the relationships involved.

Academic Skills

Academic competence or proficiency is an area which the psychologist is a general practitioner and at best can do only crude screenings. Of relevance are measures of actual reading ability, computational skills and grasp of arithmetic problems, spelling, and knowledge of grammar. In an effort to save time, many psychologists rely on tests which actually do not yield appropriate or reliable information (Williamson, 1979). A reading test should involve actual physical reading over an extended period of time—a minimum of 10 minutes. Measures of comprehension, language study skills, new word attack skills, knowledge of phonics, and memory for the sound of words should be included. Any of the standardized silent reading tests which meet these requirements can be used. In addition, oral reading tests or tests which have subtests in which the child does oral reading and then recalls the material should also be used.

Arithmetic skills should be checked for oral problem solving as well as written computations. If a child has difficulty with reading, it makes little sense to conduct an involved arithmetic test in which there is much material to be read and deciphered. Many standardized arithmetic tests will do for this measure, in that it is more important to determine the skills that have been acquired than the particular grade level, since curricula vary and different skills may be taught in different grades.

Simple tests of spelling or syllabication will also yield information as to the child's capacity to distinguish, remember, and integrate letter-sound combinations. And if time permits, a test for the child's sense of the English language appropriate at his or her age is also helpful. This can be evaluated from the ITPA as well as from standardized tests relating to grammar and language usage. If there is not enough time for a test, the psychologist should at least listen to the way in which the child uses the English language.

The child's functioning on all of the tests must be evaluated in the light of the child's cultural and economic background. If the family is bilingual, if an ethnic form of English is spoken in the home, or if the parents are functionally illiterate, then the psychologist must evaluate how much of the child's difficulties reflect lack of opportunity alone or to what extent they also represent deficits for which the child will need specialized kinds of help (Alley, Solomons, & Opitz, 1971; Kealy & McLeon, 1976; Sapirstein, Bopp, & Bak, 1978).

Personality

Children with a chronic neurophysical difficulty also develop secondary, reactive personality disturbances. These disturbances then interact with the primary difficulty, often exacerbating it at times of emotional stress. Such disturbances include psychotic or psychoticlike reactions, near-chronic impulsivity, or rigid compulsivity—or violent vacillations between the impulsive and the compulsive or from open expression of inadequacy and helplessness to blandness or defensive grandiosity. The form these secondary disturbances take, and how pervasive they are throughout the total personality, will reflect many elements, such as the family's support of the child, the role of school as either a chronically demeaning or facilitating experience, and the presence of compensatory personal strengths (Berlin, 1974; Rutter, 1978; Silver, 1958; Tarnopol, 1970).

It is a truism that personality is not a set quality established at birth but manifests itself in different ways as the child grows and copes with various life experiences. For example, denial, so common a defense in young "normal" children, diminishes in its frequency as children reach ages six and up, but denial may remain a large component in the personality structure of MBD children and even become stronger as they reach school age. Confronting tasks beyond their capabilities, which they know are expected for adult approval and social status among peers, makes denial the only tolerable way of coping with school. Meanwhile, as these children grow older, they develop certain compensatory devices, including overcompliance, distractibility, rationalization, and occasionally projection. A frequent compensatory device for older children is hypervigilance; they may become intent on discovering "tricks" in the expectancies of others and also develop hypervigilance of a self-monitoring type, so that their disabilities will not be "found out." Yet many MBD children also retain a quality of naivete and helpless dependence upon the adult (Bender, 1956; Silver 1958). The MBD child frequently needs rigid mental sets in order to make sense of the world and will use undeviating ways of categorizing relationships as well as knowledge. The contradiction between fear of his inadequacies being unmasked and a need to throw himself at the adult's mercy and demand support and succorance is often at the crux of the child's conflicts and the adult's bewilderment.

In investigating where the emphasis lies in defense and compensation patterning, the context of the total personality, the degree of impairment, and the level of general intelligence have to be considered. The brighter children may be better aware of their patterns of shortcomings and strengths. The more limited child may simply suffer with a global sense of not meeting expectations. But bewilderment at the unpredictability of life is never entirely absent from even the keenest child's awareness.

Any study of abilities and disabilities must include the way the child himself feels about them, about himself in general, and about what he perceives to be the expectations and attitudes of the world around him. Suspicion need not emerge, cookbook style, in eyes and ears emphasized in drawings or on the Rorschach. It may be expressed by efforts to control the situation and a search for the "hidden code" to understand a task. If these attempts at mastery are blocked, the child may feel open bewilderment and experience a "catastrophic reaction" in the form of temper tantrums, crying, and the like (Goldstein, 1939; Shaffer, 1979; Silver, 1958).

A first glance at the diagnostic test material of many of the MBD children seems to reveal deficient imagination. The thematic stories may be banal to the point of dullness, concerned with routines or ordinary daily life, and lacking in plot or adventure. With some children, this reflects the innate difficulty of a task where they are linguistically or cognitively hampered. Others, however, can be quite fluent on different kinds of verbal tasks, such as defining words; the flat, dull story aids the child in achieving a sense of order through repetitive routines in an often bewildering world. The older MBD child becomes increasingly aware of and frightened of his impulsivity. He learns that he cannot modulate it easily or let a little out at a time. Thus, when a task invites the temptation to deal with feelings, he takes an all-or-nothing attitude and opts for nothing in order to keep out of trouble. Often on the Rorschach there may be more overt impulsive expressions against his will. These have a torpid, disassociated quality, as if he does not feel responsible for them.

How the child feels about his own body emerges not from any single instrument but from a full battery of psychological tests. A sense of fragmentation, imbalance, or uncertainty may be revealed in the drawings of the human figure. In the Rorschach, bits of the body may never quite join, except in a stilted, forced manner. This further reveals the child's inability to experience his functioning as a psychological-neurological-physiological being, possessing unity and coherency. Feelings of fragility of the body and vulnerability to damage are frequent. In physically normal children, these feelings might reveal neurotic guilt, expectancy of punishment as retaliation for hostile thoughts, or a similar psychological meaning. But for the MBD child, such feelings must be taken literally. The MBD child's sense of his body as fragile may be projected upon the world at large. The most seemingly neutral task in the psychological test battery may be used as a vehicle to express this sense of vulnerability or the unpredictability of the world around him.

A full personality study also reveals the gratification, delight, and power a child's skills and curiosity bring him. The behavior of the child throughout the test battery gives many, many useful cues about his receptivity toward educational and therapeutic methods. Does he limply collapse at challenges? Does he repeatedly respond with a sense of helplessness and despair? Or is he able to enjoy praise and external concrete evidence of success? Is he able to separate his areas of inferiority and ineptness? Does he have some sense of a potential within himself, so that mastery of one task is seen as leading to another success?

TESTING FOR THE HIDDEN POTENTIAL

With MBD children, it is very easy to discover what they *cannot* do. But the responsibility of the true clinician is to find out, in addition, what the child may become. Impairments do exist, and a frank recognition of them is the first step in helping the child alter impairments or find tolerable ways of living with them. The child needs to find a baseline of successful functioning and to become conscious of succeeding instead of failing.

Practically all of the tests within the battery, if approached differently, can be used to reveal what the child could do under more optimal conditions. First, the MBD child's typically short attention span makes two or three sessions markedly preferable to only one. Next, drawings can be repeated and varied. Sometimes, at a second session, when anxiety is less, a repetition will show considerably better motor control and perceptual organization. A shift from the standard no. 2 pencil to a crayon and then to a large magic marker, or altering the size of paper to a very large drawing sheet, may make for a greater ease in a child's expressing himself. For the MBD child with difficulty in creating an image within his own mind and then depicting it, an excellent supplement to the usual drawing task is the Stanford-Binet Incomplete Man, Year 5, or its expanded version by

Ilg and Ames. The support of a partially done picture, particularly if it is combined with use of a magic marker rather than a pencil, may produce results a good two or even three years above the level at which the child originally seemed able to function in drawing the human body.

Perseveration is common among MBD children. On a second try, this may be cut through, for example, by telling the child after the Rorschach, "Let's take another look at those cards; but this time, try as hard as you can to see something different. *No*—this time, tell *whatever else* you see."

While rigorously employing standard timing to get scores, one may treat many tests as power tests, thus obtaining two scores: the minimum scores with strict timing and then the potential score when time is ignored. The latter may be markedly higher, raised from, for example, the defective level to the low average level. In mental arithmetic, where many children with school failures are at first so paralyzed by fear they cannot even hear the question, this approach is of great value. Also, the mental arithmetic can be followed by repeating the same problem in written form. On standard achievement tests, the key gives either right or wrong answers and no partial successes. However, many children with a capacity to understand the task and the process may make only marginal errors, such as failing to carry a digit or omitting a decimal point. In spelling, there is a difference between words that are technically wrong but intelligible, recognizable, and usually overly phonetic, and words that have no resemblance to the stimuli word. In assessing responses, it is useful to distinguish between these differing levels of appropriateness.

Also, changing the test level can bring quite startling results. When a child is working with a task within his interest level and craftsmanship, his pride in his result will bode well for his benefiting from remedial help. With other children, while the mood may improve considerably with an easier task, impaired functioning may be just as evident.

Appendix: Psychological Tests Cited in Chapter 6

Author(s)	Name of Test	Publisher
Bellak, L.	Children's Apperception Test (CAT) and Children's Apperception Test-Human (CAT-H)	New York: Psychological Corporation
Bender, L.	Bender Visual-Motor Gestalt Test	New York: American Orthopsychiatric Association or Psychological Corporation
Benton, A.	Visual Retention Test	New York: Psychological Corporation
Buck, J. N.	The House-Tree-Person Technique	Los Angeles: Western Psychological Service
Durrell, D. D.	Durrell Analysis of Reading Difficulty	New York: Harcourt, Brace and Jovanovich, Inc.
Frostig, M., Lefever, W. & Whittlesey, J.	Marianne Frostig Developmental Test of Visual Perception	Palo Alto: Consulting Psychologists Press
Gates, A. I., & MacGinitie W. H.	Reading Tests	New York: Teachers College Press
Gray, W. S.	Gray Oral Reading Tests	New York: Bobbs-Merrill Co., Inc.
Kelly, T., Madden, R., Gardner, E. F., & Rudman, H. C.	Stanford Achievement Tests	New York: Harcourt, Brace and Jovanovich, Inc.

Appendix: Psychological Tests Cited in Chapter 6 (continued)

Author(s)	Name of Test	Publisher
Kirk, S. A., McCarthy, J. J., & Kirk, W.	Illinois Test of Psycholinguistic Ability	Urbana: University of Illinois Press
McCarthy, D.	McCarthy Scales of Children's Abilities	New York: Psychological Corporation
Murray, H. A.	Thematic Apperception Test (TAT)	New York: Psychological Corporation
Raven, J. C.	Raven Progressive Matrices	New York: Psychological Corporation
Rorschach, H.	Rorschach Psychodiagnostic Plates	New York: Psychological Corporation
Slingerland, B. H.	Screening Tests for Identifying Children with Specific Language Disability	Cambridge, Mass.: Educators Publishing Service, Inc.
Terman, L. M., & Merrill, M.	Stanford-Binet Intelligence Scale L-M	New York: Houghton Mifflin
Wechsler, D.	Wechsler Intelligence Scale for Children Revised (WISC-R)	
Wechsler, D.	Wechsler Pre-School and Primary Scale of Intelligence (WPPSI)	New York: Psychological Corporation
Wepman, J.	Auditory Discrimination Test	Los Angeles: Western Psychological Services

SUMMARY

The purpose of all testing is basically to highlight the child's adequacies and proficiencies in a wide range of areas, to determine what kinds of specialized help, remedial or therapeutic, the child needs and to help establish some order of priorities so that neither the child nor the family is so overwhelmed that nothing will be accomplished. The appropriate approach to diagnostic testing of children with MBD is to evaluate not only what the child cannot do but what he *can* do, what he is like and what he may become.

REFERENCES

Adelman, H. S. Diagnostic classification of learning problems: Some data. *American Journal of Orthopsychiatry,* 1978, *48*(4), 717–726.

Allen, M. J. The role of vision in learning disorders. *Journal of Learning Disabilities,* 1977, *10*(7), 411–415.

Bender, L. *A visual motor gestalt test and its clinical use* (Research Monograph No. 3). New York: American Orthopsychiatric Association, 1938.

Bender, L. *Psychopathology of children with organic brain disorders.* Springfield, Illinois: Charles C. Thomas, 1956.

Berlin, I. N. Minimal brain dysfunction: Management of family distress. *Journal of the American Medical Association,* 1974, *229*(11), 1454–1456.

Black, W. F. Cognitive, academic, and behavioral findings in children with suspected and documented neurological dysfunction. *Journal of Learning Disabilities,* 1976, *9*(3), 182–187.

Bryan, T. H. Learning disabled children's comprehension of nonverbal communication. *Journal of Learning Disabilities,* 1977, *10*(8), 501–506.

Buck, J. N. *The house-tree-person technique.* Los Angeles: Western Psychological Service, 1966.

Cantwell, D. P. *The hyperactive child: Diagnosis, management, current research.* New York: Spectrum Publications, 1975.

Cruickshank, W. *The brain-injured child in home, school and community.* Syracuse: Syracuse University Press, 1966.

Cruickshank, W. Learning disabilities: Perceptual or other? *Association for Children with Learning Disabilities Newsbriefs,* 1979, No. 125, 7–10.

Davis, B. J. Differential language behavior patterns and diagnostic evaluation. *Journal of Learning Disabilities,* 1970, *3*(5), 264–275.

Denckla, M. B. Research needs in learning disabilities: A neurologist's point of view. *Journal of Learning Disabilities,* 1973, *6*(7), 441–450.

Di Leo, J. H. *Children's drawings as diagnostic aids.* New York: Brunner/-Mazel, 1973.

Flax, N. The clinical significance of dominance. *American Journal of Optometry,* 1966, Monograph 347.

Fuller, P. Attention and the EEG alpha rhythm in learning disabled children. *Journal of Learning Disabilities,* 1978, *11*(5), 303–312.

Gesell, A., Ilg, F. L., & Bullis, G. E. *Vision: Its development in infant and child.* New York: Paul B. Hober, Inc., 1949.

Getman, G. N. *How to develop your child's intelligence* (8th ed.). Wayne, Pa.: Research Publications, 1974.

Gold, P. Suspected neurological impairment (SNI) and cognitive abilities: A longitudinal study of selected skills and predictive accuracy. *Journal of Clinical Child Psychology,* 1979, *8*(1), 35–38.

Golden, C. & Anderson, S. *Learning disabilities and brain dysfunction.* Springfield, Ill.: Charles C. Thomas, 1979.

Goldstein, K. *The Organism.* New York: American Book Co., 1939.

Gross, M. D. & Wilson, W. C. Behavior disorders of children with cerebral dysrhythmias. *Archives of General Psychiatry,* 1964, *2,* 610–619.

Harris, D. B. *Children's drawings as measures of intellectual maturity.* New York: Harcourt, Brace and World, 1963.

Henderson, F. *Disability in childhood and youth.* New York: Oxford University Press, 1974.

Ilg, F. & Ames, L. *School Readiness.* New York: Harper & Row, 1965.

Ireton, H., Thwing, E. & Currier, S. K. Minnesota child development inventory - identification of children with developmental disorders. *Pediatric Psychology,* 1975, *3*(4), 15–19.

Knobloch, H. & Pasamanick, B. (Eds.), *Gesell and Amatruda's developmental diagnosis: The evaluation and management of normal and abnormal neuropsychologic development in infancy and early childhood* (3rd ed.). New York: Harper & Row, 1974.

Machover, K. *Personality projection in the drawings of the human figure.* Springfield, Ill.: Charles C. Thomas, 1949.

Millman, H. L. Psychoneurological learning and behavior problems: The importance of treatment considerations. *Journal of Clinical Child Psychiatry,* 1974, *3*(1), 26–30.

McGrady, H. J. Language pathology and learning disabilities. In H. R. Myklebust (Ed.), *Progress in learning disabilities* (Vol. 1). New York: Grune and Stratton, 1968.

McNeill, D. The development of language. In P. H. Jussen (Ed.), *Carmichael's manual of child psychology.* New York: John Wiley, 1970.

Optometric Extension Program Foundation Inc. Section on Children's Vision Care and Guidance. *Educator's guide to classroom vision problems.* Duncan, Oklahoma, 1968.

Osgood, C. E. & Miron, M. S. (Eds.) *Approaches to the study of aphasia.* Urbana: University of Illinois Press, 1963.

Pick, H. L. & Pick, A. D. Sensory and perceptual development. In P. H. Mussen (Ed.), *Carmichael's manual of child psychology.* New York: John Wiley, 1970, 773–848.

Pollack, C. Neuropsychological aspects of reading and writing. *Bulletin of the Orton Society,* 1976, *26,* 19–33.

Rawson, M. B. Dyslexia and learning disabilities: Their relationship. *Bulletin of the Orton Society,* 1978, *28,* 43–60.

Rie, H. E. Hyperactivity in children. *American Journal of Diseases of Children,* 1975, *130* 738–789.

Rourke, B. P. & Strang, J. D. Neuropsychological significance of variations in patterns of academic performance: Motor, psychomotor and tactile-perceptual abilities. *Journal of Pediatric Psychology,* 1978, 3(2), 62–66.

Rutter, M. Brain damage syndromes in childhood: Concepts and findings. In C. Chess & A. Thomas (Eds.), *Annual progress in child psychiatry and child development 1978.* New York: Brunner/Mazel, 1978.

Safer, D. J. & Allen, R. P. *Hyperactive children: Diagnosis and management.* Baltimore: University Park Press, 1976.

Shaffer, M. Primal terror: A perspective of vestibular dysfunction. *Journal of Learning Disabilities,* 1979, *12*(2), 89–92.

Silver, A. A. Behavioral syndromes associated with brain damage in children. *Pediatric Clinics of North America,* 1958, Aug., 687–698.

Silver, L. B. Familial patterns in children with neurologically-based learning disabilities. *Journal of Learning Disabilities,* 1971, *4*(7), 349–358.

Stone, N. W. & Levin, H. S. Neuropsychological testing of developmentally delayed young children: Problems and progress. *Journal of Learning Disabilities,* 1979, *2*(4), 271–274.

Suchoff, I. B. *Visual-spatial development in the child: An optometric theoretical and clinical approach.* New York: State College of Optometry, State University of New York, 1974.

Tarnopol, L. Delinquency and minimal brain dysfunction. *Journal of Learning Disabilities,* 1970, *3*(4), 200–208.

Usprich, C. The study of dyslexia: Two nascent trends and a neuropsychological model. *Bulletin of the Orton Society,* 1976, *26,* 34–48.

Weinstein, M. A rationale of vision and visual behavior. *Journal of the American Optometric Association,* 1961, *38* (12), 1030.

Wender, P. H. *Minimal brain dysfunction in children.* New York: John Wiley & Sons, 1971.

Werry, J. S. Studies on the hyperactive child: An empirical analysis of the minimal brain dysfunction syndrome. *Archives of General Psychiatry,* 1968, *19,* 9–16.

Williamson, W. The concurrent validity of the 1965 Wide Range Achievement Test with neurologically impaired and emotionally handicapped pupils. *Journal of Learning Disabilities,* 1979, *12*(3), 201–202.

BIBLIOGRAPHY

Ames, L. B., Metraux, R. W., & Walker, R. N. *Adolescent Rorschach responses, developmental trends from ten to sixteen years.* New York: Brunner/Mazel, 1971.

Ames, L. B., Metraux, R. W., Rodell, J. L. & Walker, R. N. *Child Rorschach responses, developmental trends from two to ten years.* New York: Brunner/Mazel, 1974.

Bellak, L. *The Thematic Apperception Test and the Children's Apperception Test in clinical use* (2nd Ed.). New York: Grune and Stratton, 1960.

Boyd, L. & Randle, K. Factor analysis of the Frostig Developmental Test of Visual Perception. *Journal of Learning Disabilities,* 1970, *3*(5), 253–255.

Coles, G. S. The learning-disabilities test battery: Empirical and social issues. *Harvard Educational Review,* 1978, 48(3), 313–340.

Ford, M. *The application of the Rorschach Test to young children. Minneapolis: University of Minnesota Press, 1946.*

Gaddes, W. H. The neuropsychology of reading disorders. *Journal of Learning Disabilities,* 1978, *11*(9) 571–575, (10) 639–646.

Goh, D. S., & Youngquist, J. A comparison of the McCarthy Scales of Children's Abilities and the WISC-R. *Journal of Learning Disabilities,* 1979, 12(3), 344–347.

Goodenough, F. L. *Measurement of intelligence by drawing.* Yonkers, New York: World Book Co., 1926.

Gunderson, B. V. Diagnosis of learning disabilities—The team approach. *Journal of Learning Disabilities,* 1974, 4(2), 107–113.

Halpern, F. Child case study: A troubled eight year old. In E. F. Hammer (Ed.), *The clinical application of projective drawings.* Springfield, Ill.: Charles C. Thomas, 1958.

Hutt, M. L. *The Hutt adaptation of the Bender-Gestalt Test* (3rd ed.) New York: Grune and Stratton, 1977.

Kaufman, A. S. & Kaufman, N. L. Research on the McCarthy Scales and its implications for assessment. *Journal of Learning Disabilities,* 1977, *10* (5), 284–291.

Koppitz, E. M. *The Bender Gestalt Test for young children.* New York: Grune and Stratton, 1963 (1), 1975 (2).

Koppitz, E. M. *Psychological evaluation of children's human figure drawings.* New York: Grune and Stratton, 1967.

McIntosh, W. J. The use of a Wechsler Subtest Ratio as an index of brain damage in children. *Journal of Learning Disabilities,* 1974, *7*(3), 162–164.

Miller, M., Stoneburner, R., & Brecht, R. WISC subtest patterns as discriminators of perceptual disability. *Journal of Learning Disabilities,* 1978, *11*(7), 449–452.

Myklebust, H. R. (Ed.) *Progress in learning disabilities* (Vol. 1). New York: Grune and Stratton, 1968.

Paraskevopoulos, J. N. & Kirk, S. P. *The development and psychometric characteristics of the Revised Illinois Test of Psycholinguistic Abilities.* Urbana: University of Illinois Press, 1969.

Sapir, S. G. & Wilson, B. *A professional's guide to working with the learning-disabled child.* New York: Brunner/Mazel, 1978.

Tierney, R. J. & Ames, W. S. An examination of the diagnostic claims of the Revised Illinois Test of Psycholinguistic Abilities. *Journal of Learning Disabilities,* 1978, 11(9), 586–589.

Part III

INTERVENTIONS

Chapter 7

THE "CASE" FOR THE CASE MANAGER
Ruth Ochroch

A gap exists in the network of both evaluation and intervention services needed by children with minimal brain dysfunction and their families. This gap is the absence of one central person to work with the child and family in guiding them through the maze of evaluations. This work entails helping the child and family understand the child's areas of difficulties and competencies and set up some order of priorities for the various kinds of aid needed, referral to the resources, and long-term support and consultation for the family.

The idea of a "case manager" was presented at the institute on working with children with minimal brain dysfunction at the 1975 Annual Conference of the American Orthopsychiatric Association and at a panel on working with families of such children at the 1978 Annual Conference of the New York Association for the Learning Disabled. A review of the literature over the past 10 years fails to yield any discussion of this concept, even though there is a growing recognition of the parents' need for such long-term, sustained support. Parents can and frequently do manage to deal with their children's crises and disturbances if they are not too severe or too long-drawn. However, the huge majority of parents cannot by themselves cope with the child who has a diagnosis of hyperactivity, learning disabilities, or minimal brain dysfunction, because the child usually presents a myriad of problems and difficulties in maturation, social activities, educational achievement, and physical and/or emotional areas. Thus, the family usually needs one central person who is familiar with all of the information about the child and the implications of this for the child and the parents. This central person can be a member of any of the child health or mental health disciplines and may or may not additionally function with the child and family in his or her own discipline. The case manager can be the first professional to whom the family has come for help—the pediatrician, a school or community center nurse, a school counselor, a social worker, a psychologist, a psychiatrist, and so forth. Or, the family may be referred by any of the above to a case manager who may be a professional in private practice, or a clinic, or a service that specializes in such work.

The case manager should have a good knowledge of the role of the various disciplines and be able to help the family make sense of contradictory or fragmented findings and recommendations. The case manager should know what previous records, if any, should be gathered, and, should also be able to take a meaningful history of the child's development if not previously done. The case manager should know the resources and to whom the child should be referred for further diagnostic clarifications and for needed intervention.

It is crucial that such a central person work with the family to set up a plan with some order of priority and pace for referral to both the diagnostic as well as the remedial and therapeutic services, so that the child and family do not become physically exhausted or psychologically and/or financially overwhelmed and give up. It is also crucial to set up some general timetable for when the parents or the professional to whom the child and family were referred should again be in contact with the case manager. It is further crucial that the case manager be available to the child and parents for interpretation, reinterpretation, and application of the findings and recommendations, and for general progress evaluations and discussions through informal telephone calls and through scheduled regular formal conferences. Phone calls can be used to support the family and child through the long, drawn-out diagnostic and remediation services and through minor crises. Formal case conferences can be used for yearly evaluations, to plan next steps, and for major crises.

The other major need that can be met by a case manager is to act as a central repository for all the information available on the child. This will ensure the parents that valuable information is available and convenient and can be easily transmitted to any professional whom they may wish to consult. Such continuous information will also provide a record of the child's growth and development and serve as an important base for long-term planning. Of course, all the safeguards relating to confidentiality of information would be observed.

As the child goes through each developmental stage and achieves greater independence and self-sufficiency, the parents rejoice, think about the child's future, but generally have ambivalent feelings about the child's growing up, eventually leaving home, and being on his or her own. This normal progression does not apply in the same way to the child with minimal brain dysfunction. Just as the child goes through prolonged struggles, so do the parents, and the final separation from the parents can probably never really take place in the way that it does with a child without these difficulties. The follow-up studies on children with these disabilities (cited in the first chapter of this volume) indicate that the psychological patterns they developed in response to their disability persist and make adjustments as adolescents and young adults more difficult. The relationship of dependence on the parents continues as does the parents' level of anxiety about the child. It is very rare for a parent of a child with these difficulties, even after the child is grown up, to be able to say, "Things are great; the kids are all settled in their own lives, and I've stopped worrying about them."

Naturally, the symptoms of minimal brain dysfunction range from the very mild to the fairly severe, and probably the professional only comes in contact with the children who have the moderate to severe symptoms. Most of the other children pass by unnoticed, although some of the early screening tests are probably calling a much higher proportion of young children to professional attention than previously. The children who are seen frequently are immature for their age; are less able to cope effectively; seem to lack a whole range of normal social skills; may have difficulty in controlling motility, impulsivity, and gratification; may be physically awkward or clumsy; and may have a range of allergies and food intolerances which further inhibit their social adjustment. These characteristics usually exist independently of, but interact with, specific learning disabilities reflecting difficulties in the cognitive, visual-perceptual, auditory, and language processing areas, and to whatever extent these disturbances are neurophysiologically based, they tend to run in families.

As anyone who has worked with these children and their families knows, the parents and the child have been aware of differences in the child's development and of difficulty in the child's adjustment but were hoping that somehow the child would outgrow it. By the time parents come for professional help, frequently on the recommendations of the school, they are frightened for the child and themselves and want to know what is really the matter with the child and what can be done in specific concrete terms to help the child and themselves. Despite all of this, most parents have great difficulty accepting the diagnosis and the implications of it, and they need a period of time just to accept the nature of the child's difficulties. Then, the parents seem to go through a crucial period in which they have to reappraise the child, shift their expectations, and accept or reaccept the child. The family counselor or case manager has to focus on two processes that are going on simultaneously. One is to explain the child's difficulties, what kinds of help the child needs, where the resources are; to act as a central information and report repository for the child; and to help the parents and child take the necessary steps to get help in some order of priority that makes sense in terms of the family's financial and energy levels. The other process is to help the parents struggle with the many contradictory feelings they have about the child and arrive at some perspective on the child.

A dominant group of feelings that parents express reflects their concern, their efforts to accept the present and future limitations that the child must endure, and a sense of closeness and tenderness for their child. The other set of feelings represents their disappointment in the child, their sense of personal injury and loss, and their struggles with their own set of standards that the child may never meet. Adolescence, with its upsurges of changes and challenges, frequently reopens many of these areas of contradictions for the parents. The professional person, in working with the family, must be aware of the parents' anxiety, pain, and ambivalence and be empathetic with the parents' struggles with their own feelings if he or she is to help the parents to help the child. The professional must also be aware that the parents are under great pressure because of the child's difficulties. Just "telling" parents what has to be done rarely helps them deal with the problems.

It is a truism in working with children that what happens in the matrix of the family will determine the outcome for the child, and this applies even more profoundly to children with these disabilities. The families are in need of help for a whole variety of reasons which do not appear to be directly related to the child's difficulties but can be triggered by them. It has been frequently stated that there is a higher divorce rate for families with children with learning disabilities than for the population as a whole. This has been a difficult statistic to track down, but parents find themselves under greater tension and facing sharp differences between them over understanding, handling, and planning for the child. There is also a great deal of pressure placed upon the other siblings, who, frequently in the first flush of the family's grappling, tend to get overlooked and who then develop their own ways of communicating their sense of loss to the parents, which then increases the general level of the family tension. This tension will frequently reach a point where the whole family equilibrium is shattered. Another disturbing issue which builds the tension is the parents' realization that they are in for a long-term struggle and that there are no guarantees that the child will ever be able to "make it" in whatever terms the parents may have. This does not negate the fact that many middle-class children with learning disabilities do eventually meet their families' expectations, go to college, and pursue certain careers. However, it is more of a struggle, it takes longer, it costs more money, and the process taxes the strength and endurance of everyone.

Unfortunately, there are no known antidotes to the pain that the child and the parents have to endure in this long struggle. There are ways, however, of helping the parents get through, and one important one is the provision of a family counselor or case manager, so that the parents have a sense that there is one person who has all of the facts and findings and who will really be available to them. In defining this role and in urging professional people of many disciplines to function in this way, there has to be a shift in the sense of the professional's purpose with the family. The professional needs a great deal of flexibility and competence in a variety of areas in order to function as a case manager. One has to learn to be a good interpreter, have full knowledge of the meaning of the various disabilities, be a good resource person, but above all be available as a professional person to the parents. Also, one needs to adapt the techniques and procedures to the needs of the family. One may see a family only once a year but have monthly telephone calls.

As crises arise and if the child or family is being seen for psychological treatment by someone other than the case manager, the case manager, therapist, and family would confer as to who should see the family. If the child or family is not in psychological treatment with anyone else or is in treatment with the case manager, then the case manager and family would decide how to proceed. In either event, there will be times when the whole family or just the parents should be seen for a number of sessions. There will be times when it is necessary to see the child alone for weekly sessions and see the parents on a monthly basis. Also, at times, the child and one or both of the parents (excluding other family members) can be seen. The important consideration is flexibility.

There are many different settings in which this type of long-term service can be made available. First are the community-based clinics in hospitals and agencies for children with learning disabilities. There are also parents' organizations, such as the state and local chapters of the Association for Children with Learning Disabilities, and the parent/ professional organizations, such as the Orton Society. The schools have been suggested as such a resource, but this is a potentially conflictful situation. The school is an authority to the parents, and the parents frequently need neutral outside opinion to evaluate the school recommendations. Also, the school counselor's role can continue only as long as the child is in that school, and it is frequently when the child changes schools that stress occurs and the family and child need the help of the familiar person with whom they have been working. Any professional in private practice can function in this capacity and to do so will have to put aside a certain amount of time for these families.

The author has been working as the case manager with a number of such children and families. The contacts have so far run from three years for some families to 12 years for others. As part of this group, four families have been seen, surprisingly enough, with three children each, two boys and one girl. In each of these families, all three children showed evidences of minimal brain dysfunction or some perceptual deficit. Also, either one or both of the parents or the parents' siblings or parents had such difficulties. In one family, the daughter was the most seriously affected. In the other three families, the daughters, while having some specific perceptual deficit, were not seriously impaired. But in each of these families, at least two of the children exhibited marked psychological difficulties. All the families needed a great deal of support and availability to get through the shock and pain of these discoveries and to begin to provide the children and themselves the needed help.

The important focus for the case managers is to see the family as composed of people who are struggling to grapple with the psychological problems that having a child or children with minimal brain dysfunction has created for them; to be aware that any family who has a child so afflicted is faced with a lifetime commitment that goes beyond that which is required of parents with children without such difficulties; and to help the families learn to deal with this on a practical as well as on a psychological basis.

BIBLIOGRAPHY

Adams, R. R., Lerner, L., & Anderson, J. Children with learning problems: A developmental view for parents. *Journal of Learning Disabilities,* 1979, *12* 3, 315–319.

Baldauf, R. J. Parental intervention. In H. R. Myklebust (Ed.), *Progress in learning disabilities,* New York, Grune and Stratton, 1975.

Caplan, P. J. Living with children in home and classroom—helping parents help their children. *Bulletin of the Orton Society,* 1976, *26* 108–123.

Dembinski, R. J., & Mauser, A. J. What parents of the learning disabled really want from professionals. *Journal of Learning Disabilities,* 1977, *10* (9), 578–584.

Doernberg, N. J. Some negative effects on family integration of health and educational services for young handicapped children. *Rehabilitation Literature,* 1978, *39* (4), 107–110.

Gardner, R. A. *MBD: The Family Book About Minimal Brain Dysfunction.* New York: Jason Aronson, Inc., 1973.

McLoughlin, J. A., Edge, D., & Strenecky, B. Perspective on parental involvement in the diagnosis and treatment of learning disabled children. *Journal of Learning Disabilities,* 1978, *11* (5), 291–296.

Ozer, M. N. The assessment of children with developmental problems. *Exceptional Children,* 1977, *44* (l), 37–38.

Ozer, M. N. The assessment of children with learning problems: A planning process involving the teacher. *Journal of Learning Disabilities,* 1979, *11* (7), 422–426.

Rockowitz, R. J., & Davidson, P. W. Discussing diagnostic findings with parents. *Journal of Learning Disabilities,* 1979, *12* (1), 2–7.

Chapter 8

PSYCHOSTIMULANT THERAPY FOR BEHAVIOR DISORDERS
A Status Review

Bertrand G. Winsberg
Janet A. Camp

The minimal brain dysfunction (MBD) syndrome in children consists of a set of behavioral symptoms including, among others, restlessness/motor overactivity, short attention span, distractibility, poor impulse control, and learning disabilities (Clements, 1966). Diagnosis is typically based on the concomitant presence of a number of these behaviors. By definition, the syndrome occurs in children of normal intelligence and in the absence of *overt* central nervous system dysfunction.

The term *minimal* brain dysfunction derives from the observation that many of the above symptoms are characteristic of children and adults with known brain damage (Campbell, 1976). This symptom correspondence has led to the suggestion that the MBD symdrome results from minor, albeit nonspecifiable, brain damage or dysfunction. Although there is no unequivocal evidence to support this suggestion (cf. Shaffer, 1978), investigations have shown that adverse pre- and perinatal circumstances can result in impaired function in infants and preschoolers (Knobloch & Pasamanick, 1974). These authors have proposed the notion of a continuum of reproductive casualty, namely that pre- and perinatal complications can produce clinical disorders ranging from severe brain dysfunction (e.g., cerebral palsy, seizures, and/or mental retardation) to more minor conditions such as the behavioral disturbances subsumed under the MBD syndrome.

Recent advances in neurochemistry and electrophysiology are beginning to allow for a direct investigation of possible organic impairment in MBD children. For example, studies of neurotransmitter concentrations in cerebrospinal fluid may provide evidence for a neurochemical imbalance, and studies of stimulus-evoked brain responses recorded from the scalp may provide evidence for a functional disorganization in brain processing. Although the data that presently exist are still too preliminary to interpret (cf. Ornitz, 1978; Winsberg, Hurwic, Sverd, & Klutch, 1978), continuing refinements in both neurochemistry and electrophysiology may eventually yield direct evidence for the presumed organic dysfunction.

The provision of this evidence has practical as well as theoretical value. Physicians generally provide treatment based on the medical or disease model, namely that dysfunction derives from an impaired organ system and that pharmacotherapy modifies dysfunctional tissue. Consequently, the use of drugs to treat the behavioral symptoms of the MBD child is based on the implicit assumption of a dysfunctional nervous system. Yet even without this assumption, psychostimulant medications have proven to be a useful therapy for behavioral disorders in children.

PSYCHOSTIMULANT PHARMACOTHERAPY

Therapeutic Indication and Efficacy

An MBD diagnosis per se is not an adequate indication for psychostimulant therapy. Based on the available literature, the only positive clinical indication for these drugs in children is the presence of socially disruptive behavioral symptoms, such as hyperactivity and conduct disorders/aggressivity; the MBD child whose sole symptoms are learning disabilities and/or home and classroom inattention is at present an inappropriate candidate for pharmacotherapy (cf. Barkley & Cunningham, 1978; Fish, 1975). The two psychostimulants commonly prescribed—methylphenidate (Ritalin) and dextroamphetamine (Dexedrine)—are generally equivalent for reducing behavioral symptoms in MBD children (Barkley, 1977; Winsberg, Press, Bialer, & Kupietz, 1974). However, since some children will respond idiosyncratically to only one psychostimulant (Cantwell & Carlson, 1978; Winsberg et al., 1974), both should be tried prior to concluding that a child is a psychostimulant nonresponder.

The efficacy of the psychostimulants for treating socially disruptive behavior in children has a long and consistent history (see Barkley, 1977; Cantwell & Carlson, 1978; Conners & Werry, 1979 for recent reviews). Clinical research demonstrating this efficacy has employed a wide variety of psychometric scales (Cantwell & Carlson, 1978; Werry, 1978) which rely on judgmental evaluations of the child's behavior as perceived by teachers, parents, and/or medical professionals. In some cases, direct observational methods (Cantwell & Carlson, 1978; Werry, 1978) have also been used. On the basis of countless investigations using these scales and observational techniques, it has been clearly established that psychostimulant therapy is highly effective in reducing the socially disruptive behavioral symptoms of a majority of MBD children. At the present time, "no rational, knowledgeable individual can dispute the efficacy of short-term stimulant treatment in the management" of these children (Gittelman-Klein, Klein, Abikoff, Katz, Gloisten, & Kates, 1976, p. 361).

The psychostimulants have also proven efficacious for improving performance on a wide variety of discrete laboratory tasks. These include tests of sustained attention, short-term memory, learning, and reaction time, all of which require that the child pay attention in order to perform optimally. Laboratory data have consistently demonstrated that the psychostimulants significantly reduce the MBD child's symptomatic inattentiveness (Barkley, 1977; Cantwell & Carlson, 1978; Sroufe, 1975). Despite this laboratory success, however, there exists no convincing evidence that pharmacotherapy directly facilitates classroom learning or improves academic performance (Aman, 1978; Barkley & Cunningham, 1978; Whalen & Henker, 1976). Given this lack of evidence and the tenuous relation between discrete laboratory measures and classroom learning, it is clearly premature to posit that psychostimulant-facilitated laboratory performance can translate to improved classroom learning. Consequently, pharmacotherapy is at present not indicated for the learning disabled child who does not concomitantly display socially disruptive behavioral symptoms.

Side Effects

Because of the extensive use of psychostimulant therapy, the side effects of these drugs have been carefully evaluated. Some good behavioral responders will experience such minor short-term side effects as headache, stomachache, dizziness, loss of appetite, and insomnia. These effects are of minimal severity and are easily controlled by dose manipulation. A small percentage of psychostimulant-treated children will show a severe exacerbation of their symptoms, notably increased motor activity and increased irritability. In exceedingly rare instances, a toxic psychosis (Winsberg, Yepes, & Bialer, 1976), tics (Denckla, Bemporad, & MacKay, 1976), or an allergic reaction (Sverd, Hurwic, David, & Winsberg, 1977) may occur. Fortunately, these severe sides effects are typically of short duration (2–6 hours), consistent with the rapid metabolism of these drugs (Cantwell & Carlson, 1978; Hungund, Perel, Hurwic, Sverd, & Winsberg, 1979).

Additional sequelae to psychostimulant therapy include their effects on the cardiovascular system and on height and weight. Some investigations of the cardiovascular effects of psychostimulants have indicated statistically significant increases in heart rate and/or blood pressure (cf. Cantwell & Carlson, 1978). This group effect is small, however, and of doubtful clinical significance (Aman & Werry, 1975). Clinically significant increases in individual cases are rare (Katz, Saraf, Gittelman-Klein, & Klein, 1975). Concern has also been voiced regarding the possibility that chronic psychostimulant use may interfere with normal height and weight growth. A recent, carefully controlled longitudinal study has shown that these concerns are unwarranted (McNutt, Boileau, & Cohen, 1977). The pediatric advisory panel of the Food and Drug Administration has reviewed the literature on height and weight suppression associated with psychostimulant therapy and concluded that when minor suppression does occur, it is temporary with no apparent long-term effects (Lipman, 1978).

In summary, for most psychostimulant responders, the prescribed doses are generally quite safe. Minor side effects can usually be eliminated by dose manipulation. Although there is no strong evidence for long-term adverse effects, common sense dictates using the minimal dose necessary to achieve clinical efficacy and incorporating regular drug holidays.

Clinical Issues

Unfortunately, child psychiatrists and pediatricians have been very poorly trained in developmental psychopharmacology. It is all too common for drugs to be prescribed without an adequate evaluation of the child, and too many children receive inadequate or excessive medication doses without follow-up to ascertain initial or continued responsivity. Since the result of this mismanagement is often a poor clinical response or excessive side effects, some nonmedical professionals and parents have developed a skeptical attitude toward the use of psychostimulants. This skepticism is misdirected, however, since the drugs can be highly effective *if* they are appropriately titrated and monitored by a trained physician.

Some concerned professionals have argued that the use of drugs to control behavior is socially irresponsible. This argument derives from the sociopolitical climate associated with the use of mind-altering drugs and has unfortunately gained credance from the misuse of medication in children. Clearly, there is no justification for medicating a well-behaved active child or for overmedicating any child into a trancelike state. On the other hand, when a child is medically evaluated, displays the behavioral disruption for which psychostimulants are indicated, and is treated with the smallest clinically effective dose, the use of pharmacotherapy to alleviate symptoms is no different from any other pharmacologic intervention, for example, anticonvulsants to control the symptoms of seizures.

Finally, some have argued that given the current epidemic of drug abuse, the daily administration of psychostimulant drugs to children should be proscribed. Yet after 40 years of use, there is no evidence either that these children abuse their medication or that they develop an addiction in later years (Beck, Langford, MacKay, & Sum, 1975).

THERAPY SELECTION

The practitioner's choice of therapy depends in large measure on his training. Consequently, a variety of treatments have been employed with behaviorally disordered MBD children, the most prevalent of which are psychotherapy, behavior modification, and pharmacotherapy. One means for comparing these therapies is the conceptual index known as the risk/benefit ratio, which weighs the biological and fiscal disadvantages of a treatment against its potential benefits for the patient.

Insight Psychotherapy

Although the biological risks of psychotherapy are virtually nonexistent, the temporal and fiscal disadvantages are quite high. Psychotherapy is time consuming and can be a very expensive treatment, particularly when provided by physicians. In addition, "seeing a psychiatrist" can be stigmatizing, since the child, the child's family, and peers typically assume that there is "something wrong" with the child's mind. All these disadvantages might be considered a necessary evil if the treatment were successful. However, there is no real evidence that insight psychotherapy diminishes behavioral deviance (cf. Aman, 1978). Without this evidence, it seems pointless to submit children and their parents to the major disadvantages of this therapy.

Behavior Modification

As with insight psychotherapy, behavior modification can often be a time-consuming and expensive endeavor. Its success is highly dependent on systematic training of parents and teachers, and both should be active participants in the therapy program. Unlike psychotherapy, however, recent research has demonstrated the efficacy of the behavioral approach, either alone (O'Leary & Pelham, 1978) or in combination with pharmacotherapy (Gittelman-Klein et al., 1976). Consequently, behavior modification may provide an important alternative therapy when parents have strong reservations regarding the use of drugs. In addition, there is some suggestion that a combined pharmacotherapy/behavior modification regimen may represent the best treatment for the behavioral symptoms of the MBD child (Gittelman-Klein et al., 1976). Although the long-term efficacy of behavior modification in altering prognosis remains to be demonstrated, the apparent inability of pharmacotherapy to do so (Weiss, Kruger, Danielson, & Elman,

1975) argues in favor of continued research on combined therapy programs.

Pharmacotherapy

Despite initial concerns, the biological risks associated with psychostimulant therapy appear to be minimal. For most children, minor side effects can be eliminated by careful dose titration, and cardiovascular and height/weight side effects can be avoided by minimal doses and drug holidays. Social concerns have proven unwarranted when medication management is provided by well-trained physicians. One unavoidable disadvantage, however, is that the stigma of daily "pill-taking" may be a problem for some children (Ross & Ross, 1976). Against this must be weighed the consistent observation that 75 percent of MBD children with behavioral deviance respond favorably to psychostimulant therapy (Barkley, 1977). From a fiscal perspective, the relative costs of medication and regular follow-up examinations are small. Thus, the well-documented efficacy of pharmacotherapy, coupled with its minimal disadvantages, should render it the treatment of choice at the present time.

TREATMENT IMPLICATIONS

On the basis of carefully conducted scientific research, only two therapeutic interventions—psychostimulant pharmacotherapy and behavior modification—have proven effective for treating the behavioral symptoms of the MBD child. Despite its acceptance, insight psychotherapy cannot make this claim.

In recent years, a number of new approaches to treating MBD children have achieved popularity, for example, the Feingold diet (which prescribes certain foods and food additions) and orthomolecular (vitamin) treatment. The acclaim afforded these so-called therapies by many parents probably derives from current concerns regarding the effect of environmental and chemical pollutants on the quality of human life. In addition, some parents would prefer to believe that the behavioral problems are not intrinsic to their child, or their interaction with the child, but rather are attributable to some outside factor, such as food additives.

Unfortunately, neither popularity nor the most fervent desire for a "better" cure can alter the fact that there are no scientific data to support the efficacy claims of any of these modish interventions. In the absence of such data, the routine use of these treatments cannot be ethically justified. Until the efficacy of any new treatment is scientifically documented, it must be considered experimental, no matter how popular or appealing it might be. As responsible professionals, it is in our best interest and in that of the behaviorally disordered MBD child to treat these children in the best possible manner, which, for the present, is psychostimulant therapy and/or behavior modification.

REFERENCES

Aman, M. G. Drugs, learning and the psychotherapies. In J. S. Werry (Ed.), *Pediatric psychopharmacology: The use of behavior modifying drugs in children.* New York: Brunner/Mazel, 1978.

Aman, M. G., & Werry, J. S. The effects of methylphenidate and haloperidol on the heart rate and blood pressure of hyperactive children with special reference to time of action. *Psychopharmacologia,* 1975, *43,* 163–168.

Barkley, R. A. A review of stimulant drug research with hyperactive children. *Journal of Child Psychology and Psychiatry,* 1977, *18,* 137–165.

Barkley, R. A., & Cunningham, C. E. Do stimulant drugs improve the academic performance of hyperkinetic children? *Clinical Pediatrics,* 1978, *17,* 85–92.

Beck, L., Langford, W. S., MacKay, M., & Sum, G. Childhood chemotherapy and later drug abuse and growth curve: A follow-up study of 30 adolescents. *American Journal of Psychiatry,* 1975, *132,* 436–438.

Campbell, S. B. Hyperactivity: Course and treatment. In A. Davids (Ed.), *Child personality and psychopathology: Current topics* (Vol. 3). New York: Wiley, 1976.

Cantwell, D. P., & Carlson, G. A. Stimulants. In J. S. Werry (Ed.), *Pediatric psychopharmacology: The use of behavior modifying drugs in children.* New York: Brunner/Mazel, 1978.

Clements, S. D. *Minimal brain dysfunction in children.* Department of Health, Education, and Welfare, Publication No. 1415, 1966.

Conners, C., & Werry, J. Pharmacotherapy of psychopathology in children. In H. Quay & J. Werry (Eds.), *Psychopathological disorders of childhood* (2nd ed.). New York:Wiley, 1979.

Denckla, M. B., Bemporad, J. R., & MacKay, M. C. Tics following methylphenidate administration: A report of 20 cases. *Journal of the American Medical Association,* 1976, *235,* 1349–1351.

Fish, B. Stimulant drug treatment of hyperactive children. In D. P. Cantwell (Ed.), *The hyperactive child: Diagnosis, management, current research.* New York: Spectrum/Halstead/Wiley, 1975.

Gittelman-Klein, R., Klein, D. F., Abikoff, H., Katz, S., Gloisten, A. C., & Kates, W. Relative efficacy of methylphenidate and behavior modification in hyperkinetic children: An interim report. *Journal of Abnormal Child Psychology,* 1976, *4,* 361–379.

Hungund, B. L., Perel, J. M., Hurwic, M. J., Sverd, J., & Winsberg, B. G. *Pharmacokinetics of methylphenidate in hyperkinetic children.* Manuscript submitted for publication, 1979.

Katz, S., Saraf, K., Gittelman-Klein, R., & Klein, D. F. Clinical pharmacological management of hyperkinetic children. In R. Gittelman-Klein (Ed.), *Recent advances in child psychopharmacology.* New York: Human Sciences Press, 1975.

Knobloch, H., & Pasamanick, B. (Eds.). *Gesell and Amatruda's developmental diagnosis. The evaluation and management of normal and abnormal neuropsychologic development in infancy and early childhood* (3rd ed.). New York: Harper & Row, 1974.

Lipman, R. S. Stimulant medication and growth in hyperkinetic children. *Psychopharmacology Bulletin,* 1978, *14* (4), 61–62.

McNutt, B. A., Boileau, R. A., & Cohen, M. N. The effects of long-term stimulant medication on the growth and body composition of hyperactive children. *Pharmacology Bulletin,* 1977, *13* (2), 36–38.

O'Leary, S. G., & Pelham, W. E. Behavior therapy and withdrawal of stimulant medication in hyperactive children. *Pediatrics,* 1978, *61,* 211–217.

Ornitz, E. M. Event related potential investigations in children with psychopathology. In E. Callaway, P. Teuting, & S. Koslow (Eds.), *Event related brain potentials in man.* New York: Academic Press, 1978.

Ross, D. M., & Ross, S. A. *Hyperactivity: Research, theory, and action.* New York: Wiley, 1976.

Shaffer, D. Longitudinal research and the minimal brain damage syndrome.

In A. F. Kalverboer, H. M. van Praag, & J. Mendlewicz (Eds.), *Advances in biological psychiatry (Vol. 1). Minimal brain dysfunction: Fact or fiction.* Basel (Switzerland): S. Karger, 1978.

Sroufe, L. A. Drug treatment of children with behavior problems. In F. D. Horowitz (Ed.), *Review of child development research.* Chicago: University of Chicago Press, 1975.

Sverd, J., Hurwic, M. J., David, O., & Winsberg, B. Hypersensitivity to methylphenidate and dextroamphetamine: A report of two cases. *Pediatrics,* 1977, *59,* 115–117.

Weiss, G., Kruger, E., Danielson, U., & Elman, M. Effect of long-term treatment of hyperactive children with methylphenidate. *Canadian Medical Association Journal,* 1975, *112,* 159–165.

Werry, J. S. Measures in pediatric psychopharmacology. In J. S. Werry (Ed.), *Pediatric psychopharmacology: The use of behavior modifying drugs in children.* New York: Brunner/Mazel, 1978.

Whalen, C. K., & Henker, B. Psychostimulants and children: A review and analysis. *Psychological Bulletin,* 1976, *83,* 1113–1130.

Winsberg, B. G., Hurwic, M. J., Sverd, J., & Klutch, A. Neurochemistry of withdrawal emergent symptoms in children. *Psychoparmacology,* 1978, *56,* 157–161.

Winsberg, B. G., Press, M., Bialer, I., & Kupietz, S. Dextroamphetamine and methylphenidate in the treatment of hyperactive/aggressive children. *Pediatrics,* 1974, *53,* 236–241.

Winsberg, B. G., Yepes, L. E., & Bialer, I. Pharmacologic management of children with hyperactive/aggressive/inattentive behavior disorders. *Clinical Pediatrics,* 1976, *15,* 471–477.

Chapter 9

ORTHOMOLECULAR TREATMENT OF CHILDREN WITH LEARNING DISABILITIES
Allan Cott

Learning disabilities constitute the most prevalent and urgent medical problem afflicting children not only in the United States but in most countries of the world. The number of children involved is staggering, when one considers that 5 percent of the nonretarded children population is affected. Physicians must be made aware that children suffering from learning disabilities will not "outgrow it," that their condition is not "a phase they are passing through." If adequate intervention is not made into these disabilities, the children's potential will never be realized and the effects on their lives will be more devastating than those of most other childhood disorders with which they might be afflicted. The earlier the diagnosis is made, the more rewarding will be the response to orthomolecular therapy or to pharmacotherapy and hence the more successful the results of remedial effort. Delayed diagnosis or treatment exposes the child to improper assessment by school personnel, peers, and parents, increasing the probability of permanent psychological damage.

Recent research suggests that learning disabilities are associated with minimal brain dysfunction. This term refers to children of near- or above-average intelligence, with certain learning or behavioral disabilities, ranging from mild to severe, which are associated with deviations of function of the central nervous system. There is growing recognition that the child with a learning disability may indeed be suffering from a biochemical disorder. The characteristic sign most often observed is hyperactivity—the one sympton common to all children suffering from severe disorders of behavior, learning, and communication. Other symptoms may include perceptual-motor impairments, impulsive behavior, general coordination defects, inability to concentrate, short attention span, and disorders of speech. Many children diagnosed as having minimal brain dysfunction seem normal or near normal until they enter a classroom. Then despite being endowed with average or above-average intelligence, they will have difficulty in one or more areas of learning.

In humans, brain damage due to trauma before, during, or after birth is now believed to be responsible for many cases of learning disability. The state of the mother's health and her general nutrition prior to conception and during pregnancy are of the utmost importance, for subtle or gross disasters occurring during these periods or during labor and delivery can compromise the child in learning and behavior (Pasamanick, Rogers, & Lillienfeld, 1956). Evidence is also accumulating that learning disabilities are frequently of genetic origin. Case studies further reveal that more than one learning disabled child frequently occurs in a family.

The author presents for consideration a most important variable in the learning process—the biochemical disorders which interfere with learning and a new adjunct to treatment which involves the use of large doses of vitamins and minerals and the maintenance of proper nutrition to create the optimum molecular environment for the brain. Drugs are being used widely as the primary intervention for the treatment of learning disabilities and are of importance in helping many children.

On 11–12 January, 1971, the Office of Child Development and the Office of the Assistant Secretary for Health and Scientific Affairs, Department of Health, Education, and Welfare, called a conference to discuss the use of stimulant medications in the treatment of elementary school-age children with certain behavioral disturbances. The conference concluded that: stimulant medications are beneficial in only about one-half to two-thirds of the cases in which use of the drugs is warranted; stimulant drugs are the first and least complicated of the medicines to be tried, while other medications—the so-called tranquilizers and antidepressants—should be generally reserved for a smaller group of patients; and the medications did not "cure" the condition, but made the child potentially more accessible to educational and counseling efforts (Department of Health, Education, and Welfare, 1971). Over the short term and at a critical age, stimulant medications can provide the help needed for the child's development.

The author agrees in essence with the conference report. Early intervention is of the utmost importance if the hyperkinetic learning disabled child is to have an opportunity to learn and achieve. It is true that in about half of the instances the hyperactivity will subside spontaneously by age 12 or 13, but those parents who accept the advice that their child will "outgrow" the condition may find that by the time they seek treatment, it is too late for the child. His academic career is gone, and opportunities for work later in life are indeed limited, since there are very few jobs left which do not require a degree of literacy.

It is unfortunate that the panel quoted above, while it did point out that drugs were not the only effective treatment, was not convened to report on effective alternatives to drug treatment or effective treatment for that one-third to one-half of 5 million children who are not helped by drugs. In the author's experience with the use of the orthomolecular intervention into the hyperkinetic learning disabled child, better than 50 percent are helped. These statistics achieve greater significance because the children treated have failed to improve with the use of methylphenidate or amphetamines. Many parents are searching for an alternative to drug therapy because their children were experiencing the side effects of insomnia, loss of appetite with concomitant weight loss, or a reaction of fatigue and sedation when the drug was given in doses large enough to control the hyperactivity. Many children had been tried on a regime of various psychotropic (tranquilizer) medications which failed because they produced the paradoxical effect of overstimulation and increased the hyperactivity and disturbed behavior. Since the orthomolecular approach is compatible with all other substances used in the drug intervention and since the megavitamins potentiate the action of most drugs, the treatments can be combined. This is frequently done early in treatment while the vitamin doses are gradually being raised to the optimal maintenance level and more rapid control of the hyperactivity is required. At times, tranquilizer medication is added at the request or insistence of the school authorities to bring the hyperactive, disruptive behavior under more rapid control.

The large majority of children treated by the orthomolecular approach improve without the use of drugs. Fortunately, very few parents accept the cliches with which their concerns about their child's development are met by so many of their pediatricians and family physicians. It has been the author's experience that the mothers most often were first in noticing their child's problems, while in a very low percentage of cases their pediatrician was first to make the diagnosis. Many parents, after reading about the orthomolecular approach, instituted the recommended dietary changes or purchased vitamins and reported marked improvement in their children.

Improvement under the orthomolecular treatment is directing the attention of the scientific community to the central nervous system processes and to closer scrutiny of the biochemical processes of the learning disabled child. In this means of intervention, remedial efforts are directed toward both brain function and body chemistry. In addition to the employment of perceptual-motor techniques and pharmacotherapy, attempts should be made to improve the child's biochemical balance through the use of orthomolecular techniques (Cott, 1971)

Orthomolecular treatment has been described by Linus Pauling, in his classical paper on orthomolecular psychiatry (1968), as treatment of illness by the provision of the optimum molecular composition of the brain, especially the optimum concentration of substances normally presented in the human body. The implications for much needed research in the more universal application of orthomolecular treatment are clear. There is rapidly accumulating evidence that a child's ability to learn can be improved by the use of large doses of certain vitamins and mineral supplements and by improvement of his general nutritional status through removal of "junk foods" from his daily diet.

With orthomolecular treatment, initial results are frequently quick and the reduction in hyperactivity often dramatic, but in most instances several months elapse before significant changes are seen. The child exhibits a willingness to cooperate with his parents and teachers. These changes are seen in the majority of children who failed to improve with the use of the stimulant drugs or tranquilizer medications. The majority of the children seen by the author have been exposed to every form of treatment and every known tranquilizer and sedative with little or no success even in controlling the hyperactivity. Through orthomolecular treatment, concentration and attention span increases, and the child is able to work productively for increasingly longer periods of time. He ceases to be an irritant to his teacher and classmates. Early intervention is of the utmost importance, not only for the child, but for the entire family, since the child suffering from minimal brain dysfunction is such a devastating influence on the family constellation. He is the matrix of emotional storms which envelop all members of the household and disrupt both their relationships to him and to each other.

Based on empirical data, the application of orthomolecular principles can be successful in helping many learning disabled children. Positive results have been obtained when the treatment regimen consisted of the following vitamins: niacinamide or niacin, 1–2 g daily depending upon body weight; ascorbic acid, 1–2g daily; pyridoxine, 200–300 mg daily; calcium pantothenate, 200–400 mg daily; B-Complex 50, 1/2 tablet. The vitamins are generally administered twice daily. Magnesium is frequently used for its calming effect on the hyperactivity and to prevent a depletion of this important mineral by the large doses of pyridoxine.

These are starting doses of the vitamins for children weighing 35 pounds or more. If a child weighs less than 35 pounds, 1 g daily of niacinamide and ascorbic acid are used in 1/2 g doses administered twice daily. If the child shows no signs of intolerance after two weeks, the dose is increased to 1 g twice daily. In the smaller child, the pyridoxine and calcium pantothenate are started at 100 mg twice daily and gradually increased to twice the amount. In a child weighing 45 pounds or more, an optimum daily maintenance level of approximately 3 g of niacinamide and 3 g of ascorbic acid is reached. Frequently, vitamin B-12, vitamin E, riboflavin (B-2), thiamine (B-1), and folic acid can be valuable additions to the treatment. No serious side effects have resulted in any of the hundreds of children treated with these substances. The side effects which occur infrequently (nausea, vomiting, increased frequency of urination or bowel movements) are dose related and subside with reduction of the dose (Buckley, 1977; Cott, 1971, 1972, 1974; Jani & Jani, 1974; Krippner, 1975; Powers, 1973, Rimland 1971; Wunderlich, 1973).

It has been shown that proper brain function requires adequate tissue respiration (Wendle, Faro, Barker, Barsky, & Guteirrez, 1971). O. Warburg (1966), Nobel laureate in biochemistry, described the importance of vitamins B-3 and C in the respiration of all body tissues in the maintenance of health and proper function. Further, laboratory findings with animals have shown a direct relationship between vitamin intake and learning enhancement (Scherer & Kramer, 1972). It has been found by some researchers that injections of vitamin B-12 markedly enhanced learning in rats (Lindenbaum & Mueller, 1974).

Control of the child's diet is an integral part of the total treatment, and failure to improve the child's nutritional status can be responsible for achieving minimal results. Greater concern must be shown for the quality of the child's internal environment in which his cells and tissues function if we are to help him attain optimal performance. The removal of offending foods from, and the addition of essential nutrients to, the diet of disturbed and learning disabled children can result in dramatic improvement in behavior, attention span, and concentration.

Children or adults suffering from hypoglycemia must eat a diet which is richest in protein, moderate in fat, and low in carbohydrates. Cane sugar and those carbohydrate foods which are quickly converted to glucose must be eliminated because they exert a definite influence on brain chemistry and over-stimulate the pancreas to overproduce insulin. Wurtman (1975) reported a study at the Massachusetts Institute of Technology which revealed the relationship in brain tissue in rats between the amounts of neurotransmitters present in the brain and the presence or absence of protein in each meal. The daily increases or decreases in the dietary intake of certain amino acids found in foods affect the production of neurotransmitters which stimulate impulses from one brain cell to the next. It was also reported that insulin apparently sequesters some amino acids.

Since many disturbed and learning disabled children are found to have either hypoglycemia, hyperinsulinism, or dysinsulinism, cane sugar and rapidly absorbed carbohydrate foods should be eliminated from their diets (Yaryura-Tobias & Neziroglu, 1975). It has been the universal observation of those investigators who have assessed the nutritional status of hyperactive and learning disabled children that they eat a diet which is richest in candy, sweets, and other foods made with sugar. The removal of these foods results in a dramatic decrease in hyperactivity. Most children do not drink milk unless it is sweetened with chocolate syrup or some other syrupy additive. All the beverages which they consume every day are spiked with sugar—soda, caffeinated cola drinks, highly sweetened "fruit juices," and other concoctions which are sold to them through television commercials. The child who drinks any water at all is indeed rare.

The appalling fact about the constant consumption of these "junk foods" is the parents' belief that these foods are good for their children. Parents must realize that they litter their children's bodies by making these unnatural junk foods available to them and incorporating them in their daily diet. The children will not voluntarily exclude these foods from their diet, they must be helped to accomplish this. These foods should not be brought into the house. The child must learn the principles of proper nutrition and proper eating from his parents. The dissemination of this knowledge is far too important to entrust it to the writers of television commercials whose aim is to sell rather than educate.

Jean Mayer (1970), professor of nutrition at Harvard University, speaking at a symposium on hunger and malnutrition, stated that "studies at Harvard among resident physicians suggest that the average physician knows little more about nutrition than the average secretary, unless the secretary has a weight problem and then she probably knows more than the average physician." Dr. Mayer (1970) pointed out that "only a half dozen or so medical schools in the U.S. include a nutrition course in the curriculum. Nutrition education should be centered on foods—their size, shape, color, caloric value, etc. —we must relate such vital information to the everday uses of all people."

The author has taken many dietary histories which revealed that the usual "nutritious" breakfast for some children consists of a glass of soda or "coke" and a portion of chocolate layer cake! At best, the breakfast menu of the majority of learning disabled children is poorly balanced and varies from this extreme by the substitution of sugar-frosted cereals. For the child with hypoglycemia, such food assures a drop in blood glucose level for several hours, during which time that child's brain function is impaired so that he cannot learn well even if he does not suffer from learning disabilities. The glucose in the bloodstream is one of the most important nutrients for the proper functioning of the brain, and the maintenance of a proper glucose level is essential in the creation of an optimum molecular environment for the mind.

An increasingly greater awareness of the importance of the role of nutrition in maintenance of health led to more research, which revealed that, beyond malnutrition due to lack of food or of a proper diet, there were illnesses or conditions produced by perfectly good foods which are for many children or adults offending foods for their brain chemistry. These foods may be the basic staples in the daily well-balanced diet of a hyperactive child, yet they produce disturbed, hyperactive behavior or physical symptoms. Many wholesome foods can for many children with minimal brain dysfunction be offending foods. Their response is an allergic one, but the symptoms produced by the allergy are not the usual allergic symptoms but a disturbance in behavior. This response must be considered the result of a cerebral allergy. The foods most often productive of cerebral allergies are wheat, milk, eggs, corn and corn products (the latter is almost as ubiquitous as sugar), and beef. Since these foods are consumed daily and many are used several times each day, dramatic changes in behavior can be seen when the offending food or foods are removed from the diet. The reduction in hyperactivity can in many cases be immediate. This can be accomplished by an elimination diet. The foods most often responsible are those which the child eats or drinks with greatest frequency and in the largest amounts. There have been few instances in which a half-gallon-a-day milk drinker was not benefited by being withdrawn completely from milk. Other liquids consumed in prodigious amounts are apple juice and soda. There are many children whose daily allotment of 48 oz. of soda is consumed by noon each day. These are the sodas whose labels listing the chemical additives and artificial colors, flavors, and preservatives Jean Mayer has described as reading like a qualitative analysis of a water sample drawn from New York's East River. In some children, the major allergies are not foods but inhalants to which they are constantly exposed.

Ben Feingold's work with salicylate sensitive children and their response to the removal from their diet of foods with artificial colors and flavors and with naturally occurring salicylates is well known (Feingold, 1974). This subgroup of children with minimal brain dysfunction respond dramatically to the elimination of these additives, which occur in sodas, most frankfurters, and other luncheon meats as well as in such wholesome foods as apples, oranges, peaches, grapes, raisins, cucumbers, and pickles (Feingold, 1974; Hawley & Buckley, 1974).

Other important contributors to disturbed brain functioning are the environmental pollutants of heavy metals, such as lead, mercury, or cadmium (Bryce-Smith & Waldron, 1974). The pollution of our environment, and particularly the cities, with lead has already reached a disturbingly high level (Caprio, Margulis & Jaslow, 1974; Kasowski & Kasowski, 1976). Prof. D. Bryce Smith of the University of Reading (1971) wrote in *Chemistry in Britain* that no other toxic chemical pollutant has accumulated in man to average levels so close to the threshold for overt clinical poisoning. Millar & Hernberg (1970) referred to research done in 1964 by Sir Alan Moncrieff and others at the Institute of Child Health in London. They found that a group of mentally retarded children had distinctly more lead in their blood than a group of normal children.

It is now a well-known clinical fact that susceptibility to the harmful effects of lead is highly variable. Lead in heavy concentrations in the tissues (and some of the hundreds of children examined by the author have concentrations as high as 85 parts per million) can interfere with metabolic reactions which activate such other metals as copper, iron, manganese, and potassium. Children accumulate lead from sucking their dirty fingers and toys, from inhaling road dust, and automobile and airplane exhaust, and from many other sources. Children can absorb dangerous quantities of lead from chewing newspaper or color-printed pages in magazines. At present one-quarter of several hundred thousand children tested and living in cities have blood levels at the borderline of toxicity.

Orthomolecular treatment has many advantages which make it especially suitable for large numbers of children. Treatment can be directed by parents and paraprofessionals, reducing to a minimum the occasions when the child must be brought to a specialist for therapy. It is inexpensive, since it does not depend upon complex machinery or equipment or upon the long-term use of psychotropic drugs. Of great importance is the role it could serve as a preventive as well as a therapeutic measure, because it could easily be included in prenatal and infant care programs everywhere. These are important considerations in view of the evidence that neurologically based and biochemically based learning disabilities are especially frequent amount children from low-income areas. U. Bronfenbrenner (1969) points out that a low-income mother's "exposure to nutritional deficiency, illness, fatigue, or emotional stress can be far more damaging to her child than was previously thought. The neurological disturbances thus produced persist through early childhood into the school years, where they are reflected in impaired learning capacity."

Even, though research cannot at this time give an unequivocal or full answer to the question of what effect malnutrition or malnourishment has on intellectual development this is not a valid reason to delay programs for improving the nutritional status and eating practices of mothers and infants. Information demonstrating the benefits of good nutrition in improved health, physical growth, and improved learning already justifies such efforts.

We cannot afford the luxury of waiting until the causes of learning disabilities can be unquestionably established by techniques yet to be developed. We cannot postpone managing as effectively and honestly as possible the 5 million or more children who desperately need help now.

REFERENCES

Bronfenbrenner, U. Dampening the unemployability explosion. *Saturday Review*, January 4, 1969, pp. 10–14.

Bryce-Smith, D. & Waldron, H. A. Lead pollution, disease, and behavior. *Community Health 6*, 1968.

Bryce-Smith, D. Lead poisoning. *Chemistry in Britain*, 1972, *7*(54).

Buckley, R. E. Nutrition, metabolism, brain functions and learning. *Academic Therapy*, 1977, *12*(3), 321–326.

Caprio, R. J., Margulis, H. L. & Joselow, M. M. Lead absorption in children and its relationship to urban traffic densities. *Archives of Environmental Health*, 1974, *28* 195–197.

Cott, A. Orthomolecular approach in the treatment of learning disabilities. *Schizophrenia*, 1971, *3*(2), 95–105.

Cott, A. Treatment of learning disabilities. *Journal of Orthomolecular Psychiatry*, 1974, *3*(4), 343–355.

Department of Health, Education and Welfare. Office of Child Development and Office of the Assistant Secretary for Health and Scientific Affairs. *Report of the Conference on the Use of Stimulant Drugs in the Treatment of Behaviorally Disturbed Young School Children*. Bethesda: 1971.

Feingold, B. F. *Why your child is hyperactive.* New York: Random House, 1974.

Hawley, C. & Buckely, R. E. Food dyes and hyperkinetic children. *Academic Therapy*, 1974, *10*(1), 27–32.

Jani, S. N. & Jani, L. A. Nutritional deprivation and learning disabilities—an appraisal. *Academic Therapy*, 1974, *9*(1), 151–158.

Kasowski, M. A. & Kasowski, W. J. The burden of lead: How much is safe? *CMA Journal*, 1976, *114*(573).

Krippner, S. An alternative to drug treatment for hyperactive children. *Academic Therapy*, *10*(4), 433–439.

Lindenbaum, E. S. & Mueller, J. J. Effects of pyridoxine on mice after immobilization stress. *Journal of Nutrition and Metabolism*, 1974, *17*, 368–374.

Mayer, J. World wide report. *Medical Tribune*, January 19, 1970.

Millar, J. A. & Hernberg, S. Lead and d'Aminolevulinic acid dehydratase levels in mentally retarded children and in lead poisoned suckling rats. *Lancet,* 1970, *2,* 695–698.

Pasamanick, B., Rogers, M. E. & Lillienfeld. A. M. Pregnancy experience and the development of behavior disorder in children. *Journal of the American Psychiatric Association,* 1956, *112,* 613–618.

Pauling, L. Orthomolecular psychiatry. *Science,* 1968, 169–256.

Powers, H. W. S., Jr. Dietary measures to improve behavior and achievement. *Academic Therapy,* 1973, *9*(3), 203–214.

Rimland, B. High dosage level of certain vitamins in the treatment of children with severe mental disorders. In L. Pauling & D. Hawkins, Eds. *Orthomolecular Psychiatry.* San Francisco: W. H. Freeman Co., 1971.

Scherer, B. & Kramer, W. Influence of niacinamide administration on brain 5-HT and a possible mode of action. *Life Science,* 1972, *1,* 189–195.

Warburg, O. The prime cause and prevention of cancer. 1966 Linden Lecture, presented for the Nobel Peace Committee.

Wendle, F., Faro, M. D., Barker, J. N., Barsky, D., & Gutierrez, S. Developmental behaviors: Delayed appearance in monkeys asphyxiated at birth. *Science,* 1971, *171*(3976), 1173–1175.

Wunderlich, R. C. Treatment of the hyperactive child. *Academic Therapy,* 1973, *8*(4), 375–390.

Yaryura-Tobias, J. & Neziroglu, B. A. Violent behavior, brain dysrhythmia, and glucose dysfunction. *Journal of Orthomolecular Psychiatry,* 1975, *4*(3), 182–188.

BIBLIOGRAPHY

Hoffman, M. S. Early indications of learning problems. *Academic Therapy,* 1971, *7*(1).

Michaelson, K. A., & Sauderhoff, M. W. Lead poisoning. *Medical World News,* 7 September, 1973, p. 8.

Montagu, A. *Life before birth.* New York: New American Library, 1964.

Pfeiffer, C. C. Observations on trace and toxic elements in hair and serum. *Journal of Orthomolecular Psychiatry,* 1974, *3*(4), 259–264.

Silbergeld, E. K. & Goldberg, A. M. Effects of lead ingestion on mouse behavior. *Medical World News,* 7 September, 1973, p. 7.

Williams, R. J., Heffley, J. D., & Bode, C. W. The nutritive value of single foods. Paper presented to the National Academy of Sciences, Washington, D.C., 28 April 1971.

Wunderlich, R. C. *Kids, brains and learning.* St. Petersburg, Florida: Johnny Reads Inc., 1970.

Chapter 10

THE RATIONALE FOR OPTOMETRIC INTERVENTION IN LEARNING DISABILITIES

Harold N. Friedman

Optometry has long been concerned with visual function. An optometric diagnostic evaluation goes beyond a determination of ocular integrity or the need for glasses. The evaluation probes the ability of the visual system to gather and interpret information.

There are those professionals, both in and out of the eye care field, who still relate the visual function of the eye only to that of a camera. Yet current research indicates that the eye and the camera are more unlike than similar. The focusing system of the eye consists of a complicated neuromuscular system which changes the curvature of a protein capsule called a lens. This focusing system is not absolutely perfect and cannot produce a clear image throughout the retina. Even if it could produce such an image, the retina is not capable of responding to such an image. The retina is a relay station which changes light energy into neural signals. Information is transmitted to the brain neuroelectronically rather than in picture form. Only the central 2 or 3 degrees of the retina (foveal area) responds to fine contour, and it is at the center (macular) of this area that a human is capable of 20/20 eyesight. On the other hand, the peripheral retina has nerve cells capable of transmitting blurred information. This information involves directional orientation, movement, and intensity contrasts transmitted not pictorially but neuroelectronically.

Since clear resolution is achieved only in the very center of the eye, it is dependent on the precision of fixation or aiming of the eye. Therefore, the control of or lack of eye movement skills directly affects the quality of information received by the brain. The interaction between the peripheral retina and the complex eye movement system also affects the information received by the brain. Improper or inaccurate visual information transmitted to the brain can create a learning confusion.

A second important ocular function related to learning is the focusing capability of the eye. Change in focus is achieved by a lens system controlled primarily by the involuntary motor system. Generally, the system is capable of focusing through all the distances until about 40 years of age. However, the ease and efficiency of maintaining adequate focusing is most important to determine. It is not unusual for a school-age child to experience intermittent blurring and excessive effort to maintain clear vision.

Finally, a human has two eyes. If there is no wandering eye, a person must use the two of them together as team. In other words, he is binocular. It is important to know if there is any stress in the oculomotor system which would mean extra stress for maintaining binocular vision. This stress could result in physical pain, general ocular discomfort, and occasional blurring and/or double vision and would certainly detract from attention span and ease of concentration when reading. There is a physiological connection between the focusing and the binocular fusion system, which means that stress in one area probably will affect the other.

To summarize, there are three ocular skills which seem to have a relationship to efficient visual information gathering: eye movement and fixation control, focusing, and binocular eye teaming skills. Inefficiency in these areas may be unrelated to ocular pathology or the need of glasses for clear eyesight. Testing for adequacy in these oculomotor areas requires more than a standard eye evaluation for pathology and glasses.

The oculomotor system does not function independently of other motor systems. Information about spatial localization, movement, and directional orientation comes from gross motor skills of balance, body image, locomotion, and bilaterality. It is therefore necessary to investigate the level of development and ease of function of bilateral motor skills since the child's whole motor system may be involved in faulty information processing.

Another important part of optometric investigation involves the ability of the brain to recognize, reproduce, and remember visual coded data. Obvious examples of visual coded data are letters and numbers. These figures also have an auditory code. The ability of the brain to "crack" these codes affects reading and mathematical skills. Coding immaturities are consistently mentioned in the literature describing learning disabled children. While it is not the purpose of this paper to discuss the causes of learning disabilities, it should be noted that within the learning disabled population, there are children who exhibit symptoms of visual coding confusions. These children confuse and/or misinterpret visual coded data. The confusion could be in recognition (reading), reproduction (writing), spelling (memory), or any combination, and could be severe or minimal. Adaptation to these confusions depends on intelligence, proper educational and supportive intervention, and emotional stability. Optometrists feel that a sequenced visual perceptual training program supported by a proper educational approach contributes to a more positive adaptation of the learning disabled child with visual coding immaturities.

Clearly, one can have stress in the oculomotor system without being learning disabled. Almost every human being at one time has put too much stress on this system, resulting in eye strain, blur, or headache. Most people can adapt to this stress without the need for intervention. If, however, there is stress in the oculomotor system and other indications of a learning disability, then the adaptation becomes difficult and in some cases nonexistent. There is no other profession that examines the visual system from a functional point of view and then attempts to improve this function.

An optometric visual training program attempts to deal with increasing the function of the oculomotor system as well as providing a positive adaptation approach for those children with visual coding immaturities related to poor academic performance. The oculomotor goals include: (1) the efficient control of eye movement skills of tracking and fixation; (2) the ability to use both eyes as an efficient team; and (3) the ability to sustain and adjust focusing for any viewing distance. These goals are often achieved by the use of training lenses and/or orthoptic instrumentation. This instrumentation was originally designed for children with deviating eyes but has been adapted for use to increase the oculomotor skills described above. The instruments provide visual and motoric feedback, so that users are aware of whether they are using their eyes correctly and, if not, how to go about correcting themselves. The instrumentation allows for steriopis and involvement of the hands, so that there is an enhancement of eye-hand coordination. In many instances, the office training is reinforced by home exercises. These exercises may look easy and sometimes irrelevant, but in truth they are carefully sequenced in order to increase oculomotor efficiency.

When necessary, an optometric training program attempts to increase the efficiency of the child to extract appropriate information from visual stimulation. These mothods involve the use of commercial materials, tachistoscopic instruments and techniques, and individually designed procedures. The program is individualized and sequenced for each child. Many of these techniques have been written up and are used by schools and special education therapists. The optometric approach involves the sequenced learning of these techniques, the coordination of visual coding skills with other sensory motor learning, and the relationship of acquiring these skills to the functioning of the apparatus necessary to acquire the incoming information —the physical oculomotor system.

BIBLIOGRAPHY

Adler, F. H. *Physiology of the eye,* C. V. Mosby Co., New York: 1965.

Barsch, R. *Achieving perceptual motor efficiency,* Seattle: Special Child Publications, 1967.

Barsch, R. *Enriching perception and cognition,* Seattle: Special Child Publications, 1968.

Boynton, R. M. Retinal contrast mechanisms, In F. A. Young and D. B. Lindsley (Eds.), *Early experience and visual information processing in perceptual and reading disorders.* Washington, D.C.: National Academy of Sciences, 1970, 95–118.

Chalfanit, J. & Scheffelin, M. P. *Central processing dysfunctions in children —Review of the research,* (NINDS Monograph No. 9). Washington, D.C.: U.S. Government Printing Office, 1969.

Clements, S. D. *Minimal brain dysfunction in children,* (NINDS Monograph No. 3). Washington, D.C.: U.S. Government Printing Office, 1966.

Doty, R. W. Modulation of visual input by brain stem systems. In F. A. Young & D. B. Lindsley, Eds., *Early experience and visual information processing in perceptual and reading disorders.* Washington, D.C.: National Academy of Sciences, 1970, 143–150.

Eames, T. H. Visual handicaps to reading. *Journal of Education,* 1959, *141,* 1–35.

Flax, N. Visual functions in learning disabilities. *Journal of Learning Disabilities,* 1968, *1*(9), 551–556.

Flax, N. The contribution of visual problems to learning disabilities. *Journal of the American Optometric Association,* 1970, *41*(10), 841–845.

Friedman, H.N. A classroom oriented visual perceptual training program. In R. Woldod, Ed. *Visual and Perceptual Aspects for the Achieving and Underachieving Child.* Seattle: Special Child Publications, 1969.

Friedman, H.N. *Perceptual training manual.* Unpublished Manuscript, 1975. (Available from 7 Park Avenue, New York, New York 10016.)

Frostig, M., & Horne, B. *Teachers guide—Frostig program.* Chicago: Follet Publishing, 1973.

Getman, G. N. *Techniques and diagnostic criteria for the optometric care of children's vision.* Duncan, Oklahoma: Optometric Extension Program, 1959.

Harmon, D. B. *Notes of a dynamic theory of vision.* Austin, Texas: by author, 1958.

Jung, R. & Spillman, L. Receptive-field estimation and perceptual integration in human vision. In F. Young & D. B. Lindsley (Eds.), *Early experience and visual information processing in perceptual and reading disorders,* Washington, D.C.: National Academy of Sciences, 1970, 181–197.

Kephart, N. *Slow learner in the classroom.* Columbus, Ohio: Charles Merrill.

Marg, E. A neurological approach to perceptual problems. In F. A. Young and D. B. Lindsley (Eds.), *Early experience and visual information processing in perceptual and reading disorders,* Washington, D.C.: National Academy of Sciences, 1970, 151–156.

Michael, C. R. Retinal processing of visual images. *Scientific American,* 1969, *220* (5), 104–114.

Myers, S. & Hammill, D. *Methods for learning disorders.* New York: John Wiley, 1976.

Neisser, U. The processes of vision. *Scientific American,* 1968 *219* (3), 204–214.

Nichols, J. V. Ophthalmic disturbances. In J. L. Keeney, M. B. Keeney, & C. V. Mosby, Eds. *Dyslexia, diagnosis and treatment of reading disorders.* New York, 1968, 49–52.

Portage Guide to Early Education. Portage, Wisc.: Cooperative Education Service Agency.

Rosner, J. *Perceptual skills curriculum,* New York: Walker Book Co., 1968.

Silver, A., Hagin, R., Beecher, R. Scanning, diagnosis, and intervention in prevention of learning disabilities. *Journal of Learning Disabilities,* 1978, *11,* 5–18.

Spache, G., *Toward better reading.* Champaign, Ill.: Garrard Publishing Co., 1963.

Thomas, E. L. Movements of the eye. *Scientific American,* 1968, *219* (2), 88–95.

Vernon, M. D. *Backwardness in reading.* Cambridge, England: Cambridge University Press, 1957.

Chapter 11

DANCE/MOVEMENT THERAPY WITH THE MBD CHILD

Claire Schmais
Florette Orleans

The literature is replete with references to the importance of addressing the movement behavior of the child with minimal brain dysfunction (MBD) (see, for example, Frostig, 1975; Kephart, 1975). Dance therapy deals directly with this component within the context of a child's total development. Observation and analysis of the child's movement patterns form the baseline for creative therapeutic intervention using dance.

Dance as an educational medium can be traced to antiquity. Its recent emergence as an integrated part of the educational system can be attributed to the work of Emile Jacques-Dalcroze in Switzerland and Rudolph Laban in England (Laban & Laurence, 1947). Both stressed the need for variability and flexibility in body functioning prior to teaching specific skills. Based on Laban's educational philosophy, British children of all ages engage in dancelike activities to preserve their spontaneity and to develop their natural inclinations.

Creativity—the ability to search out new, unique solutions

to presenting problems—is the means through which everyone learns and copes throughout life. It has been shown that acquisition of specific information is predicated on the successful integration of a wide range of generalized skills and information (Frostig, 1975; Kephart, 1975).

Ideally, in working with all children, and in particular with MBD children, it is important to keep in mind that "learning requires opportunities to practice, organize and refine during the process of integrating them for everyday use. Consequently, creativity is directed at housing the required practice in as many different games and enjoyable experiences as possible" (Rappaport, 1975).

Too often, specialists in the field focus narrowly on one area of deficit—either the social, cognitive, or motor deficit—of the MBD child. To avoid this "tunnel vision," which Morse (1975) views as a hazard in the field, and to approach work with each child as a complex, unique individual, the dance therapist must pay attention to each child's dynamics, motivations, and aspirations. To that end it is crucial that, as part of a remedial program, every child have ample opportunity to explore his own needs and desires in the context of flexibly structured, open-ended, creative activities, such as those provided by dance therapy.

The authors agree with Morse (1975) that the dance therapist must be truly involved in "the total life experience of the special child. . . . To help a child is to study a life" (p. 337). The dance therapist undertakes this life study through the medium of movement. Dance therapy with the MBD child builds from the premise that movement is the infant's first mode of communication and remains the substrate of subsequent developmental processes.

Despite divergent theories and approaches in the field, MBD children are consistently described in terms of a specific spectrum of movement behavior. According to Gosling and Palonis (1978), McCarthy and McCarthy (1971), and Wender (1971), components of the spectrum are:

1. Hyperactivity
2. Poor eye-hand coordination
3. Clumsiness
4. Poor orientation to personal and environmental space
5. Distractibility and impulsivity
6. Emotional lability

The dance therapist recognizes these behaviors in the context of a child's total functioning and transmutes these so-called negatively valenced patterns into positive, creative dance experiences.

The work in dance therapy with MBD children blends therapeutic practices used with mentally retarded and emotionally disturbed children with principles inherent in modern educational dance. Dance therapists working with the retarded are particularly sensitive to the need for understanding developmental processes—from primitive reflex behavior to the emergence of automatic postural and adaptive reactions. It is generally accepted that a minimal level of sensorimotor functioning is necessary before a child is ready to master efficiently higher cognitive skills. Ayres (1975), for example, writes "that certain perceptual or sensory integrative development associated with motor concomitants must occur before a child is optimally prepared to read" (p. 311). Therefore, it is critical that the appropriate movement activities and environmental stimuli are available for children who have developmental lags.

Hatcher (Hatcher & Mullin 1967), a dance therapist who has worked extensively with such children in kindergarten, describes movement activities within four developmental stages:

1. Birth to 3 months—activities for the total body;
2. 3–9 months—activities emphasizing hands and feet;
3. 9–15 months—activities for multisensory awareness;
4. 15–24 months—activities for body-image concepts.

While emphasizing the motor component of development, it is important to remember that the child's cognitive and social skills are likewise progressing through various developmental stages.

On the other hand, dance therapy with emotionally disturbed children has highlighted the importance of developing a positive relationship through movement interaction and has taught the importance of accepting the existing emotional state of the child. Kalish (1968), who pioneered in dance therapy with autistic children at the Philadelphia Developmental Center, describes her goals as follows:

> The initial aim of movement therapy is to reach the autistic child at the level where he seems to be functioning . . . a primitive, sensory-motor level; and to explore with him rhythms, vocalizations and body action, in an attempt first to gain his attention, and hopefully lead to an emotional relationship and second, and equally important, to help him form a body image. . . .The therapist tries to engage the child's interest, using her own movements as stimuli, while offering the opportunity for reciprocal interaction. (p. 51)

While the autistic child represents one end of the spectrum of emotional isolation, most children with disabilities have secondary emotional problems.

Laban's work (Laban & Laurence, 1947) was instrumental in shifting the focus in movement education from task accomplishment to process in performance. Today, the dance therapist is concerned with process rather than product and looks at the child's perceptual-motor functioning, expressivity, and interaction within the context of his development. The child's perceptual-motor function can be seen during his/her performance in games, dances, and dramatic play. It is generally recognized that the major issues with MBD children include body awareness, spatial orientation (laterality and directionality), balance, eye-hand and eye-foot coordination, and arhythmicity (Ayres, 1975; Frostig, 1975; Radler & Kephart 1960).

For example, the therapist might note the child's body awareness in a mirror dance. Does he hesitate, use the wrong body parts, engage the opposite limb, or reverse his partner's pattern? Spatial or directional awareness is closely associated with body awareness. A child's internalized sense of left-right, up-down affects his perceptual efficiency in dealing with environmental constraints. The inability to follow verbal directions, such as "turn your head to the right," "raise your left arm," "walk backward," clearly indicates the child's lack of an internal map. Without such an internal design, the child is unable to orient himself to the external world.

According to Lashley (1969), the "motor schema" depends on internalized spatial representations of body axes, gravity, and the space coordinate systems derived from vision, audition, and touch. For example, the lack of an internalized body schema becomes apparent when a child is required to negotiate an obstacle course. He/she will be unable to correctly estimate heights or distances or shape his/her body to go under a low object or through a narrow space.

Another problem, that of balance, can be seen as the child walks an imaginary tightrope or quickly freezes into a position in space. The therapist here observes whether the child can easily shift his/her weight, how the child uses his arms to maintain balance (does the child use both arms or favor one?).

The problem of eye-hand-foot coordination becomes apparent in the use of props. For example, the child may be unable to kick a stationary object. As a Nerf ball approaches his midline he may be unable to keep his eye on the ball; some children close their eyes as the ball approaches, follow the ball with their heads rather than their eyes, or bend their heads backward. Additionally, a child may be unable to alternate feet in a predesigned floor pattern of stepping-stones.

Rhythmicity involves a number of subissues, such as synchrony, organization, and sequencing. In a simple dance, it is easy to discern whether the child can be self-synchronous (i.e., move the entire body in a single rhythm) or move in rhythm with others. Children may encounter difficulty duplicating the accents and temporal arrangement of an uneven phrase, such as skip, or of an even pattern, such as a step-hop. Phrases may lack preparation, follow-through, or recovery.

Whereas perceptual-motor function is seen in specific tasks, expressivity—the child's preferred behavioral style—is seen across tasks in his/her consistent movement characteristics and present emotional state. For this information, the dynamics of the movement—how an action is performed—is observed. For example: Does the child characteristically initiate an action with excessive exuberance that quickly dissipates into disorganization (agitated chaos?), or does he/she initiate activity with indifference and lethargy, gradually shifting into focused, concentrated attention?

Information about a child's personal style is derived by using Laban's observational system called "Effort" (Laban & Laurence, 1947). He identified eight dynamic elements which define a child's attitude to flow (free, bound), time (quick, slow), force (strong, light), and space (indirect, direct).

Flow, the primary motion factor, operates on a continuum from free to bound. A simple example of free flow is the continuous random movement of the infant (behavior often characterizing the MBD child). As the infant begins to fret, the emergence of controlled, tense motion—termed bound—is often seen.

The time factor describes a person's temporal preferences. It refers to the quickness or slowness typical of one's behavioral functioning and encompasses the range between these two polarities.

Force refers to the use of body weight in its relation to gravity. One is equally involved with one's weight when lightly handling a china cup or forcefully moving a car forward.

Space can be either direct, channeling movement toward

a specific goal (threading a needle), or indirect (wringing one's hands).

In addition to considering how the child moves through space, the dance therapist likewise considers where in space the child moves. The therapist looks at spatial preferences; how much space is claimed by an individual—an element crucial to the child's continuing interaction with the environment and, consequently, the most sophisticated level of movement functioning. Observation of the child's expressivity, efforts, and use of space complements the therapist's understanding of the child's perceptual-motor functioning.

Interaction is closely connected to expressivity. In the course of tag games, folk dances, and creative activities, the dance therapist observes the child's ability to adapt to others, to touch and be touched, and to move in step with other children. For example, how the child seeks attention is noted. Does communication occur in passing with a poke or by stopping and making eye contact? Children with minimal brain dysfunction may have difficulty moving in unison with a group or moving reciprocally with another child (i.e., moving back as someone moves forward). The dance therapist looks at the child's capacity to be close to another child as well as to give others the room they require.

The resultant information about a child's perceptual-motor functioning, expressive style, and social behavior provides the gestalt of his/her functioning. The child's perceptual-motor activity yields information relevant to establishing goals; the affective (expressive and interactive) information guides the process of the therapeutic intervention. The utilization of techniques that synthesize theory and practice from the fields of dance, education, and therapy enable the dance therapist to broaden a child's range of movement, to establish a realistic body image, and to develop more effective social skills.

The physical manifestation of the "disability," colored by the emotional state of the child, is the main concern of the dance therapist. The following clinical examples[1] describe one approach to dance therapy with MBD children.

Paul[2] a large awkward 11-year-old boy, had a typical movement style characterized by peripheral, jittery gestures around a flaccid, immobile torso. He entered the dance room in a highly anxious state, gesturing frenetically with his hands, making silly sounds, and hitting his head continuously with short, quick slaps. I picked up on the flexion/extension aspect of this self-punitive action and, as he mirrored me, he involved his entire arm. As our arms reached further into space we gradually slowed down the movement and began gently touching our heads. With rhythmic repetition and stretches he came to involve more and more of his torso, enabling him to experience opening out into space and closing himself in again. For a child such as this, whose flaccid body tone reflects his low self-esteem and lack of body awareness, such simple total body involvement is an important first step in helping him support peripheral limb gestures from his body center. Sensing his body weight, he began to sense himself and to be able to use his weight to accomplish tasks requiring balance and strength. He also had to sense his weight to experience himself as capable of making an impact on others.

On days when Paul's low energy and sad affect indicated that he was depressed, I worked toward lifting his mood while addressing the same body image issues through floor work. As he lay on his back, I stretched him gently and manipulated his arms and legs to allow him a passive experience of his bodily connections. The element of touch with this youngster, who had had very little positive experience of this kind, introduced the therapeutic element of nurturance and mothering—a life-long human need of all.

When he allowed himself to be taken care of, to be pampered, he seemed to be more positive about the body that caused him so much trouble. At this point, I encouraged him to attempt simple full-body exercises, such as folding and unfolding himself

---

[1]Examples used are of children Florette Orleans worked with at Bronx Children's Hospital, Gateway School, and Mt. Sinai Hospital, New York, 1970–78.

[2]The names of the children have been changed.

while still on the floor. I occasionally saw instances of torso involvement (a sign of change in body awareness) during the floor work similar to those observed as we danced through space in Paul's active state.

Developing a sound body image is widely accepted as a necessary prelude to a sound self-concept. Managing his body was a necessary prelude before Paul could use that body most efficiently to manage the environment and relate to others.

John, a 10 year old, presented an interesting example of a child who, because of an ability to execute one very specific, albeit complex, movement—a cartwheel—his extreme deficits in body image and spatial orientation were momentarily masked. Additionally, the recognition he received for performing this virtuoso act made it very difficult for him to tolerate failure in other movement areas or to attempt new behaviors. This child's lack of a sound body-image and orientation to space was less apparent than was that of Paul's.

I sought to increase John's limited spatial range, thus providing him with movement options outside his habitual patterns. As Kephart (1975) writes, "the optimum condition is not high degrees of skill. It is minimum ability in a wide number of motor activities" (p. 119). John was resistant to change because he had effectively compensated for his deficits by learning how to do a cartwheel and being excessively rewarded for this activity by adult authorities.

On close examination, it became clear that John was unable to translate into movements simple verbal directions to move sideward, backward, and forward. Rotary movement of his arms were perserverative in that they used the vertical plane, the same spatial area used in his cartwheels. Asking him to move in the horizontal or sagittal plane precipitated anxiety (resulting in disruptive behavior), because he did not know how to orient himself in space.

Because of the complexity of his one accomplishment, the crucial work with this youngster had to recapitulate early development. It was necessary to help him to focus on the various parts of his body and their relationship to one another and to learn how to extend his entire body in various relationships to space.

Floor work for this youngster was an opportunity to allay the anxiety of needing to perform. Being exercised while passive allowed him the important experience of relaxation, "which is not complete rest but compensatory movement which must be used to avoid too-rapid fatigue" (Russell, 1958, p. 29).

John's disruptive behavior when faced with new situations was ameliorated in playful situations. Creating different shapes in space (asking him to freeze into a statue while balancing on 1, 2, 3, 4, or 5 body parts) motivated him to explore new spatial dimensions. We also jumped to capture imaginary stars, crawled around and through objects, and spread soap bubbles through the room. The use of imagery helped John to act out his ambivalence and to externalize some of his fears and anxieties.

Once he could move in a gross fashion in various planes—by jumping up and down (vertical), by crawling (sagittal), by spreading and closing (horizontal)—he was able to begin to execute more complex rotary actions, an example of which was drawing a figure 8 through space with a wand.

Gail, a small, cute winsome seven year old, lacked awareness of when her body began or ended. She clung to adults and would frequently collide with objects and people, falling suddenly. Many MBD children like Gail, who are either overprotected or avoided, are overly dependent and socially immature. These children need to develop the social skills contingent on experiencing autonomy and self-control.

The main focus in this case was on fostering body boundaries. Gail needed first to develop some sense of autonomy, so that she could clearly experience the distinction between herself and other objects and people. Her lack of clear body boundaries was apparent in the unique pattern of her jumps—she seemed to take off from nowhere and simply melt into the floor—looking as if she would just keep going down and down if the floor were not there to receive her. She had difficulty organizing her body in order to accomplish even a simple task, such as catching a beanbag. She literally had to fold herself around an object in order to feel she had it.

The use of props was instrumental in working with Gail, because they provided the transition from self to others in space. A chair, for example, provided a simple means of delimiting the high and low point of a jump. Holding firmly to its back, Gail had to push down as she prepared to jump up. As she came back down on the floor, placing her hands back on the chair served as a brake system that kept her from sinking into the floor.

A large, elastic, tubular cloth was used to experience dependency with individuation. Both she and I would step into this cloth. We faced one another and spread the cloth so that our entire back was resting against it. As we moved away from one another, the cloth would become taut and, in trying to maintain its tension, Gail experienced her weight, while at the same time experiencing the safety of being connected to someone else without actually being in physical contact with that person.

Gail enjoyed playing with a Freeka—a bright, 2-foot length of plastic hose which, when swung energetically, produces an eerie, haunting sound. The energy and spatial clarity required to produce this sound are the kind not easily activated by a child such as Gail. Seeing myself or another child playing with the Freeka often motivated her to repeat the motion until some measure of success was achieved. When she used the directness and strength necessary to accomplish this task, the noise was an auditory reward of her own achievement.

The foregoing are brief descriptions of some of the problems and their solutions that evolved during work with MBD children. They illustrate the way in which a movement dialogue develops between therapist and child, starting with the mood and strengths (as well as weaknesses) of that particular child.

As the dialogue continues, each child indicates his/her readiness to move on to a more complicated problem—for example, to explore a new space, to try a new game, or to improvise with new friends.

Within each session, a specific scenario develops as a consequence of the interaction between therapist and child. The resultant movement dialogue is an expression of communication between the two at a cognitive-affective level; it is a creative enactment of issues of importance to a specific child at a specific moment in time seen in terms of the child's ongoing life stream.

The initial thrust of each session is to provide a climate in which the child is free to risk new behaviors and to modify old patterns. The form and substance of the movement interaction with MBD children are shaped by this crucial concern. This mandates that the therapist "capitalize upon their unique strengths, rather than spend fruitless energy in trying hopelessly to compensate for so-called weakness" (Torrance, 1963, p. 25).

It is sometimes necessary to stay with the limited movement repertoire of the MBD child for some time in order to allay the youngster's anxiety and fear of failure. Accepting a child, by accepting his movements, is an important step in developing a therapeutic relationship and in promoting self-esteem.

The therapist develops the therapeutic script from the behavioral themes presented by the child. Dance therapy, by clarifying and reinforcing the chosen input through multisensory channels (repetition, mirroring, verbalization, touch), facilitates the child's faulty feedback channels. In relation to repetition, for example, Rappaport (1975) states that many learning disabled children "cannot imagine how to cope with a situation that they have not actually experienced. . . . To prevent that, the adult and the child must have continual dry runs —as many as are needed" (p. 373).

Additionally, respect for the child's level of functioning is demonstrated by engaging in activities with the child at his/her level. Mutual participation strengthens the budding relationship. As Morse (1975) puts it: "It is not to manipulate but to care and to realize that, freed from fear and distrust, the child will show the desire to learn" (p. 347).

Techniques are merely instrumental to the life goals that have been stressed. The intent is to involve actively the MBD child in a supportive environment, presenting alternatives for his/her maladaptive functioning. Dance therapy—a holistic, process-oriented, interactive modality—offers human support and creative activities at the level of each child's functioning. The dance therapist moves with the child toward healthier more effective functioning.

REFERENCES

Ayres, J. A. Sensorimotor foundations of academic ability. In W. Cruickshank & D. Hallahan (Eds.), *Perceptual and learning disabilities in children* (Vol. 2). Syracuse: Syracuse University Press, 1975.

Frostig, M. The role of perception in the integration of psychological functions. In W. Cruickshank & D. Hallahan (Eds.), *Perceptual and learning disabilities in children* (Vol. 1). Syracuse: Syracuse University Press, 1975.

Gosling, A. & Palonis, M. A scale of movement characteristics for hyper- and hypo-active children. In S. Schmais & F. Orleans (Eds.), *Dance therapy research: seven pilot studies.* New York, Hunter College, 1978.

Kalish, B. Body movement therapy for autistic children. In *Proceedings of the 3rd Annual Conference of the American Dance Therapy Association.* Columbia, Maryland: American Dance Therapy Association, 1968.

Kephart, N. C. The perceptual-motor match. In W. Cruickshank & D. Hallahan (Eds.), *Perceptual and learning disabilities in children* (Vol. 1). Syracuse: Syracuse University Press, 1975.

Laban, R. & Laurence, S. C. *Effort.* London: MacDonald Evans, 1947.

Lashley, K. In search of the Engram. In P. Tibbets (Ed.), *Perception: Selected readings in science and phenomenology.* Chicago: Quadrangle, 1969.

McCarthy, J. J. & McCarthy, J. F. *Learning disabilities.* Boston: Allyn and Backo, Inc., 1971.

Morse, W. C. The learning disabled child and considerations of life space. In W. Cruickshank & D. Hallahan (Eds.), *Perceptual and learning disabilities in children* (Vol. 1). Syracuse: Syracuse University Press, 1975.

Radler, D. H. & Kephart, N. C. *Success through play.* New York: Harper & Row, 1960.

Rappaport, S. R. Ego development in learning disabled children. In W. Cruickshank & D. Hallahan (Eds.), *Perceptual and learning disabilities in children* (Vol. 1). Syracuse: Syracuse University Press, 1975.

Russell, J. *Modern dance in education.* London: MacDonald & Evans, 1958.

Torrance, P. E. *Education and the creative potential.* Minneapolis: University of Minnesota Press, 1963.

Wender, P. H. *Minimal brain dysfunction in children.* New York: John Wiley & Son, Inc., 1971.

BIBLIOGRAPHY

Cratty, B. J. & Martin, Sister M. M. *Perceptual motor efficiency in children.* Philadelphia: Lea & Febiger, 1969.

Cruickshank, W. M. & Hallahan, D. P. (Eds.). *Perceptual and learning disabilities in children* (2 vols.). Syracuse: Syracuse University Press, 1975.

Gilliom, B. C. *Basic movement education for children.* Reading, Massachussets: Addison-Wesley, 1970.

Hatcher, C. C. & Mullin, H. *More than words.* Pasadena, Ca.: Parents-for-Movement Publication, 1967.

Millar, S. *The psychology of play.* New York: Jason Aronson, 1974.

Schilder, P. *The image and appearance of the human body.* New York: International University Press, Inc., 1950.

Tarnopol, L. (Ed.). *Learning disabilities.* Springfield, Illinois: Charles C. Thomas, 1969.

Thomas, A., Chess, S., & Birch, H. *Temperament and behavior disorders in children.* New York: New York University Press, 1968.

Chapter 12

SPECIFIC LEARNING DISABILITIES
Communication and Language Process Disturbances
Sydney Zentall

Children with specific learning disabilities (SLD) fail because there is poor correspondence between the child's learning style and environment. This failure is exacerbated by expectations of school personnel that children of average IQ and with prior opportunities to learn will demonstrate average progress in school. SLD children, by definition, have average IQ, can see and hear within normal ranges, and do not have impoverished early learning experiences due to poor homes, poor teaching, frequent moves by the child's family, or chronic illness (Hallahan & Kauffman, 1976).

Thus, there are strong expectations placed on them to learn by conventional methodologies, and tasks and in standard physical settings. However, remediation of SLD children is achieved most effectively by correctly pairing child characteristics with learning environments and tasks. There is an emphasis on modifying the setting and those events that *precede* performance and behavioral requirements. Such a treatment philosophy is at variance with the modal treatment for children with primary behavior disorders. For these children, it is assumed that inappropriate or inconsistent consequences (reinforcement and punishment) have been applied to their behavior; thus, they have learned inappropriate behavioral reactions (Haring & Phillips, 1962, pp. 9–10). Treatment for these children involves consistent reinforcement of appropriate behaviors or modifying the events that *follow* performance.

SLD children, on the other hand, because of learning style differences require modification of antecedents to task failure or behavioral deviation. To the extent that (1) behavior disordered children have inappropriate performance expectations placed on them or (2) SLD children develop secondary behavior problems (frustration), these treatment approaches are, of course, overlapping.

This chapter will briefly delineate how learning styles may be at variance with the setting and what educational implications there may be for such child/environment discrepancies. Two major types of SLD will be presented: (1) who manifest problems in language (written language; i.e., reading, math, spelling, and composition—as well as spoken language; i.e., listening and talking) due to problems with auditory learning; and (2) overriding problems of behavior as well as learning (hyperactivity). These specific learning problems, as representatives of the total range of problems and contributing factors, will be discussed in terms of appropriate antecedent modifications, for example, of the environment, physical setting, or task.

Written and Spoken Language Disorders

Written language deficits are more readily identified than are problems in spoken language. This may be due to the fact that (1) deviations in spoken language appear initially in the developing years prior to school enrollment, (2) school personnel do not require spoken language to the same extent as written expression as a measure of learning, and (3) early delays in spoken language often carry over into more significant retardation in the higher-level tasks of receptive written language (comprehension of written symbols, that is, reading and math) as well as in the highest level involving the expression of meaning (composition) and of sound symbol relations (spelling). For these reasons, the analysis of written language and associated techniques for remediation will be emphasized initially.

When a regular classroom teacher expresses concern over the performance of a child, it is because the child is not progressing as per age expectations. Such a referral typically results in a follow-up academic achievement assessment by a special educator or diagnostician in the area of the presenting or referral complaint. That is, if a teacher feels the child is not doing his or her reading assignments, it becomes necessary to objectively confirm the presence of an achievement problem in reading. If this academic problem is significant, the second task is to determine why the problem exists in order to plan an appropriate remediational approach. To the first purpose, the child is given an individual achievement test in reading, and the scores are compared with those of the child's normative age group. A deviation from age expectancy confirms the presence of a problem. To determine what factors may have contributed to the assessed problem, a number of variables are considered and tested.

Learning Process Disturbances

Probably the major contributing factor to failure for specific learning disability children is one or more problem(s) in the psychological processes or learning skills involved in perception, figure-ground, memory, and comprehension of abstract relations.

Learning begins with the reception of an impulse along one of the sensory receptor modalities (visual, auditory, olfactory, tactual, kinesthetic, and gustatory). The near receptors are used extensively by infants and toddlers in learning, while school-age children rely heavily on the visual and auditory distance-receptor systems. Sensations are organized along each modality into perceptions. For example, a visual sensation could be light, color, and line; but to be organized into a perception, it would be a yellow triangle and would be recognized as different from similar configurations. These perceptions are then ready to be recognized as distinct from a background of competing patterns (i.e., figure-ground), to be stored into memory, for comparing, contrasting, and associating with other perceptions, events, ideas, and experiences to accumulate meaning.

Using various tests, each of these process areas from perception through reasoning ability can be assessed along both auditory and visual modalities to determine reasons for learning failure. While the specific learning disabled child is defined most generally as having average reasoning abilities (either visual performance or auditory verbal IQ) and good visual and auditory sensory acuity, problems in memory, figure-ground, or perception are not uncommon.

Most would readily agree that the visual system (i.e., visual perception, figure-ground, memory, and reasoning) contributes to problems in written language, but problems in the auditory learning system are less obvious as moderators of disorders (Zigmond, 1971). For this reason, problems in auditory learning which provide the basis for spoken and written language disorders will be systematically developed.

Auditory Learning

The first auditory task of a child is listening. This task occurs under complex and highly variable conditions for all children. The auditory stimulus is ephemeral; it is here and gone in seconds. One cannot go back and scan what was presented, except through reliance or memory, or skim ahead to see what is coming. Additionally there are no spaces between spoken symbols as there are between written words. Thus the task of separating language into its component units becomes difficult even for normal auditory processing children. The spoken language of even normal children thus often denotes these listening problems with a phrase strung together into a single word like "yentoo" translating to "do you want to." When the task of separating meaning units has been accomplished, children are then ready to distinguish the separate elements within one spoken word. Such an analysis is requisite to the development of reading and spelling (Durell, 1964).

Added to these, are other general problems of the listener which require adapting to a range of individual differences in pitch, inflection, rate, volume, and dialect. All of these variations compound problems for a child with an auditory learning deficit, as described in the next section.

Auditory Perception Problems

Children with auditory perception problems hear sounds within the normal range as measured on an audiometer but do not detect differences between words. When these children are given an auditory discrimination test, they have difficulty distinguishing between such words as hat and mat, stuck and struck. Sometimes they have problems in articulation simply because they do not hear these small differences between words (Van Riper, 1963). Children with such difficulties rarely have problems in math but more readily manifest reading and spelling problems. If they are placed with a teacher who teaches through the auditory modality (i.e., through a concentration on sounds), their problems are exacerbated. Books presenting content through this modality are similar to those written by Dr. Suess, in which all the vocabulary involves similar sounding words or families (e.g., at, rat, hat, mat, fat, sat, bat). However, if the words all sound the same, the stories are meaningless to children with auditory perception problems.

Auditory Figure-Ground Problems

Problems with auditory figure-ground occur for children in the presence of background noises such as conversations, television, classroom noise, or traffic. Unlike visual stimulation, auditory stimulation is continuous. While it allows us to maintain contact with our environment even during sleep, it is also *not* possible to turn it off or turn it down during the day. Some children are at the mercy of their auditory environment because they are unable to selectively focus their attention on relevant conversations while ignoring background noises and thus do not learn well from class discussion or group projects.

Auditory Sequential Memory

Problems in the area of auditory sequential memory determine a large number of spoken and written language problems. Young children typically evidence spoken sequential memory problems such as mixing or reversing letters in words ("psghetti" for "spaghetti"), parts of compound words ("sitter-baby" for "babysitter"), words within sentences, and sentences within stories or paragraphs. For older children such signs may be symptomatic.

Because of poor memory, spoken and written language often lacks production, with children expressing sentence fragments, single words only, syntax problems, or a confused sequence of ideas. Children with this disability typically exhibit reading problems, because many experience problems recalling the equivalence between the sound and the written symbol that is representative of the sound. Similarly, they have problems recalling the sequence of events in a story. Spelling errors that are characteristic of poor auditory learners bear little resemblance to the word, (e.g., "tairl" for "table"), reflect loss of memory for a part of a word (e.g., "together" spelled "tother"), or involve reliance on words the child has already visually memorized (e.g., "monkey" for "machine") (Zigmond, 1976).

Problems with auditory memory may account for some math difficiencies such as remembering the sequence of steps involved in math operations or even recalling number facts which have been drilled auditorally.

Auditory Comprehension

The ability to reason, that is, to comprehend meaning and abstract relations from auditory stimuli, is often informally measured by a child's ability to express meaning verbally. Initial indicators of problems in this area can be seen in the child's use of single words and parts of speech. A child who has difficulty naming objects (using nouns), for example, may not understand that more than one thing can have the same name. Difficulty with verbs may be noted by a child's insistence that waving connotes only a hand and that pointing refers specifically to a finger.

Adjectives become even more abstract, because the understanding that words can represent attributes must be recognized. Children have been noted to say "no, no, that not sharp —that knife." Prepositions are similarly abstract, since the same auditory symbol can represent a number of unlike objects or experiences depending on context. For example, the preposition "on" can connote (1) in a position above, as with "put your pencil on the paper"; (2) near to, as in "cottage on the lake"; (3) at the time of, as in "on time"; (4) to engage in, as in "on a trip"; (5) in the state of, as in "on parole"; (6) as a result of, as in "a profit on the sale"; (7) in the position of covering, as in "put your shoes on"; (8) continuously, as in "she sang on," and so on.

Additionally, there are words or phrases that refer directly to concepts which may be particularly problematic, for example, use of puns, absurdities, humor, and directional words (e.g., before-after, same-different, beside, around). When a child has difficulty with single words and phrases, it is assured that meaning derived from sentences, paragraphs, and stories will be impoverished.

Some of these children with auditory comprehension problems have difficulties with even the most basic components of attaching meaning to auditory stimuli, that is, the prosodic features of language involved in meaning communicated through inflection (e.g., questions typically are communicated with a raise in voice). Other children cannot attach meaning to such social sounds as fire engines, telephones, or a knocking. Where a child has difficulty understanding meaning, there is an associated severe retardation involved in the verbal and written expression of meaning (i.e., talking and composition).

Treatment Implications

Children who experience difficulty with some of these auditory skills will probably have problems learning the sounds of individual letters, blending sounds into words, and sounding out words. These latter skills are necessary for certain auditory approaches to reading and spelling instruction (Zigmond, 1976). Problems in processing, recalling, and associating auditory stimuli quite apparently suggest educating children through a reliance on visual experiences whenever possible. That is, math facts, spelling words, and reading words can all be learned with a visual perception and memory emphasis, for example, by using flash cards or tachistoscopic presentations (Johnson & Myklebust, 1967). Ideally children should learn material through their strong input modalities, and once an asymptotic level of achievement is reached, they can practice through their weak modalities. Where this is not possible, both auditory and visual stimuli can be paired; for example, directions for a task could be both written and verbally presented.

However, while much of reading, math, spelling, and listening can be compensated for by a reliance on an alternative stimulus input mode, spoken language and composition as types of expressive language are primarily auditory, requiring good auditory memory to achieve any measure of fluency or organization. In these instances practice in the weak modality will be necessary, for example, by listening to longer and longer taped stories and then recounting the events. Additionally, teaching such children various mnemonics, such as imagining visual images that correspond to the auditory material, may be an aid to recall or to storytelling.

It has been assumed above that a child will present consistent modality deficits. However, if more than one learning process is involved, this may not always be the case. Children have been observed to recall auditory events poorly but to reason exceptionally well from verbally presented material. In such instances, discussion groups or lectures involving new material may be appropriate while recall of associated facts may be undertaken by visual memory techniques.

Such a match of children's learning styles with tasks and teaching methodology will prevent failure for these children; as well, it may obviate reactions to failure often exhibited by SLD children who assume, as their teachers often do, that they are lazy or dumb.

HYPERACTIVE CHILDREN

While most SLD children demonstrate academic problems in their initial school years which result in later problems of adjustment (outcomes of failure and frustration), some hyperactive children evidence behavioral control difficulties prior to school enrollment. They later demonstrate problems in written language, and not until adolescence do secondary and new problems involving antisocial behavior occur (Minde, Lewin, Weiss, Lavigueur, Douglas, & Sykes, 1971). Thus, in terms of chronology of referral complaints, behaviors are the primary problem. Ratings summed across a number of these behavioral problems (hyperactivity, impulsivity, variability, short attention span, etc.) provide a reliable basis for identifying these children (Zentall & Barack, 1979). Hyperactive children, like children with auditory learning disorders, do not exhibit problem behavior or deficit performance in all school settings nor with all tasks.

Environmental Antecedents

The antecedent conditions demonstrated to exacerbate hyperactivity are decreases in environmental stimulation (Zentall, 1975; Zentall & Zentall, 1976). This suggests the increased activity, precipitated by low environmental stimulation, functions to increase auditory, visual, and kinesthetic stimulation to children thereby increasing their arousal. That is, activity serves as a regulatory mechanism to maintain optimal arousal; so when a child experiences insufficient stimulation resulting in reduced arousal, increases in activity supplement the available environmental stimulation. Where the situation or activity provides sufficient stimulation (e.g., on the playground), measurable differences between hyperactive children and their normal counterparts have not been observed (Zentall, 1975). Increases in distal visual plus auditory stimulation have been presented to hyperactive children when they are in the context of a boring task (sitting and waiting), producing significant reductions in activity (Zentall & Zentall, 1976). Similarly, the chemical introduction of stimulation (amphetamine drug therapy) reduces the need for response-produced stimulation (i.e., hyperactivity).

Treatment Implications

Because increases in environmental stimulation appear to normalize hyperactive children, suggestions for treatment involve adding novelty to environments while maintaining structure, as outlined in greater detail elsewhere (Zentall, 1977). While it may be that hyperactive children "take in" stimulation in novel condtitions (i.e., look around the class), they appear to work more efficiently while on task. Shores and Haubrich (1969) demonstrated that hyperactive children spent 10 percent less time maintaining visual attention to tasks while in a classroom relative to time spent in a nonstimulating cubicle. Still, they did not demonstrate faster, more accurate performance in the cubicle as a result of increases in time on task. Thus, it may be hyperactive children use the time off task to take in stimulation, allowing for more concentrated and productive time on task.

Task Antecedents

The learning style of hyperactive children has received less systematic study. Tasks have been identified which elicit poorer performance in hyperactive relative to normally active children with equivalent IQs. These tasks appear to cluster into several areas. Hyperactive children perform poorly on tasks requiring (1) eye-hand fine motor coordination, (2) rapid reaction times, (3) choice of or search for a correct response among similar visual alternatives, (4) analysis of a relevant visual image from a confusing visual background, and (5) sustained performance and attention to a repetitive rote task (see list of specific tasks in Douglas, 1974).

Simple rote tasks may consistently disrupt the performance of hyperactive children, because they provide insufficient stimulation resulting in disruptive stimulus-seeking behavior often called distraction and hyperactivity. This is supported by findings of increases in activity as a function of time on such tasks, especially for hyperactive children (Cohen & Douglas, 1972). This increased activity is thought to substitute for reductions in task novelty over time (Cohen & Douglas, 1972; Reardon & Bell, 1970). When increases in relevant stimulation were added to this type of easy rote task, reduced motor activity and increased performance were reported (Rugel, Cheatam, & Mitchell, 1978). These findings have been interpreted by Rugel et al. as consistent with the underarousal theory of hyperactivity (Zentall, 1975).

However, performance disruptions and increased activity resulted for hyperactive children when stimulation was added to tasks that (1) tapped areas of possible learning deficit (e.g., visual-motor tasks or visual search tasks) or (2) were not repetitive, boring tasks (Zentall, Zentall, & Barack, 1978; Zentall, Zentall, & Booth, 1978). Here, adding stimulation embedded the relevant features of an already problematic visual attention task, thus rendering it an embedded task which is a noted problem area for hyperactive children (Douglas, 1974).

Overall stimulation is beneficial for hyperactive children when it is added (1) to the distal environment; (2) to the period following task completion, especially for complex visual tasks; or (3) possibly within the task itself if the task is overly familiar or involves rote practice. We are just beginning to understand the complex antecedent task and environmental moderators of hyperactivity. Many of these factors appear to relate to the low level of arousal for these children, particularly with overly familiar environments and tasks. Other precipitating factors, however, may be more specific to learning process deficits primarily evidenced in visual- (1) attention, (2) analysis (figure-ground), (3) search, and (4) motor-tasks. While there is some incipient evidence that similar attention problems are evidenced with auditory tasks (Douglas, 1972), this area is even less developed in terms of available empirical data.

CONCLUSION

What appears to be most confusing about specific learning disabled children is the variability of their behavior. This sometimes good, sometimes poor behavior communicates to the teacher that this child with average intelligence and experiences is just lazy. It is, however, just this variability that promises a good prognosis in time. Use of the term variability expresses the present lack of overall predictability concerning behavior of SLD children that sometimes appears to be normal. It may be that task, time, and environmental factors have converged to produce this normalization. Therefore, to examine the temporal, physical, spatial, and task variables within which we place these children and to compare these with the child's assessed learning style appears to be the strongest approach for specific learning disabled children.

REFERENCES

Cohen, N. J., & Douglas, V. I. Characteristics of the orienting response in hyperactive and normal children. *Psychophysiology,* 1972, *9,* 238–245.

Douglas, V. I. Stop, look and listen: The problem of sustained attention and impulse control. *Canadian Journal of Behavioral Science,* 1972, *4,* 259–282.

Douglas, V. I. Sustained attention and impulse control: Implications for the handicapped child. In J. A. Swets and L. L. Elliott (Eds.), *Psychology of the Handicapped Child.* Washington: U.S. Government Printing Office, 1974.

Durrell, D. D. *Teaching young children to read.* in W. G. Cuffs (Ed.), *U.S. Department of Health, Education, and Welfare Conference Proceedings,* 1964.

Hallahan, D. P., & Kauffman, J. M. *Introduction to learning disabilities.* New Jersey: Prentice-Hall, Inc., 1976.

Haring, N. G., & Phillips, E. L. *Educating emotionally disturbed children.* New York: McGraw Hill, 1962.

Johnson, D. J., & Myklebust, H. R. *Learning Disabilities: Educational Principles and Practices.* New York: Grune and Stratton, 1967.

Minde, K., Lewin, D., Weiss, G., Lavigueur, H., Douglas, V. I., & Sykes, E. The hyperactive child in elementary school: A 5-year controlled follow-up. *Exceptional Children,* 1971, *38,* 215–221.

Reardon, D. M., & Bell, G. Effects of sedative and stimulative music on activity levels of severely retarded boys. *American Journal of Mental Deficiency,* 1970, *75,* 156–159.

Rugel, R. P., Cheatam, D., & Mitchell, A. Body movement and inattention in learning disabled and normal children. *Journal of Abnormal Child Psychology,* 1978, *6,* 325–337.

Shores, R. E., & Haubrich, P. A. Effect of cubicles in educating emotionally disturbed children. *Exceptional Children,* 1969, *36,* 21–24.

Van Riper, D. *Speech correction: Principles and methods* (4th ed.) Englewood Cliffs: Prentice-Hall, 1963.

Zentall, S. S. Environmental stimulation model. *Exceptional Children,* 1977, *43,* 502–510.

Zentall, S. S. Optimal stimulation as theoretical basis of hyperactivity. *American Journal of Orthopsychiatry,* 1975, *45,* 549–563.

Zentall, S. S., & Barack, R. S. Rating scales for hyperactivity: Concurrent validity, reliability, and decisions to label for the Conners and Davids abbreviated scales. *Journal of Abnormal Child Psychology,* 1979, *7,* 179–190.

Zentall, S. S., & Zentall, T. R. Activity and task performance of hyperactive children as a function of environmental stimulation. *Journal of Consulting and Clinical Psychology,* 1976, *44,* 693–697.

Zentall, S. S., Zentall, T. R., & Barack, R. S. Distraction as a function of within-task stimulation for hyperactive and normal children. *Journal of Learning Disabilities,* 1978, *11,* 540–548.

Zentall, S. S., Zentall, T. R., & Booth, M. E. Within-task stimulation: Effects on activity and spelling performance in hyperactive and normal children. *Journal of Educational Research,* 1978, *71,* 223–230.

Zigmond, N. K. Auditory processes in children with learning disabilities. In L. Tarnopol (Ed.), *Learning disabilities.* Springfield, Illinois: Charles C. Thomas, 1971.

Zigmond, N. K. *Teaching children with special needs.* Dubuque, Iowa: Gorsuch-Scarisbrick, 1976.

LIFE AFTER DIAGNOSIS
Schooling

Betty S. Levinson
Claire D. Nissenbaum

Diagnosis of the MBD child, more commonly known in education as the child with specific learning disability (SLD), leaves
the question unanswered: what is the best prescription for the
child; what treatment plan best suits the child's unique needs?

The terms *minimum brain dysfunction, diagnosis, treatment, prescription* reflect the earlier dominant orientation of
most parents and professionals to the medical model and imply
medical management, especially through drugs. Research and
practice, however, show increasingly that the basic problems
are psychoneurological; they arise from neurophysiological
processes markedly different from the norm (Cruickshank,
1978). Now there is virtual unanimity among the professions
that the syndrome demands clinical management by an interdisciplinary team, with the major focus on educational programming. Less often do educators "diagnose and prescribe";
more frequently, they use psychoeducational tests and other
measures to assess a child's strengths and deficits to determine
ability to function in school and to plan the child's individual
educational program.

The SLD syndrome (which goes by many names and which in the United States is legally defined as an educational handicap) is a culturally imposed disability. Children in nonliterate, more primitive cultures have no such "learning disability." In advanced cultures where the spelling of the language is phonetically regular, as in Italy, there is little dyslexia (Critchley, 1975). For many U.S. children, the specific learning disability operates visibly only in the academic setting—the school (Rawson, 1968, p. 28). It has been demonstrated that in classes where the instructional technology is suited to the students' learning styles and individual needs, SLD children learn (Reynolds & Birch, 1977, pp. 448, 449). Much attributed to *learning* disability is the result of inadequate teacher training. It is *teaching* disability, a defect of the system (Keogh, 1976, p. 33).

In the United States, with few exceptions, schools reward conforming students with "left-brain" skills—reading, spelling, math computation, logic, writing ability—skills that are currently attributed to dominance of the left hemisphere. Few schools reward, and most penalize, the "right-brained" person: wholistic, creative, intuitive, more inclined to challenge and to question, whose strengths are in nonverbal conceptual thinking in math and science, and in music, art, architecture and other nonlinear, nonsequential skills. This is clear from the biographies of such creative geniuses as Albert Einstein, Leonardo da Vinci, Auguste Rodin, Thomas Edison, Harvey Cushing, Winston Churchill, and Woodrow Wilson. All had serious school problems (Lynn, Glucking, & Kripke, 1978, p. 7). It is also clear from current case records of bright SLD children whose academic skills are significantly discrepant from expected achievement.

Don (not his real name), 15, was advised by his counselor to avoid careers which involved mathematics and to forget about math in high school. Soon after, Don was employed as a part-time research assistant in a university physics lab, using sophisticated mathematics. He also used a calculator, to compensate for his inability to memorize basic math facts. His unique needs may be seen from the discontinuity of his school and work experience.[1]

Since 1975, U.S. public schools have been required by federal law to provide "free, appropriate education for all handicapped children, *which emphasizes special education and related services to meet their unique needs.*" The federal regulations governing implementation of the *Education for All Handicapped Children Act,* Public Law (PL) 94–142, stress placement of handicapped children in programs with nonhandicapped students:

> Each public agency shall ensure that *to the maximum extent appropriate, handicapped children are educated with children who are not handicapped* and that special classes, separate schooling or other removal of handicapped children from the regular educational environment occurs *only when the nature or severity of the handicap is such that education in regular classes with the use of supplementary aids and services cannot be satisfactorily* achieved (PL 94–142, 20 U.S. Code § 1401 et seq., 42 *Federal Register* 42474 et seq., 23 August 1977, emphasis added).

Defined in the federal regulations as placement in the " *least restrictive environment,*" this administrative practice has become known popularly as "mainstreaming." Current mainstreaming practices, however, often are administrative expedients dictated by economics and available resources, presented to parents with underemphasis on the nature and consequences of specific learning disability and overemphasis on the benefits of placement with nonhandicapped children. This is understandable, though not acceptable, as a result of the misunderstanding of the syndrome by teachers, administrators, and school psychologists because of serious inadequacies in professional training (O'Donnell & Bradfield, 1976, p. 51).

Often the outcome is the unwitting subversion of the intent

[1]Case file, TRI=Services Center, Rockville, Maryland, 1977.

of the handicapped children act, specifically stated as "full educational opportunity for handicapped children"; and constitutes "the denial of an appropriate education"(McCarthy, 1978, p. 56). The difficulty is in the interpretation of the phrase ". . . to the maximum extent appropriate."

The regular classroom teacher, legally designated the executor of mainstream educational programs for handicapped children, has had litle preparation in undergraduate, i.e. preservice training as preparation for teaching the student with special needs, the "exceptional" student. Little effective in-service training has been made available since the passage of the handicapped children act, though it holds regular classroom teachers responsible to deliver the program. (Parks & Rousseau, 1977; See also Cruickshank, 1978; Lynn et al., 1978, p. 98) Mainstreaming is therefore an issue in contract negotiations with union leaders of both the National Education Association and the AFL-CIO American Federation of Teachers, who demand appropriate in-service training, lower pupil-teacher ratios, and supportive professional and clerical services for classroom teachers.

Ninety percent of the 49 million U.S. school children attend public schools (*PTA Today,* 1979, p. 4). Conservative estimates calculate that from 2 to 4 million are handicapped by specific learning disability (Smith, 1978, p. 3). Obviously, educational solutions for SLD children must be effected largely in the public schools. But current administrative response to the law is constrained by the ratio of handicapped children to available trained personnel by the state's interpretation of the PL94–142 and the federal regulations, by court decisions, by preexisting state law, by preexisting state and local programs, by existing physical plants, by fiscal resources, and by political support for (or opposition to) programs for handicapped children (Stannard, 1976, pp. 141 ff). Where school boards do not control local financing of public schools, these constraints are especially serious. Equally serious is the widespread administrative resistance to change (Meisgeier, 1976, p. 102).

Parents have the legal right to choose private special school placement at their own expense, if public schools decline to pay for it, but the cost is prohibitively expensive. This alternative is possible only for the affluent.[2]

Parents adivsed by competent medical, psychological, and educational specialists find the decision about school placement a difficult one to make.[3] Indeed, it is not an easy question for noneducational professionals on multidisciplinary teams. Even education specialists are frequently uncertain about answers to the programmatic questions for a given child. On what bases, then, is the decision made? A written Individual Educational Program (IEP) is mandated by PL94–142.

The appropriateness of an IEP to meet an SLD student's unique needs depends on:

1. sophisticated understanding of the behavioral manifestations of the disability, social-emotional as well as academic; more precisely of its underlying neurophysiological bases (sic) and the implications for placement and for classroom practice;
2. accurate knowledge of PL94–142 and the federal regulations, especially of the due process provisions and parents' rights;
3. detailed, current and first-hand knowledge of existing school programs and services and other community resources;
4. accurate assessment of the student's strengths and deficits, thus of the student's unique needs;
5. well-developed local criteria for classification, placement, programming, and re-evaluation;

---

[2]Private special school placement in the D.C. area ranges from $3,000 to $6,000 a year, with residential schools charging around $8,000–12,000.

[3]PL94–142 requires written parental consent to the Individual Education Program.

6.   the availability of skilled teachers with appropriate special training and experience.

The SLD student was virtually unknown in U.S. public schools prior to the mid-1960s. Because of the presenting symptoms, such children were considered retarded, emotionally disturbed, or slow learners. Less often they were thought (correctly) to be language impaired. Until recently, it was possible for them to be passed illiterate up through the grades by "social promotion," until they were graduated or until they dropped out. Some were dealt with in the mainstream in remedial reading classes or "catch-up" classes for tutoring.

The legal ancestry of the Education for All Handicapped Children Act can be traced to the Supreme Court decisions rejecting the constitutionality of "separate-but-equal" schools for blacks, to civil right and due process decisions, and to court rulings supporting the right of the mentally ill to appropriate treatment (i.e., to more than warehousing) (Reynolds & Birch, 1977, p. 3; see also Bancroft, 1976, p. 11 ff). The trend is one of "progressive inclusion" (Reynolds & Birch, 1977, p. 40).

The provisions of the act are very specific:

> Special education means specially designed instruction, at no cost to the parent [or guardian] to meet the unique needs of a handicapped child, including [but not restricted to] classroom instruction, instruction in physical education, home instruction, and instruction in hospitals and institutions . . . with supplementary services such as a resource room or itinerant instruction to be provided in conjunction with regular placements. . . .
>
> Related Services means transportation and such developmental, corrective, and other supportive services as are required to assist a handicapped child to benefit from special education, and includes [but is not restricted to] speech pathology and audiology, psychological services, physical and occupational therapy, recreation, early identification and assessment of disabilities in children, counseling services, and medical services used for diagnostic or evaluation purposes. (PL94 = 142, Rules and Regulations, § 121 a.14, § 121 a.13)

The act further provides that a multidisciplinary team of professionals must write the IEP jointly with parents. The team includes a school administrator, special educators, the classroom teacher, the school psychologist and physician, and other school personnel. Older students are included when possible. (PL94 = 142, Rules and Regulations § 121 a.344). The IEP must state the child's present achievement levels, short-term and annual goals, the specific special services to be provided (with starting date and duration) and an indication of "the extent to which the child will be able to participate in the regular school program" (PL94 = 142, Rules and Regulations, § 121 a.346).[4]

Clearly the law stresses the goal of placement of the handicapped in classes with nonhandicapped children; it places a premium on mainstreaming. To decide which child may benefit from mainstreaming, and more important, which may suffer there, parents and professionals must understand the SLD syndrome, the child's unique needs, and the kinds of programs and practices appropriate to meet those needs. At the present time, this is highly problematical.

Few classroom teachers, relatively few other professionals, and fewer parents have a correct understanding of either the SLD syndrome or its implications. Classroom teachers generally view the SLD student as a slow learner or as manipulative, a "con artist," emotionally disturbed, or overindulged. They may resent such a student in the class. At best, they may consider the student not truly handicapped. They can and do misuse information provided (Jones, 1978, p. 10 ff). SLD is an invisible handicap; because of this, the legitimacy of the child's needs is often denied. Rarely can parents or teachers without special training and experience comprehend the implications of the sensorimotor bases of the child's difficulties, the profound problems the child has with symbolic language as a result, or the pervasive effect of these perceptual and cognitive difficulties

[4]Parents should also be aware of provisions in § 121 a.401 and § 121 a.506.

on personality and behavior (Smith, 1978). Most teachers, including special teachers, regard as the emotional consequences of the SLD those behavioral symptoms which are in fact its manifestations, "stubbornness" for example, which is actually rigidity or involuntary perseveration.

Descriptions of successful programs have not been widely disseminated. Those which have been were poorly replicated, with the subsequent failure ascribed to the model. Few SLD programs stress teaching basic academic skills—reading, spelling, written English, and mathematics. Yet the law expressly guarantees "full educational opportunity" (PL94–142, Rules and Regulations, § 121 a.304). "Above all, [the] child is entitled to effective instruction in the basic skills needed to become self-sufficient: Reading, writing, speaking, and arithmetic" (Yohalem & Dinsmore, 1978, p. 2 (1) and 6 (3.1)).

Because of limited teaching repertoires, elementary SLD programs rely heavily on audiovisuals and other nonprint aids. That children in the program do not acquire basic skills is presented consistently as proof that they cannot learn, or, at best, can learn only "survival" skills. The enormous problem of the ability of individuals to function in the world of work on the level of their intellectual and personal competencies, is deferred to high school. This is why secondary school programs, largely tutorial, or work-release programs and alternative schools emphasize vocational training and counseling even for students with superior intelligence.

A Pandora's box of confusion has characterized the field since 1963 (Kirk, 1977; see also Cruickshank, 1978) frustrating parents, teachers, and students and generating one program after another which has failed to meet the academic and social needs of the SLD student. It is not surprising that:

- No research currently exists to validate mainstreaming as appropriate educational treatment for an SLD student (McCarthy, 1978).
- SLD students appear to have improved behavior and

better attitudes toward school when mainstreamed but show no gains in academic skills (Keogh, 1976, p. 28 ff).
- Social isolation may be the result simply of the valid perception of real differences by nonhandicapped children and not of segregated programs or categorical labels (Keogh, 1976; see also McCarthy, 1978).
- White, female SLD students are in significant danger of being rejected by students in regular classes (Thurman, 1979, p. 468).
- SLD students in some situations are vulnerable to physical assault and violence by other students (Bader, 1975, p. 26).

The law does not state specific criteria for classifying children SLD; this is left to the local education agency. Psychoeducational testing is done by school psychologists and educational diagnosticians, most of whom have had no special training in the administration and interpretation of tests to SLD children. Too often, the findings as reported in the I.Q. score reflect not the true intellectual potential or real skills but the child's disability. This is a violation of due process (Cruickshank, 1978; see also PL94—142, Rules and Regulations, § 121a.532, especially (a)(3) and (c)). Many SLD students are mislabeled borderline, low-average, or, in the case of the superior IQ child, average at best. The IEP is scaled down accordingly, placement becomes misplacement, and teachers' expectations for the child are low. The program is scaled to the low expectations, and the child is educationally underfed.

The law does not specify criteria for placement or for preservice and in-service teacher training. It does mandate the latter and a continuum of special and ancillary services to the child. Permutations and combinations include among others:

- In-service training for the teacher only;
- Placement in regular classes for the full day with no special services;

- Placement in regular classes with consultant services to the teacher, for example, by reading specialists, psychologists, curriculum specialists;
- Placement in regular classes with special services to the student, in or out of class, from classroom aides, remedial reading, resource room, math or speech teachers, for example;
- Placement in a resource room half day, with placement in regular class(es) for art, music, physical education, science, math, etc;
- Placement in a self-contained noncategorical class for children with any handicapping condition;
- Placement in self-contained categorical classes for children with "mild" learning problems, usually a combination of SLD, the emotionally disturbed, the mildly mentally retarded and slow learners;[5]
- Placement in resource rooms or self-contained classes plus any combination of adjunctive services, including academic tutoring (in school);
- Placement in a special public school, with or without adjunctive services;
- Placement in a private special school, with or without services;
- Placement in a private special residential school for SLD students[6]

Secondary schools may not offer the alternatives described above. Most U.S. adolescents receiving supportive academic services are in remedial classes for basic skills (45 percent);

[5]Such placements are usually incompatible with the SLD student's emotional, social, and academic needs; the gifted LD student is especially misplaced here. For all SLD students, there are negative consequences for the self-concept and self-esteem.

[6]Some older children with severe LD problems and secondary or independent severe emotional problems require a residential psychotherapeutic placement which also offers a good LD school program.

tutoring classes for content subjects, such as math (24 percent); low-track classes which stress functional reading and math ("survival" skills) (17 percent); work-study programs (5 percent), and classes which stress learning strategies (4 percent) (Deshler, Lowrey, & Alley, 1979, p. 389).

The states have various responses to the law. An early model, the diagnostic-prescriptive teacher model, has been discontinued in many areas. The d/p teacher bases recommendations for the IEP on the results of formal and informal assessments, usually tests of perceptual-motor and reading ability. The reading, speech and language, physical education and classroom teachers, one or more, were to implement the recommendations, often with no further support or consultation. Theoretically, the building principal had the responsibility to coordinate and manage the several facets of the program. SLD children (who have difficulties adjusting to change) might be referred to four separate teachers under such a prescription: the reading teacher, the speech teacher and the P.E. teacher for physical development, all of which required the child to be out of the classroom frequently, thus causing problems for the fourth teacher, the regular classroom instructor. This gave rise to sharp "territorial disputes" and teacher resistance. The consultant-teacher model . . . has been used with greater success (in Hartsdale, New York; Monroe County, Indiana; and Vermont) (Truesdell, 1979; see also Reynolds & Birch, 1977, pp. 377 ff, 441 ff.). Montgomery County, Maryland employs the continuum model, with the range of services as described above. In this model, special teachers provide systematic back-up support to the classroom teachers. California mainstreamed thousands of children through transition programs, resource learning centers, consulting teachers, ancillary teacher assistants (classroom aides), in-service training programs, and pupil personnel consultants, with many variations. Research on the California program suggests that mainstreamed students remained as much as three years below grade level in basic skills (Keogh, 1976; McCarthy, 1978).

The current U.S. taxpayers revolt, the shrinkage in available revenue sources, spiraling inflation, and the skyrocketing costs of operating schools together mitigate against the expansion of special services. Currently, the Montgomery County, Maryland School Board has cut over half a million dollars for projected expansion of special education, eliminating 58 teachers requested to staff special classes and resource rooms, and for projected in-service training programs (Montogmery County ACLD, 1979, p. 2). A parents' lobby for improved regular education programs at the expense of special services, is developing a phenomenon which will affect existing programs, pupil-teacher ratios, and all supplementary services. Most critical, while PL94–142 requires expensive procedures and expanded programs, appropriations for the handicapped for 1980 and 1981 are $1.4 billion less than the authorization; putting states in a "dammed-if-they-do, damned-if-they-don't" double bind.[7]

Some authorities have declared all the alternatives described inadequate to the need, they predict a total reorganization of schools, school management systems, and teacher preservice and in-service training (Bradfield, 1976, p. 130, 131; Meisgeier, 1976, pp. 99, 100).

The experience of the Bloomington, Minnesota, public schools may point to more adequate solutions. Primary teachers were trained by consulting teachers in their classrooms during the school day. The "Project Read" teachers demonstrated instructional techniques and materials with children who had reading problems. The children were simply treated as one of the several traditional reading groups, with

> Remarkable results . . . (a) The number of children scoring low on reading tests have been reduced sharply; for example, as compared with earlier years, the proportion of children falling below the 25th percentile on nationally normed reading tests was

---

[7]Personal communication from Don Sodo, executive director, Foundation for Exceptional Children, received 2 April 1979.

reduced by *71% in the first year,* and by 83% and 85% in the following years. . . . (d) The cost of the new program was less than half that of a traditional tutoring program. (e) Among the regular teachers, 96% agreed that the program should not be discontinued. (f) All of the school principals agreed that the program had been successful in their buildings. (g) More than 90% of the parents whose children were in the program wanted it continued. (Reynolds & Birch, 1977, p. 448–449)

In this program, synthetic rather than analytic phonics was used, taught by simultaneous multisensory techniques and materials and highly systematic instruction, basically an Orton-Gillingham approach to acquiring language skills (Reynolds & Birch, 1977, p. 448 ff.)

All of this is background to answer the question; how are the IEP decisions made for a given child? The questions are whether to mainstream; or not; if so, how and to what extent; what ancillary services are needed? If not, which special placements should be recommended? public or non-public? day or residential? Factors which must be taken into account are derived from the various assessments specified by PL94–142, conversations and conferences with parents and teachers, classroom observations, psychoeducational tests and other measures, medical examinations, interviews with the student, information from health and school records, and others (PL94–142, Rules and Regulations, § 121a.13). Specifically, information should include the following.

About the student: Sex, age, current grade placement. Intellectual potential. Current achievement in basic skills. Physical and emotional health and stamina. Personality and temperament. Self-awareness, general information, sophistication. Special talents and skills. Competencies in nonacademic areas. Interests and hobbies. Personal preferences. Job or career goals. Peer relationships. Child's perception of his or her relationships with parents and siblings, perception of support from family and teachers. School history, especially of failure. Retentions. Learning style, coping strategies. Motivation, ability to persevere with difficult tasks. Ability to focus and to attend; work habits. Capacity to anticipate, to organize and to plan. Severity of perceptual-motor deficits and cognitive dysfunction, especially memory, receptive and expressive language difficulties, and abstract thinking. Speech problems. The child's view of his current predicament. Outlook (e.g., optimistic). It is vital that one or more team members have observed, met with personally, and interviewed the child.

About the school: Structure and organization of the current school and class placement. Structure and organization of possible alternative placements. Order, consistency, routine, predictability of daily class program. Student population—range of ability, behavior (acting-out or disruptive?). Pupil-teacher ratio. Teacher assistants or aides, if any. Demands for outside reading, written work, homework. Criteria for grading classwork, tests. Teacher general philosophy, teaching style, and professional training.[8] Teacher style in giving correction, praise, criticism. Teacher flexibility. Teacher attitude toward SLD children in general, understanding the characteristics of SLD students, attitude about SLD child mainstreamed in regular classes, willingness to have SLD child in his or her class, willingness to modify curriculum for SLD child. Ancillary services available. Scheduling problems between regular and special services. Size of groups in small group instruction. Opportunity for and frequency of immediate feedback. Success orientation? Emphasis on cooperation and mutual support? Focus on quality and accuracy, not quantity and speed. Nature and frequency of professional support to the teacher. Support from building and district administrator(s). Prospect of social acceptance of SLD child by the group(s). Will child be expected to return to a less restrictive environment? How soon? By what criteria?

A critical point in this consideration is the state interpretation of the federal regulations. Does the IEP specify only what

---

[8]This requires some knowledge of the adequacy of the training programs.

the state or local agency has to offer and not what the child's unique needs require?[9] The ideal program should be specified to parents and other professionals, as well as actual available programs and services. Finally, what is the probable life of the program, given local fiscal and political realities?

About the community: Do regular, nonspecial schools exist whose structure, organization, curriculum, pupil-teacher ratio, and staff can serve mildly or moderately handicapped students, with or without supplementary services? What special schools exist? What is the training of the director and staff in each? What is the record of success of the school? To what schools and programs do students go afterward? What is the licensing status and accreditation? What is the cost of the program? Is the school staff and financial base stable? What is the socioeconomic and educational "match" of the children with the SLD student? What recreational and nonacademic programs are available in the community (4H, Y, athletic teams, physical development programs, gymnastics, programs for the gifted, drama groups, art centers, prevocational, vocational, and technical training programs)? Are there businessmen, professionals, artists, or scientists interested in working with SLD students through formal or informal apprenticeships? Does the junior college offer special programs for LD students?

About the family: Do both parents agree on the problem? What is their view of the child and of the way the child functions in the family? (Is he or she seen as a burden?) What are the demands on the family—emotional, financial, time? How many other children are there, how old? Are there other problems, chronic illnesses, infirm elders, unemployment? Can the family transport children to nonpublic special services or schools? What are the family support systems in times of crisis?

Direct, personal, current, and detailed knowledge of the program components and of every adult involved is necessary.

---

[9]One Mid-Atlantic state specifies only the best alternative the system has to offer, not what the child's best interests require.

This requires observations on site, interviews, continuous involvement, and information-gathering and monitoring through feedback from parents and students. Parents should visit classes and programs which have been suggested. Transportation is an issue. Long bus trips are difficult for the SLD child, especially for the physically (motoric) hyperactive child and the socially rejected child.

Consideration of special schools also should weigh the following: humanistic over mechanistic approaches to instruction—an emphasis on children as responsible for their own progress, as active agents in their development; personal interaction between teachers and students; direct personal teaching; absence of teaching machines, dittoes and other busy-work papers, and self-instruction programs; constant reteaching, repetition, review, representation, demonstration, and feedback; close monitoring of student progress; clear expectations for the class, clearly stated to the child. Explicit criteria, firm limits, firmly and fairly enforced; liberal, simultaneous use of multisensory materials; new learning presented concretely; opportunity for students to demonstrate knowledge orally; reading material on a wide range of levels of difficulty; taped text books; absence of time pressure; general attitude among the staff that each teacher shares in the responsibility for every child; active and effective measures to capitalize on and display children's talents, skills, and strengths, including those in nonacademic areas.

Nothing has been said of the management of hyperactivity. In the experience of the TRI-services Center for Children with Learning Disabilities,[10] which serves public and nonpublic school children from widely different backgrounds, the problem of (motoric) hyperactivity is not as frequent or as difficult to

[10]A private, nonprofit, tax-exempt agency in Rockville, Maryland that serves the metropolitan Washington, D.C. area. Cited as a "model that works" in the private sector by the Task Force on Learning Failure and Unused Learning Potential of the President's Commission on Mental Health, 1978.

resolve as is generally thought. Almost all children seen at the center are described as hyperactive by their teachers. Much of what is called hyperactivity is situational, operative only in the school, where the child's continuous experience is of failure and frustration. The restlessness, distractibility, and inattention are often the consequence of being "imprisoned" in a failure situation in which they are constantly asked to do what they cannot do.

In appropriate educational programs, with supportive teachers who understand the SLD syndrome and who are skilled in teaching SLD children basic skills so that students see concrete evidence of their own progress, many so-called hyperactive children show no more unfocused excessive activity than is found in the general population.

Medication should be a last resort when all else has failed. If parents and teachers understand fully the reasons for the child's problems and are assisted to manage them well, anxiety, stress, and conflict lessens all around; the child's anxiety and tensions are further reduced, and the child can begin to become invested in the job at hand and to realize beginning successes. It should be noted that there are cyclical pressure periods just before the end of the term, when teachers begin to push children to finish their work and set up demands for classwork and homework dramatically. Often the students are reported as "hyper" or upset during these periods. Parents and professionals who realize what is occurring can do much to relieve the child at these times (children themselves usually do not understand what is happening).

References

Bader, B. W. *Social perception and learning disabilities.* Des Moines, Iowa: Moon Lithographing and Engraving, 1975.

Bancroft, R. Special Education: Legal Aspects. In P. O'Donnell & R. Bradfield, (Eds.) *Mainstreaming: Controversy and Consensus.* San Rafael: Academic Therapy Publications, 1976, pp. 11–21.

Bradfield, R. How to Fail in Mainstreaming without Really Trying. In P. O'Donnell & R. Bradfield (Eds.) *Mainstreaming: Controversy and Consensus.* San Rafael: Academic Therapy Publications, 1976, pp. 129–138.

Critchley, M. Developmental Dyslexia: Its History, Nature and Prospects. In D. Duane & M. Rawson (Eds.), *Reading, perception and language.* Baltimore, Maryland: The Orton Society by arrangement with York Press, 1975, p. 12.

Cruickshank, W. *Learning disabilities: Perceptual or other?* Paper presented at the meeting of the Special Education Association, Amsterdam, The Netherlands, May 1978. (Reported in *Newsletter* of the National Association for Children with Learning Disabilities, Winter 1979.)

Deshler, D., Lowrey, N., & Alley, G. Programming alternatives for LD adolescents: A nationwide survey. *Academic Therapy,* 1979, *14:*(4).

Kirk, S. Learning Disabilities: Pandora's Box. A paper presented at the International Conference of the National Association for Children with Learning Disabilities, Washington, D.C., March 1977.

Keogh, B. What Research Tells Us about Mainstreaming. In P. O'Donnell and R. Bradfield (Eds.), *Mainstreaming: Controversy and Consensus.* San Rafael: Academic Therapy Publications, 1976, pp. 25–36.

Lynn, R., Gluckin, N., & Kripke, B. *Learning disabilities: The state of the field 1978.* New York: Social Science Research Council, 1978.

McCarthy, J. The learning disabled in the mainstream of education. *Devereux Forum,* 1978, *13:*1.

Meisgeier, C. The Houston Plan: A Program that Works. In P. O'Donnell and R. Bradfield (Eds.) *Mainstreaming: Controversy and Consensus.* San Rafael: Academic Therapy Publications, 1976, pp. 99–112.

Montgomery Country Association for Children with Learning Disabilites. *Newsletter,* April 1979, p. 2.

O'Donnel, R., & Bradfield, R. (Eds.). *Mainstreaming: Controversy and consensus.* San Rafael: Academic Therapy Publications, 1976.

Parks, A. L., & Rousseau, M. K. *The public law supporting mainstreaming: A guide for teachers and parents.* Austin: Learning Concepts, 1977.

PTA Today, March 1979, *4*(8), p. 4.

Rawson, M. *Developmental language disability: Adult accomplishments of dyslexic boys.* Baltimore: Johns Hopkins Press, 1968.

Reynolds, M., & Birch, J. *Teaching exceptional children in all America's schools: A first course for teachers and principals.* Reston, Virginia: Council for Exceptional Children, 1977.

Smith, S. *No easy answers: The learning disabled child.* Rockville, Maryland: U.S. Department of Health, Education, and Welfare, 1978.

Stannard, R. Mainstreaming: Some Basis for Caution. In P. O'Donnell and R. Bradfield (Eds.) *Mainstreaming: Controversy and Consensus.* San Rafael: Academic Therapy Publications, 1976, pp. 141–149.

Thurman, S. & Lewis, M. Children's Responses to Differences: Some Possible Implications for Mainstreaming. *Exceptional Children,* 45 (6), 1979, p. 468.

Trusdell, M. L. *Various Service Delivery Models for SLD Students.* Paper presented at Sixth Annual Meeting of the New York Orton Society. March 19, 1976.

Yohalem, D., & Dinsmore, J. *Special education 94–142 and 504: Numbers that add up to educational rights for handicapped children: A guide for parents and advocates.* Washington, D.C.: Children's Defense Fund of the Washington Research Project, Inc., 1978.

BIBLIOGRAPHY

Brutten, M., Richardson, S., Mangel, C. *Something's wrong with my child: A parent's book about children with learning disabilities.* New York: Harcourt Brace Jovanovich, Inc., 1973.

The Council for Exceptional Children. *The education of all handicapped children act: A free appropriate public education for all handicapped children.* Washington, D.C.: Bureau of Education for the Handicapped, U.S. Office of Education, 1976.

D'Alonzo, B., D'Alonzo, R., & Mauser, A. Developing resource rooms for the handicapped. *Teaching Exceptional Children,* 11 (3), 1979.

Duane, D., & Rawson, M. (Eds.) *Reading, perception and language: Papers from the World Congress on Dyslexia Sponsored by the Orton Society in cooperation with the Mayo Clinic.* Baltimore, Maryland: The Orton Society by arrangement with York Press, Inc., 1975.

Frostig, M., & Maslow, P. *Learning problems in the classroom: Prevention and Remediation.* New York: Grune & Stratton, 1973.

Gearhart, B. R. *Learning disabilities: Educational strategies.* St. Louis: V. C. Mosely Co., 1973.

Johnson, D. J., & Myklebust, M. R. *Learning disabilities: Educational principles and practices.* New York: Grune & Stratton, 1967.

Kirk, S. *Educating exceptional children.* Boston, Houghton Mifflin Co., 1962.

Meyen, E., Vergason, G., & Whelan, R. *Alternatives for teaching exceptional children: Essays from focus on exceptional children.* Denver: Love Publishing Co., 1975.

New Jersey Association for Children with Learning Disabilities, *Handbook on learning disabilities: A prognosis for the child, the adolescent, the adult.* R. E. Weber (Ed.) Englewood Cliffs: Prentice-Hall, Inc., 1978.

President's Commission on Mental Health. *Report to the President* (Vol. 1). Washington, D.C.: U.S. Government Printing Office, 1978.

President's Commission on Mental Health. *Task Panel Reports* (Vol. 3). Washington, D.C.: U.S. Government Printing Office, 1978.

Rosenthal, J. *Hazy . . .? Crazy . . .? and/or Lazy . . .? The maligning of children with learning disabilities.* San Rafael: Academic Therapy Publications, 1973.

Sapir, S., & Nitzburg, A. (Eds.) *Children with learning problems: Readings in a developmental-interaction approach.* New York: Brunner/Mazel, 1973.

Siegel, E. *Special education in the regular classroom.* New York: John Day Company, 1969.

Winter, S. Mainstreaming: The impact of the Public Law 94–142. *FOCUS The Psychiatric Institute,* Winter-Spring, 1979.

Part IV

PSYCHOTHERAPEUTIC APPROACHES

Chapter 14

SPECIAL PROBLEMS IN THERAPY WITH CHILDREN WITH CENTRAL NERVOUS SYSTEM DYSFUNCTION

Archie A. Silver

The child with Central Nervous System (CNS) dysfunction is not exempt from the forces which create anxiety in any of us, whether these arise from cultural, environmental, or intrapsychic sources. The difference in the child with CNS defect lies in the biologic substrate upon which these pressures impinge. The biologic substrate may be disturbed in four major areas of function: (1) an interruption of normal maturation with delay in the acquisition of new functions and retention of more primitive ones; (2) problems in muscle tone, posture, and equilibrium; (3) problems in the initiation and control of impulses; and (4) distortions in perception and in cognition.

Distortions in perception create frustration and confusion, difficulty in learning, and reactive pressures at home and at school. Psychological reaction to repeated academic failure may of course vary with the resources of each child, the nature and extent of the dysfunction, and the parental and school support the child may receive. At best, a pervasive sense of inadequacy results, a feeling that the world is a harsh and difficult place, demanding the impossible. Many children give up and withdraw, some so completely as to present a picture of autism. Others give up and become suspicious and rebellious in their efforts at achieving recognition and self-esteem and easily fall into aggressive and sexual difficulties. Midway are those who stagger along academically, clowning in school, but depressed, demanding, and rigid at home. Where parental disappointment and disapproval accentuate the problem, children add to their sense of inadequacy a bewilderment and a guilt that they cannot please their parents, that their parents think so little of them. The psychological sequelae of perceptual and cognitive defect have been frequently described (Bender, 1956; Eisenberg, 1957; Silver, 1958; Wender, 1971).

While the anxiety attendant upon perceptual defects is not to be minimized, there is a more basic source of anxiety in children with brain damage: an intrinsic change in the biologic substrate which reflects itself in the subjective sensation we call anxiety.

The prototype of this anxiety is found in two primitive responses of the child with CNS dysfunction—namely, the Moro response and the reaction to antigravity play. The former relates to the initiation and control of impulses, the latter to problems in muscle tone, posture, and equilibrium.

The Moro response is evoked by any sudden stimulus "such as a loud noise or quick passive movement" (Ford, 1937). The usual stimulus is a hard slap against the supporting bed on either side of the dorsal recumbent child. The reaction consists of an initial adduction and extension of all extremities, followed by adduction and flexion, especially of the arms. It is normally present during approximately the first three months of life and normally disappears by about the fifth month. This is the so-called startle response. In the child with central nervous system dysfunction, this startle response persists beyond the fifth month, is evoked with a minimal stimulus, is exaggerated in its intensity, and is prolonged in duration. This is the prototype of the child's reaction to any sudden stimulus throughout life.

Most of us, even as adults, will startle at a sudden loud noise or a sudden change in equilibrium; our reaction, however, is largely a controlled one, and we achieve equilibrium quickly on our recognition of the source and nature of the stimulus. For the child with brain dysfunction, this return is not as rapid. The physiological concomitants of the startle response—increased heart rate, sweating, changes in gastrointestinal tone, pupillary dilation, increased muscle tone, metabolic changes—all reverberate in persistent waves which subjectively reach awareness as anxiety.

The result (Wender, 1973) is that the organism is flooded with stimuli which it cannot control. This may well be the "predisposition to anxiety," "the physiological sensitivity which heightened the anxiety potential," which Phyllis Greenacre (1941) describes in patients with a history of organic insult at or before birth.

The stimulus, however, need not always be external, as in the startle response. It may arise from within the organism at any and every level of function from the automatic reflex level to that involving complex psychic stimuli.

At a reflex level, autonomic lability is characteristic of cerebral dysfunction. This can be detected clinically in vasomotor responses, in pupillary responses, and sometimes in visceral responses. The entire homeostatic mechanism is alert and sensitive. In the framework of Hans Selye (1956), this individual is more vulnerable to stress, overreacting initially but reaching the stage of stress exhaustion more readily.

Theoretically, we may also postulate that the inability to inhibit autonomic stimuli makes the nerve pathways easily accessible to conditioning and that a pattern, once established in response to a specific stimulus, may readily appear in response to a nonspecific stimulus. This ready autonomic conditioning was noted also by Cattell & Scheier (1961) and Cattell (1963) to be a significant loading factor with anxiety and may offer clues to the tenacity with which patients cling to their somatic symptoms.

The child with central nervous system dysfunction not only has difficulty in screening and dampening autonomic activity but also has difficulty in screening and dampening voluntary motor and psychological stimuli. The child with cerebral dysfunction, as we have stated, is not exempt from the psychological problems of growing up. The difference here is that repression is not readily achieved, and impulses appear undisguised in motor action or in conscious thoughts. The classic motor restlessness of brain damage may well be the result of inability to screen motor impulses.

The child with CNS dysfunction not only has a labile physiological homeostatic mechanism but also a labile mechanism for emotional homeostasis. The inadequate ability to repress or dampen psychological impulses results in what has been termed a child with "ego defects." Psychologically, there is a primitive quality to children with CNS dysfunction. They cannot quite control their instinctual needs; their demands are immediate and incessant. As the personality develops, however, the uncontrolled instinctual needs run headlong into superego restraint. Because instinctual demands are repressed with difficulty, guilt and its subsequent anxiety are easily aroused. Phobias also plague the organic child. Fears of the dark, of animals, and of imaginary monsters as well as hypochondriasis are frequent.

In other children, the most rigid type of psychological defense is attempted. Just as impulses are controlled with difficulty, so guilt is controlled with difficulty. Rigid defense systems are set up, rigidity not only in limiting the daily routine of living but in controlling anxiety by ritualizing the world. Obsessions and compulsions are defenses of choice in organic disturbance (Schilder, 1938). The obsession or compulsion is "stimulus bound," just as is the perseveration. Unfortunately, the compulsion never really relieves the anxiety which provokes it, so that the ritual must be repeated over and over again.

The Moro response then is the prototype of a reaction from which subsequent anxiety develops, an inability to inhibit or dampen stimuli whether they are external or internal, auto-nomic, voluntary motor, or psychological. Autonomic lability, lack of control of voluntary motor activity, difficulty in repres-sions of instinctive drives, and psychological conflicts become the biological substrate for anxiety and may be the basis for psychophysiological reactions and for obsessive-compulsive patterns into adult life.

A third source of anxiety is epitomized by the child's reaction to antigravity play. Being held upside down, being swung from side to side, and being tossed and bounced evoke delight in the normal child. Disturbance of equilibrium is nor-mally pleasurable. This is not true of the child with central nervous system dysfunction. Here, disturbance of equilibrium evokes panic; a clinging, frantic resistance; an attempt to re-align the physical orientation of the body with the world. Sub-jectively and objectively, this is fear (Shaffer, 1979).

Children with structural brain damage, therefore, have a basic biologic problem in maintaining spatial orientation and in muscle tone relative to posture. They cannot automatically and smoothly adjust to changes in posture and equilibrium (Silver, 1952). Phylogenetically, this is a fundamental necessity for food getting and for defense. Actually, the survival of an individual may depend upon the ability to orient head and limbs with respect to the world. Behaviorally, the clinging of the organic child may be understood as an attempt to maintain physical support and to obtain reference points for position in space. Psychologically, the need for physical support could well be the basis for dependency needs, needs which are often so very great that they cannot be met and in themselves then become a source of secondary anxiety. It is thus suggested here that CNS dys-function makes the child more susceptible to any stress—prena-tal, perinatal, or environmental.

In each area of function described in this chapter—distor-tions in perception and cognition; difficulty with the initiation and control of impulses; problems in muscle tone, posture, and equilibrium—the organism has retained a primitive stamp. The sequence of normal maturation in these areas is slowed down, and behaviors suitable for earlier stages in development are still seen as the individual grows older and is forced to cope with the world with an immature physiological apparatus.

Maturation alone is not sufficient to overcome these physiological deficits. These dysfunctions persist into adult life profoundly influencing adjustment and creating a precarious equilibrium easily upset by psychological and physical stress.

For these patients, dynamic psychotherapy is for the most part a long and arduous process; interpretation frequently becomes only an intellectual exercise. A supportive relationship, however, is of help, with the therapist stepping out of the traditional role, if need be, to help remove realistic stress situations, to work with the family and school. The remediation of perceptual deficits is an important aspect in removing frustrating, chronically stressful experiences in learning. For somatic symptoms, behavior modification is helpful. This may be the desensitization described by Wolpe (1973), the reduction of tension under hypnosis, progressive relaxation, and an attempt at creating new conditioned responses which may be less destructive than established ones. It may be that newer therapies, such as biofeedback, may indeed affect autonomic conditioning and eventually find some clinical validity.

These diverse therapeutic considerations suggest the complexities in management of these children and the need of dissecting out their source of anxiety and their defenses to it.

SUMMARY

Children with central nervous system dysfunction are not exempt from the forces which create anxiety in any of us, whether these arise from endogenous or exogenous sources. These children are different, however, in that their biologic defects make them vulnerable to any stress and create specific intrinsic sources of anxiety. These sources spring from distortions in perception and in cognition, from difficulty in the initiation and control of impulses, and from problems in muscle tone, posture, and equilibrium.

Distortions in perception create frustration and confusion, difficulty in learning, and reactive pressures from school and home. The psychological reaction may run the gamut from autistic behavior to outgoing, clowning behavior, from submission to aggression—all are underlined with a pervasive sense of inadequacy and suspicion.

Defects in the initiation and control of impulses has as its prototype the Moro or startle response, in which the organism is flooded with stimuli which it cannot control. The inability to screen and dampen stimuli may be found at every level of function, from the autonomic reflex to that involving complex psychic stimuli. At the autonomic level, homeostatic dysequilibrium is the rule, with physiological symptoms easily conditioned. At the voluntary motor level, increased motor activity is frequent. At the psychic level, instinctual demands are repressed with great difficulty, creating, on the one hand, children who demand immediate gratification and, on the other, children responding with anxiety and guilt as they struggle with only partially successful repression and sublimation. Introjections, obsessions, and compulsions are typical psychological defenses.

Anxiety attendant upon problems in muscle tone, posture, and equilibrium is epitomized by the reaction to antigravity play, where disturbance in equilibrium evokes anxiety. Automatic adjustments to posture and equilibrium are not easily made, with physical clinging as a young child and psychological clinging, dependency, and a free-floating anxiety in the adult.

Therapeutic implications for these sources are suggested.

REFERENCES

Bender, L. *Psychopathology of children with organic brain disorders.* Springfield, Ill.: Thomas, 1956.

Cattell, R. Nature and measurement of anxiety. *Scientific American,* 1963, *208,* 96–104

Cattell, R., & Scheier, I. *Measurement of neuroticism and anxiety.* New York: Ronald Press, 1961.

Eisenberg, L. Psychiatric implications of brain damage in children. *Psychiatric Quarterly,* 1957, *31,* 72–92.

Ford, F. R. *Diseases of the nervous system in infancy, childhood and adolescence.* Springfield, Ill.: Thomas, 1973.

Greenacre, P. The predisposition to anxiety. *Psychoanalytic Quarterly,* 1941, *10,* 66–94.

Schilder, P. Organic background of obsessions and compulsions. *American Journal of Psychiatry,* 1938, *94,* 1397–1413.

Selye, H. *The stress of life.* New York: McGraw-Hill, 1956.

Shaffer, M. Primal terror: A perspective of vestibular dysfunction. *Journal of Learning Disabilities,* 1979, *12,* 89–92.

Silver, A. Postural and righting responses in children. *Journal of Pediatrics,* 1952, *41,* 493–498.

Silver, A. Behavior disorder associated with brain damage in children. *Pediatric Clinics of North America,* August 1958, 687–698.

Wender, P. *Minimal brain dysfunction in children.* New York: Wiley-Interscience, 1971.

Wender, P. Some speculations concerning a possible biochemical basis of minimal brain dysfunction. In F. de la Cruz, B. Fox, R. Roberts, & G. Tarjan (Eds.), *Annals of the New York Academy of Sciences,* 1973, *205,* 18–28.

Wolpe, J. *Practice of behavior therapy.* New York: Pergamon, 1973.

Chapter 15

PSYCHOTHERAPY WITH MBD CHILDREN AND THEIR PARENTS

Irving N. Berlin

Minimal brain dysfunction (MBD) is a widely used diagnostic term applied to many children with a variety of symptomatic behaviors. Most frequently, the diagnosis is made in school as a result of the child's (usually a boy) hyperactive, distractible, aggressive, and nonlearning behavior. Most teachers faced with disturbed and disturbing behavior prevail on parents to have a physician examine the child and prescribe a stimulant drug. In recent studies, some 20–30 percent of children so treated seem to be behaviorally improved at school and at home (Weiss, Minde & Werry, 1970). What of those who do not improve, and what of the hazards of stimulant drugs on growing organisms? These questions are rarely considered since behavior change *now* is the issue. There are some data that indicate that, when clear neurologic evidence of cerebral dysfunction exists and response to stimulants occurs, additional therapeutic help to child and parents is important if the drug is to be maximally effective (Greenberg, Deem, & McMahon, 1972; Spring and Greenberg, 1972–73).

The questions at issue are: what are some effective psycho-therapeutic strategies with parents that will be helpful early in the child's life? Later, how can psychotherapy be used to help both children and parents who need help, whether drugs are effective or not? Some studies show that, despite relevant stimulant prescription, a considerable group of children who improve with stimulants have learning and social problems in adolescence (de la Cruz, Fox, & Roberts, 1973; Mendelson, Johnson, & Stewart, 1971; Weiss, Minde, Werry, Douglass & Nemeth, 1971). These problems interfere with their adaptation in adolescence and adult life. The way in which the diagnosis is understood by the child and family and how longitudinal implications are focused on and resolved by the child and parents are critical to effective treatment of any kind.

EARLY DIAGNOSIS OF MBD AND ITS IMPLICATION FOR FAMILY ADJUSTMENT

In many instances, the hyperactive infant, whatever the etiology, has poorly organized biological rhythms. Sleep is fretful and brief, eating schedules are difficult to establish, and the hypermotility makes it difficult to cuddle and relax such an infant. It becomes important that the physician or pediatric nurse practitioner recognize the parents' distress and weariness, acknowledge the problem, and proceed to help find some solutions to help, especially the mother. Stating that "the child will grow out of it," so often heard, aggravates the problem for both child and parents.

Several demonstration projects reveal that these "driven" infants and their parents can be helped through an early regular infant stimulation program (Dmitriev, 1972; Dmitriev and Hayden, 1973). The most striking changes occur as mother (usually) is taught the techniques of light body massage, and singing and talking to the infant, and as the infant begins to quiet a bit, some cuddling occurs until the infant gets fussy. It is fascinating to watch both infants and mothers settle down. A variety of kinesthetic, auditory, and visual stimulation seems to help with regulating the infant. When the mother is doing something that clearly helps, her child is also more relaxed. In a few months, eight-to-nine-month-old-hypermotile children begin to enjoy the stimulation, and look forward to the play and singing, and their sleeping and eating schedules begin to regulate (Berlin, 1974). Both infants and mothers look more relaxed. The several-times-daily massage and general sensorimotor stimulation schedule must be reinforced at weekly meetings with professionals who can help parents assess developmental change, indicate the improvements and encourage the daily program.

THERAPEUTIC WORK DURING THE PRESCHOOL YEARS

Early intervention has very important preventive implications in many disorders. Most often, disorders are not recognized and therefore not worked with early. In the hypermotility, attentional deficit disorders, early intervention and therapeutic help to the parents may be critical to the child's entire life.

Where early stimulation programs have helped an infant or young child to settle down, to become more cuddly, to develop a close attachment to the parent, and thus to experience more normal object relations, the parents' job is easier but still difficult. The driven child, whatever the etiology of the behavior, is impulsive in his acts, in constant motion, hard to control, and difficult socially, since the behavior is so unpredictable and often is destructive (Berlin & Berlin, 1975).

Establishing Parental Authority

It is clear that parents need to be helped over time to find ways to help the child hear "No!" and respond to parental

interdictions of dangerous behavior and control over the antisocial, hyperactive behavior. Unless this happens, the parents
resign parental authority, which frightens the child and increases frenzy, since no one seems to be able to help the child
settle down. Siblings and other children become alienated and
fearful, and the MBD child begins a life of isolation from peers.
These children do not feel wanted and loved and are unable to
turn to an adult for relief from pain and distress.

Helping parents establish their authority is a difficult therapeutic job, often best done in small groups of parents with
children of the preschool age. The method discussed in this
chapter, while a variant of operant conditioning, depends primarily upon first helping the parents face their ambivalent and
often murderously angry feelings toward the child who makes
them feel so helpless and unrewarded as a parent.

Response to Authority

When parents are able to share the gamut of feelings toward their child and find them empathetically understood, they
need to face the difficulty of helping the child hear the "No!".
They need to be helped, by modeling and role playing, to learn
how the ignoring of the "No!" or "Stop it!" can be dealt with.
For instance, by stating firmly, "No you cannot cross the
street," stopping the impulsive dash, looking the child directly
in the eye and firmly grasping the child's shoulders, and repeating "I said no. You cannot run across the street! Understand.
Now let's try again!" If the parents understand the drivenness,
they will understand that behavior change will occur slowly
and take time and energy, but must be maintained until learning occurs (Berlin, 1974).

Parents learn quickly that positive reinforcement of adaptive behavior by a hug and a warm "good boy" is the most
effective tool they have, besides their firm resolve to assert
parental authority. The rewards to the child for responding
become more genuine as they become more frequent. The affectional relationship helps with learning and curiosity, extended

attention, and establishment of parental authority in other areas.

Parents also need help to understand that their child's impulsive acts of disarranging or breaking objects need to be dealt with by a firm insistence on cleaning up, rather than with recriminations about the impulsive act, whose cause may not be within the child's awareness. Similarly when their child pushes or hurts a child, and an adult has not been able to prevent that behavior, it needs to be dealt with in terms of helping the hurt child and taking care of him or her, rather than recriminations about the act itself, the cause of which may be unclear to the MBD child. MBD children need continual help to accept the impulsive acts as their own, part of their illness, and something for which they must assume responsibility.

As parents come to terms with their own anger and helpless feelings and can more freely admit how troublesome their child is and how natural a feeling it is to want to be rid of the child, they can begin to understand the necessity of spending the time and energy to establish parental authority as one way of establishing meaningful parent-child relationships.

Case vignette 1:

> Freddie, age two, had been a very hypermotile child who slept little, was always into everything, and was sometimes destructive. Mother had been sleepless and very tired for nearly two years. Father, who helped on weekends, could not understand how mother could keep it up. This was their first and, they now felt, their last child.
>
> Both parents joined a parents' group on the recommendation of a pediatrician who recognized the disorder in the child and the weariness of the parents. The pediatrician was reluctant, despite the presence of several soft signs, to begin stimulant medication.
>
> As was customary, the intake interview was done with Freddie and both parents. His hyperactive behavior and distractibility was evident in the waiting room and during the interview for the family and developmental histories.
>
> Both parents watched the developmental testing and the

diagnostic play interview through one-way mirrors. To their astonishment, Freddie responded to the unequivocal firmness of the developmental psychologist by more settled behavior. His occasional wandering about the room and sweeping test materials to the floor was countered with a firm return to the examination. Some sensorimotor deficits were tentatively outlined, but it was clear that with one-to-one attention and firmness he was quieter and attentive and carried out tasks the parents considered miraculous.

In the playroom, he was engaged in rolling first a ball and then a toy train across the floor. His distractible behavior was minimal, and he responded to the (male) therapist's laughter and enthusiastic "good boy" when he recovered the object and sent it back to the therapist, rather than flinging it around the playroom, which was promptly stopped each time. Toward the end of the half hour, when he threatened but did not throw a train, he climbed on the therapist's lap; he responded to the therapist's wrestling with him playfully with obvious pleasure, and then cuddled up to him and gave him a hug. This behavior was rarely seen at home and only in response to receiving a gift or at bedtime when ill.

The capacity to settle down and attend is frequent with MBD youngsters in a one-to-one situation, with little distraction present in the room. Freddie's playfulness and cuddling indicated positive relationships with his parents, though rarely overtly demonstrated. His enjoyment of play was enhanced when his disruptive behavior was ignored and his success and enjoyment was focused on. The fact that his cue to the therapist during the playful gesture to throw the train was correctly interpreted and led to playful physical contact in wrestling enabled the boy to sit quietly in the therapist's lap and accept and give a hug for a moment.

When the data from the various examinations were clearly described to the parents, with sufficient time to respond to questions, the parents were able to accept the diagnosis of possible MBD. They began to understand that perhaps Freddie would need stimulant medication, but at this time, for his security in living and learning and their greater ease in living, they would need to learn to help him accept his place in the home rather than dominate it. He would have to learn to accept parental authority and to learn to enjoy age-appropriate curiosity and mastery rather than random erratic hypermotile play.

In addition to participating in the parent group, all parents were seen every two weeks with their children in small groups to learn, with the help of others, how to manage their children in a variety of situations. Each parent-child group was given games to play together, and reading and puzzles to do, and engaged in some teaching of the child by the parent. Staff went from group to group demonstrating and suggesting how parents could more effectively accomplish each task with their child.

After six to eight months of work together, there were marked changes in Freddie's behavior. His affectional responses to both parents were frequent, as was his ability to hear "no" and respond to parental authority. His fun in play with children and his beginning pleasure in exploration and learning went hand in hand with a slowing down of activity and increase in capacity to attend.

On follow-up, Freddie continued to be able to cooperate and learn to interact with reduced impulsivity. When placed on stimulants in the third grade to help his concentration further, he was not in any way a behavior problem in school or at home.

THE SCHOOL-AGE CHILD AND MBD

Whatever the cause of the hyperactive behavior, by the time MBD children have been in school several years, they usually have severe learning and behavior problems. Often the stimulant medication, when it does work, helps the attention span and may decrease the hyperactive behavior, but the asocial, nonresponsiveness to social situations with children and adults remains a difficult problem. The home environment may not settle down, since the interactional patterns with siblings and parents have long been established. The issue of becoming accountable for one's behavior requires considerable help from home and school. Both child and parents must unlearn previous behavior patterns.

The data suggest that where children do benefit from stimulant medication, those children and parents who had therapeutic help did the best (de la Curz et al., 1973; Greenberg et al, 1972).

There are also data which indicate that when children with MBD treated or untreated, reach adolescence, a time when the attentional problems and hypermotility should subside; they often continue to be asocial, to have few friends, to have severe learning problems and continued behavior problems of defiance and uncooperative withdrawal, and to have little capacity to plan for their future.

Thus, no matter what the treatment, children and parents require early help to establish discipline and authoritative parental relations, with the related affectional bonds and implications for future socialization, learning, and capacity to develop into a self-motivated, responsible young adult.

Case vignette 2:

Andy was a ten-year-old white boy in the third grade in a developmental disabilities class because of his widly impulsive behavior, assaultive destructiveness, and inability to learn and to socialize. He had been on Ritalin, 60 mgm per day, for almost one year, with minimal improvement in his capacity to attend; he slowed down a bit in school and at home but had not been helped to learn very much. He was one of a family of six siblings, each from a different father; there was no father in the home at the time Andy entered treatment. Andy came to the clinic because he knocked his three-year-old sister down the stairs, causing a concussion. The probation department, in considering foster home placement, wanted him evaluated.

Mother, when seen for the initial interview, came in with a son, age two, and daughter, age three, not yet in day care because they were not toilet trained.

Mrs. T, a still-attractive woman in her midthirties, looked haggard and tired and vainly tried to get her young children to obey her. They disregarded her querulous admonitions and went their merry ways, requiring a posse of secretaries to round them up every so often as they wandered through the clinic.

Mrs. T. said Andy alone was worse than the other five. A boy and a girl, one and two years older than Andy, were doing well in school, but Andy's rages scared them and he bullied the whole family. Mother recounted the familiar story of not being prepared for a sleepless, rarely hungry, constantly-in-motion infant who would not be still in her lap and nurse. Although she was having troubles with Andy's alcoholic father during Andy's first year of life, she believed that had little to do with Andy's behavior. She was busy with the other small children as well, but they were good. She came to see Andy as the Devil. When a doctor first examined Andy, he felt Andy had some pylorospasm and treated that with drops. Phenobarbitol given to make him sleep drove him wild. Mother had very little memory of Andy's developmental milestones, except that he was slow to walk. He was always aggressive, acted impulsively. No one could make him obey, not even her fourth husband, who beat Andy severely for some of his destructiveness and tied him in bed so he would not wander the house at night. School was a nightmare. No day care center or kindergarten could keep him; they described him as an angry cyclone.

The previous year, when in the special class, an interested teacher prevailed on the welfare worker to have Andy undergo a special neurological examination. The neurologist found that Andy was clumsy in his gait and poorly coordinated and had some minor perceptual-motor problems. He prescribed the Ritalin and has followed Andy since. He is troubled that the drug has so little effect on Andy's behavior.

The evaluation revealed a normal IQ of 96, some gross motor clumsiness, and poor eye-hand coordination. His draw-a-person was very primitive, and he would not draw a family.

Andy also settled down somewhat in the diagnostic sessions and could, in the play session, spend as long as five minutes with the tinker toy trying, and finally with help making a steering wheel for a boat.

Andy, his mother, all the siblings, a colleague and the author met to discuss Andy's diagnosis. The two older siblings asked the pertinent questions about whether he would get worse, would need to be hospitalized, would die, and so on. In two such sessions, the colleague and author felt that mother and the older siblings understood Andy's illness and the goals in treatment. They also became clearer about mother's and their roles with Andy at home. The task was to help Andy to manage his impulsive aggressive behavior, and we would be working with mother and occasionally with the older siblings to find ways to help

Andy control his behavior. Both siblings had already had to assume responsibilities far beyond their ages and agreed to do anything to help if it would keep Andy at home.

Mother and siblings were frank about the fact that it would be easier for them with Andy out of the home, but they were sure he would panic and get worse with strangers, because each new teacher or class caused him to be more difficult to manage. The Probation Department deferred placement to determine the effect of psychotherapy with Andy and his family.

The treatment with Andy, mother, and siblings took place over an 18 month period with a 2 1/2 year follow-up. Andy was seen in the playroom by the author, and the colleague worked with mother and, when necessary, the siblings. The plan was first to help mother learn to attend to and control her small pre-schoolers and, in the process, to help her see herself as a more adequate and competent person.

INTRODUCTORY PHASE   The introductory phase consisted of 2 months with mother and 3 1/2 months with Andy. Mother very quickly related to her female therapist and discussed the hardships of her childhood. She was one of eight siblings born to an alcoholic mother and father; each parent had to be hospitalized and many times abandoned the family leaving the older siblings, including Mrs. T., to act as parents. At 16 Mrs. T. ran away with a high school boyfriend. They were married and had a good life for 1 1/2 years, while each worked, until the first baby was born and her husband left for a life without responsibility. Mother had always been able to attract men who needed to be taken care of. Each one left because they did not want a family burden. Bitterly, she described how the more stable men, the two she married in the last five years might have stuck it out except for their inability to control and tolerate Andy. Each stepfather was afraid he would hurt or kill Andy.

BEGINNING THERAPY WITH MOTHER   Initially, the therapist met with mother and two younger children in the playroom and began to insist that mother help her control and play with the two young children. Mother noted that the therapist's firm voice and rapid follow-up action to prevent destruction of toys or running out of the room seemed to reduce her children's wild behavior. She tried to follow suit. She was surprised when they began to obey her. Then the therapist taught mother some learning games that they could all play together with mutual pleasure.

It was clear that mother had played little as a child. The therapist helped mother tune into each child's signals that they needed to urinate or have a bowel movement. She helped mother praise the children when they said they needed to go to the toilet. In the course of the first six months of work, both children were toilet trained and able to go into day care. Mother had by then also learned to play with them and to be firm with them at home.

The issues about dealing more firmly with Andy led quickly to exploring mother's terror of her own unpredictable mother and fear that any effort to stop Andy's destructive behavior would lead to some assaultive or murderous action on Andy's part. It took mother quite a while to recognize that Andy feared no one could control his angry behavior and that Andy's escalating behavior seemed to ask for controls not punishment. The two older siblings were brought in for several of these discussions once mother could explain to them the problem and her need for their help in holding Andy when he got assaultive.

Mother was very quick to make associations from her work with her small children and the effect of her attention on them to the neglect Andy had suffered, not only because of his difficult behavior, but because she was troubled and overwhelmed.

She talked a good bit about her sense of blame that Andy was her punishment for wanting sexual pleasure and company for herself.

BEGINNING THERAPY WITH ANDY.   In the initial work with Andy, he ignored the therapist's efforts to explain his disorder and stormed the playroom. He picked something up, looked at it, used it for a moment, then threw it down and started on something else. In ten minutes, the playroom was a shambles. The therapist stopped him and said "We need to stop our time together until we can clean up." He ignored this comment. The therapist grabbed his wrist tightly and said "No more toys until we clean up." Andy struck out at him. The therapist grabbed both hands, put him in a chair, and sat beside him, his arms encircling Andy and holding his wrists firmly. Andy screamed, struggled, called the therapist names until the end of that hour and the therapist cleaned up alone. The next hour, after Andy threw three toys down, the therapist grabbed him and held him for ten minutes. After he let him go, he stood over Andy until he picked up one toy. Then the therapist picked up the other two. At Andy's gesture of throwing the toy at the therapist, the therapist grabbed his wrist. Andy found the tinker toys and made a ship's steering wheel. The therapist watched and helped him put spokes in the steering wheel when he had trouble. As the hour drew to an end, he made a dash for a shelf and the therapist stopped him.

In the next seven hours, restraint was necessary for some part of each hour, but Andy's play was more intense and longer as he made more complicated tinker toy projects. Few eye-hand coordination problems were observed.

While Andy made tinker toy constructions, the therapist would repeatedly tell him about his developmental disability. He would draw a brain and point out that some parts were not developing as fast as normal. Andy would not die or go to the hospital. Sometimes he could not control his actions, but most of the time he could. No matter what he did, even if he was not aware he had done it because it was his disorder, he would have to learn to make up for anything that happened, etc. in order to get along with others. This was said in many different ways and illustrated with each impulsive act.

This phase of treatment ended when Andy made a Batmobile out of tinker toys and spent a number of weeks as the terrible Batman destroying cities and bombing the therapist. Then he began to ask the therapist to build block cities for him to destroy. He looked much calmer at the end of each session and greeted the therapist with a warm and lively "hi" at the start.

MIDPHASE OF TREATMENT. This phase was about 12–13 months for mother and 10 months for Andy.

As mother began to make demands on Andy and stop his destructive behavior, she found it possible to ask his help in doing something for a younger child, instead of asking the oldest son. At first, Andy refused, but when he occasionally helped a child dress or fixed a toy, mother's clear pleasure seemed gratifying to him. On one occasion, after a bad day of hitting out at children in school, he struck his little sister. Mother grabbed him, and he ran away. The older brother caught him, and mother and brother contained him for an hour until he seemed more relaxed. Mother was asked by the therapist to talk to Andy about how he looked or seemed to feel to her when she was with him, to try to help him express his feelings in words and not behavior. His therapist had been doing this in their hours, with an increase in Andy's sense that others could understand his various feelings from helplessness to despondent "I don't care" when he could not learn something or perform as expected, to terrible anger when he was frustrated. Although mother's efforts were ignored or snarled at with "What do you care?" it became clear he wanted her to notice and to comment on how he seemed to feel and to find out what happened in school. Thus, very slowly began a new relationship based on mutual talk and sharing of feelings rather than reaction to Andy's destructive, assaultive behavior.

Mother began to realize she saw her hateful mother and father in Andy and that her reactions, both irrational and reactive, perpetuated her and Andy's disturbed relationship.

Thus, Andy slowly changed at home. Mother's therapist and mother began then to involve the teacher in their effort to alter Andy's environment. The teacher, to her surprise, found that Andy was ready to sit still longer and responded to her praise about his behavior and learning by trying to work harder. The teacher could not understand how the changes in Andy had occurred, though she recognized his need to be cared about and thought well of and to feel important.

WORK WITH ANDY.   Andy began a series of dramas of monsters destroying children in gruesome ways. After a particularly agonizing or cruel death scene, he would glance at the therapist who would comment "Well the poor kid sure got it. I wish I could help him." Slowly his monsters ceased killing children and began to destroy men and women in fiendish ways. He laughed with anxious pleasure and watched the therapist. When the therapist acknowledged that was a particularly terrible scene he had just directed, he would beam.

After many weeks, he then began to bring in good monsters to rescue the victims, and the good monsters could always outsmart the bad ones. Here he asked the therapist to play the evil monsters, like Dracula, and he would come flying to the rescue and destroy him.

Andy was obviously attending more easily for long periods of time, and his coordination and walking seemed better. When he was retested, his IQ showed an increase of 15 points and the scatter was less. He did much better on performance items than previously.

The therapist had been working continuously to help Andy assume responsibility for any impulsive act. When he destroyed a toy, he would reluctantly help fix it. Once he smashed a large ceramic ashtray on the therapist's desk, and they spent the next two hours with china cement gluing it back together. Andy was pleased when it looked almost as good as new. Thus, in the therapeutic relationship he made restitution more willingly for any temporary lapses. The turning point occurred when he was destroying a monster. His eyes glazed for a moment, and he slapped the therapist in the face. When he became aware of the red mark on the therapist's face, he hugged the therapist, touched his face gently, and said "I'm very sorry. I hope it doesn't hurt too much. I'm so sorry." The therapist reassured Andy and told him he was pleased Andy owned his behavior and could apologize rather than saying his usual "I didn't mean it." While such lapses sometimes occurred, Andy quickly set to making things right first in the playroom, then at home, and finally at school.

A very clear shift in cognitive process now began to occur as, instead of plots and counterplots of action, he wanted us to write a scenario so he could figure out how to go about the rescue. It was no longer a magical act but a more logical sequence of dealing with each evil act by a logical counterploy.

THE END PHASE OF WORK.   This phase lasted about 6 months. Mother tried bringing men friends home and, from her therapist, learned how to rehearse Andy in the behavior expected of him so there were no catastrophies. When Andy had a very severe flu with pneumonia and they were alone together, she found she could nurse him and enjoy taking care of him. Mother was also able to play and care for the younger children with less stress and often with pleasure. She found firmness easier. As she worked through her hatred of her parents and could look at her present behavior as efforts not to repeat the past, she began to make rapid gains in relationships with both men and women and especially her children. Termination was worked through gradually with the therapist still available to mother.

Andy, in the end phase of treatment, continued his scenarios, writing and acting them out. He now sometimes talked of his anger at mother or siblings or teacher and also recognized how he set things up.

As his teachers found he could and would concentrate and work, they took pleasure in helping him master math, history, and English. Andy would keep the therapist abreast of his progress with real pride.

Andy had a difficult time when mother began to bring male

friends home. He reverted to monsters, who first killed defenseless children, then adults and then a quick return to murder in drama, as if to recapitulate his work and consolidate it.

Separation from the therapist was very difficult for Andy. It was made easier, however, because of one of his teacher's concerns and interest in him.

Follow-up showed that with continued medication following therapy, Andy did well. He got into regular class finally at his grade level with lots of extra help. His talents with words made him a standout in English. He was quite active in high school drama and learning well in everything but math, where he continued to have troubles with concepts. His behavior difficulties gradually ceased.

RESTATEMENT.   The thesis here is that in Andy's case the medication did not help until therapy began to reduce the anxiety and improve behavior and attitudes. It is clear that without help to parents and child, MBD youngsters are at risk to continue with learning and behavior problems throughout adolescence, even if medication is of some help.

SUMMARY AND CONCLUSIONS

Since there is no single causative etiologic agent of the behavior in MBD, so there can be no single treatment in this or any other multicausal disease. Psychotherapy with child and family may be a critical factor in the efficacy of medication where otherwise the improvement is not dramatic.

The early intervention and prevention efforts with very young and preschool children are critical to their development. Helping parents learn to establish a firm authoritative relationship, which helps the child to relate socially, and to follow directions and diminish impulsive behavior, may be critical to the child's future ability to live independently. Thus, a variety of therapeutic modalities—behavior modification, modeling and instruction in early stimulation, help with establishing discipline through reduction of parent guilt about their angry murderous feelings toward an impossible child, intensive conflict-reducing psychotherapy for child and parents—may be important to successful treatment of MBD.

REFERENCES

Berlin, I. N. Minimal brain dysfunction: Management of family distress. *Journal of the American Medical Association,* 1974, *9,* 1454–1456.

Berlin, I. N., & Berlin, R. Parents' advocate role in education as primary prevention. In I. N. Berlin (ed.), *Advocacy for child mental health.* New York: Brunner/Mazel, 1975.

de la Cruz, F. F., Fox, B. H., & Roberts, R. H. (Eds.). *Minimal brain dysfunction.* New York: New York Academy of Sciences, 1973.

Dmitriev, V. *Infant learning.* Seattle: Experimental Education Unit, University of Washington, 1972.

Dmitriev, V. & Hayden, A. H. *Multidisciplinary programs for Down's Syndrome children.* Seattle; Experimental Education Unit, University of Washington, 1973.

Greenberg, L. M., Deem, M. A., & McMahon, S. Effects of dextroamphetamine, chlorpromazine, and hydroxyzine on behavior and performance in hyperactive children. *American Journal of Psychiatry,* 1972, *129,* 532–539.

Mendelson, W., Johnson, N., & Stewart, M. A. Hyperactive children as teenagers; A follow-up study. *Journal of Nervous and Mental Disorders,* 1971, *153,* 273–279.

Spring, C., & Greenberg, L. Relations between teachers' ratings of abnormal motor behavior in poor readers and performance on a reaction-time test. *Journal of Reading Behavior,* 1972–3, *5* (2), 134–139.

Weiss, C. F., Chairman, American Academy of Pediatrics, Committee on Drugs. An evaluation of pharmacologic approaches to learning impediments. *Pediatrics,* 1970, *46* (1), 142–144.

Weiss, G., Minde, K., Werry, J. S., Douglass, V., Nemeth, E. Studies on the hyperactive child: VIII. Five-year follow-up. *Archives of General Psychiatry,* 1971, *24,* 409–414.

Chapter 16

A DEVELOPMENTAL MODEL FOR TREATMENT OF HYPERACTIVE CHILDREN

Gunnar Nirk
Pamela Rubovits
Haven Miles

Our treatment of hyperactive children is designed to help them develop better self-regulatory mechanisms. We see these children as deficient in their abilities to regulate mobility, maintain sustained attention to relevant tasks, ignore irrelevant stimuli, and control internal sensations and thoughts. Our program has evolved since 1973 in a preschool unit of a community mental health center. We see preschool children and their parents with a variety of emotional and cognitive problems. Hyperactivity is, however, one of the most frequent reasons for referral.

Twenty years after the "hyperkinetic impulse disorder" was initially described (Laufer, Denhoff, & Solomons, 1957), there is still no sufficient evidence that hyperactivity in children is a definable clinical syndrome. The view that hyperactivity is a "nonspecific symptom occurring in a variety of medical and behavioral disorders and associated with a heterogenous group of etiological factors" is supported by extensive research evidence (Ross & Ross, 1976 p. 11).

In the voluminous literature on the subject, hyperactivity

is frequently associated with minimal brain dysfunction and/or learning disabilities, but these are also not clearly defined clinical entities (Ross & Ross, 1976; Wolff & Hurwitz, 1973). Regardless of the nosological ambiguities, the symptom of hyperactivity in children is very real and easily recognizable by clinical observation. It creates serious problems for the children themselves and is very troublesome to teachers and parents.

Virginia Douglas (1972, p. 260) suggests that "a core group of symptoms involving ability to sustain attention and to control impulsivity can account for most of the deficits found in the hyperactive group." Attention and impulse control are complex functions. They become more effective as the child develops. The central nervous system is continuously bombarded with a multitude of stimuli from the environment and impulses coming from within the organism. Only a few relevant stimuli are selected for sustained attention. The selection and maintenance of attention are based on cognitive and emotional factors and form the basis for purposeful self-regulated behavior (Milner, 1970).

A young child has only a limited ability to organize incoming stimuli. As the organism develops, its ability to deal with a complex environment in a purposeful and organized way increases. We all know that young children are overactive, impulsive, and distractible. We become concerned only when these behaviors do not change as the child gets older.

Hyperactivity can be viewed as a symptom indicating that a child has delayed ability to sustain attention and control impulses. This developmental delay may be caused by slow maturation of the central nervous system (CNS), by damage to the CNS tissues, by biochemical dysfunction of the CNS, or by lack of appropriate environmental stimulation which is essential to CNS development. Several of these causes may be combined (Ross & Ross, 1976). Sorting out etiological factors is often unproductive, seldom adding to a construction of a treatment plan. After active medical and neurological illness is ruled out, treatment must focus on environmental inputs which at-

tempt to provide the child with the most appropriate stimulation for psychological development. We should not forget that
the minimally injured brain is still capable of development
(Lebovici & Diatkine, 1974).

For most children, the child's home and school provide the
stimulation needed for healthy development. Parents and
teachers offer increasingly complex materials and activities and
teach children to find pleasure and satisfaction in completing
tasks which require sustained attention. What works well with
most children, however, frequently does not work with children
whose development is delayed or uneven. Adults are not always
able to disregard their expectations based on the child's chrono-
logical age and to interact with the child on his or her developmental level. Hyperactive children are frequently expected to
attend to complex tasks which are far beyond their ability;
results are failure and frustration. The child's self-esteem is
injured, and problems in parent-child relationship occur. We
have observed unresolved dependency needs in many hyperactive children; these are frequently hidden behind a dramatic
show of pseudoindependence.

Our treatment of hyperactivity does not depend on the use
of stimulants, but we also see no conflict between our therapeutic approach and the use of stimulant medication. If a child
responds to stimulants, it will make our task much easier; but
medication is no substitute for the environmental experiences
which are needed to achieve a better level of self-regulation.

THE MODEL

The goal of our treatment of hyperactivity is to stimulate
development of the following functions: (1) regulation of
motility; (2) sustained attention to relevant tasks; (3) impulse
control; and (4) self-verbalization. This therapeutic model is
derived from Santostefano's "cognitive control therapy" (Santostefano, 1978), a form of psychotherapy combining psy-

choanalytic and cognitive-developmental principles. After assessment of the child's level of functioning, the therapist provides the child with a systematic sequence of developmentally graded kinesthetic and perceptual (tactile, visual, and auditory) experiences. A variety of materials and activities are used. This process is aimed at correcting deficits in dealing with external stimuli and internal impulses. At the same time, the therapist helps the child to become aware of inefficient coping methods and emotional reactions, including feelings toward the therapist. Emphasis is placed on verbalizing feelings instead of acting them out.

We use Santostefano's theoretical framework, but our assessments of attention deficits and our treatment plans are much more flexible. We also have borrowed treatment ideas from other sources. Meichenbaum's "self-instructional training" of hyperactive and impulsive children has been particularly useful (Meichenbaum, 1977). He relies on Luria's self-verbalization techniques to decrease impulsive behavior. Similar methods have been described by Palkes, Stewart, and Kahana (1968) and Douglas (1975). Treatment techniques derived from different theoretical frameworks frequently fit well together in a treatment plan and complement each other.

Our experience in treating hyperactive children suggests the following generalizations:

1. Considering psychological problems of children as indications of developmental delay (Santostefano, 1971) is useful when dealing with hyperactive children.
2. Cognitive and emotional aspects of a preschool child's problem cannot be separated. A treatment plan has to consider both. The relationship between cognitive and emotional aspects of development is best articulated by Piaget (1962, p. 121): "at no level, at no stage, even in the adult can we find behavior without affect, nor a purely affective state without a cognitive element involved."

3. Drug treatment of hyperactivity is not enough (Douglas, 1975). Even if the child responds well to drugs, there are most likely cognitive and emotional difficulties which need remediation. Hyperactive children treated only with drugs are less hyperactive in adolescence but continue to have difficulties with sustained attention and impulse control, poor peer relationships, poor self-image, and a high risk of antisocial or delinquent behavior (Weiss, 1975).

4. Serious developmental delays will only respond to intensive intervention.

All referrals to our program are evaluated by our professional staff consisting of a psychiatric social worker, developmental psychologist, and child psychiatrist. A developmental profile and remedial plan are formulated. The child is then assigned to a paraprofessional remedial assistant, who works under professional supervision with the child and also maintains contact with the child's parents and teacher. Most children in treatment with us are seen two to four times a week for 30–45 minutes in addition to their regular Head Start or day care program. If possible, parents are also seen regularly, either to discuss child management or in more intensive treatment. If parents are not receptive to treatment, we feel we still have a chance to help the child who is in a full-day day care program.

CASE EXAMPLE

Specific remedial techniques are best illustrated by case examples. In the following presentation, we will focus on direct work with the child. Contacts with parents and teachers are based on traditional concepts of casework and consultation.

Peter's parents contacted their local community mental health center at the suggestion of their pediatrician when Peter was four years old. The pediatrician had had Peter on stimulant medication since he was two but as reports of management problems at home persisted had decided that in addition the family needed counseling. Peter had just recently been expelled from preschool because of overactivity and excessive aggressiveness toward other children and adults.

Peter's family—mother, father, Peter, and a two-year-old brother—lives in a low-income neighborhood, occupying the second floor of a three-decker tenement. Both mother and father describe themselves as the "black sheep" in their families. Father, a construction worker, left school after nine years in an ungraded class; he had repeated troubles in school because he "could't seem to sit still, was always showing off, and wouldn't take orders." He still speaks rapidly and fidgets in his chair. He has continued to have difficulty with authority and has quit many jobs because he could not get along with his bosses. Peter's mother appears to be a gentle, soft-spoken woman. She had no problems in school and graduated from high school. She became pregnant with Peter two months before graduation. She recalls with emotion the humiliation she felt about the circumstances surrounding her marriage, never having known anyone else in her family who was pregnant out of wedlock. She and Peter's father had not wanted to marry and felt they were forced to by her parents.

The marriage has been troubled. Mother and father report frequent arguments, and father has twice left the family. The family has moved four times in five years, twice having to move in with the wife's parents because they could not afford their own apartment. The family has been on and off welfare, another fact that causes the wife much embarrassment.

Mother's pregnancy with Peter and delivery were normal, although mother says she cried "all the time" while pregnant. When Peter and mother left the hospital, they went to live with maternal grandparents. Maternal grandmother became the primary caretaker of the baby. Peter was a difficult baby, according to his mother, and there were frequent arguments between mother and grandmother. Grandmother kept telling mother to let Peter alone and not "fuss over him so much." Mother used to "sneak" into his room to hold him, but Peter would scream when she touched him and that would bring in grandmother, who would reprimand mother. Mother says she feels she was not a good mother for Peter.

Developmental milestones were within normal limits. Mother reports no sleeping or eating problems. Peter was toilet trained by three with no problems. Mother thinks he talked early, was climbing out of his crib by 18 months, was running by age two, and "hasn't stopped since." Management problems began when Peter was about two. Mother and father reported incident after incident in which they were embarrassed in public or at family gatherings by Peter's resistance to discipline. Reports of how they respond to Peter's misbehavior have been vague and often contradictory.

The family sought help from a series of pediatricians. None found any neurological deficits nor any speech or hearing problems. One doctor finally prescribed stimulant medication. It was the parents' perception that initially the medication calmed Peter down, but then after a few days "he was his old self again." Different dosages were tried. With each new medication plan, the parents thought they saw an initial improvement and then a return of the old problems.

With detailed interviewing, it became apparent problems with Peter developed primarily when he was out of the house or when people came to visit. Alone, he spent most of his time watching television; but when other stimuli were added, he would run around, jump on furniture or people, talk rapidly, laugh and shriek loudly, and become aggressive when attempts were made to stop him. He rarely played with his toys; but if his brother used them, he would snatch them away and frequently wound up breaking them. He and his brother could not play together because Peter would get frustrated and physically attack his brother if he did not follow Peter's directions. This overactivity and impulsivity became extreme when Peter was placed in a preschool classroom with 20 other children and eventually led the school to decide they could not maintain him.

Our evaluation at the mental health center was done when Peter was four and a half. We saw an extremely active and anxious child who played on the level of approximately a two or two and a half year old. He was uncontrollable in the waiting room, running through the building, hiding in closets, and jumping out to scare people. In the playroom, he darted from toy to toy. He talked incessantly, but the discourse was telegraphic and disjointed. Psychological testing indicated that Peter was functioning above average in the verbal area but below average to borderline on performance tasks. Testing took three sessions, and the limits of the standardization procedures were frequently taxed.

Further observation and educational assessment revealed serious developmental delays of two to two and a half years in visual-motor skills. Peter tried to avoid visual-motor activities, becoming anxious when asked to do something, especially if it involved using his hands. He would start fidgeting then become very angry and try to run away. A home visit revealed an obsessively neat and clean apartment that showed almost no signs that two small children lived there. The doors had been removed from all bedrooms, mother said, so they could keep an eye on the boys while they slept.

We were easily able to identify a number of areas in which both Peter and his parents needed help. It was determined that initially Peter could benefit most from a cognitive therapy program, focusing on his attention and impulse control problems. He was assigned to a remedial assistant, to be seen three times a week. At this time, we had only limited insight into Peter's emotional deficits. His play was so disorganized he could not use it to act out underlying internal struggles and anxieties. He had such difficulty organizing his thoughts and maintaining a theme that he could not talk about areas of conflict. These delays made him a poor candidate for traditional play therapy.

Peter's parents, although extremely guarded in their conversations with us, had revealed enough to indicate there were serious marital problems and much underlying anger and hostility in both mother and father. They had, however, come to us specifically for help with their son and were not ready to deal with their own problems. We accepted this as a starting point and offered them weekly sessions with our psychologist to discuss child management techniques, hoping to progress to considering problems in the marital relationship and to parents' own difficulties.

Peter's therapy sessions were initially 20 minutes long, gradually increasing to 45 minutes. They were conducted in a small room, stripped bare at the beginning of therapy and gradually enriched with materials as therapy progressed. The goals for these sessions were: to teach rule and direction following, shape attending skills, improve basic visual-motor skills, and increase self-esteem. The therapist's role was to impose structure and sequence on Peter's activities, to slow down his movements and speech, and to give him opportunities to find enjoyment in attempting and completing tasks.

The order of activities for each session was always the same. Pictures signifying each activity were drawn on a daily schedule given Peter in the waiting room and carried along by him for the entire session until he was back in the waiting room. Checks were put next to the picture (initially by the therapist, later by Peter) as each activity was completed. Three rules were stated on day one; more were added as Peter began testing his therapist and the structure. Most of his misbehavior was ignored or alternatives were offered: "Here are some blocks you can bang." The use of these alternatives was verbally reinforced. Rules were stated indirectly: "Air conditioners are not for touching." Peter was encouraged to verbalize the rules himself.

Tasks were presented to Peter that at first had one or two and then three or four steps. Completion of each step was acknowledged. A star was pasted onto the "daily log" when Peter finished all the steps for a task. Activities included moving a truck down a piece of tape, picking up a few blocks, moving the truck back up the tape, and depositing the blocks in a bin. Peter learned to imitate the pattern of beats made by his therapist on a set of bongo drums. At first, it was very difficult for him to inhibit his random, fast beating, but gradually with very specific directions to "stop and listen" he was able to listen to a four- or five-beat pattern, wait for his turn, and then reproduce the pattern. Obstacle courses were constructed with bowling pins, and Peter learned to move around them going fast and slow.

Unfortunately, after nine weeks of therapy, Peter's therapist became ill and took an extended leave. Significant progress had, however, been made. Rule transgressions decreased from approximately 30 per session to one or two per session. Peter became able to follow consistently directions given two at a time without having to be reminded. He progressed from staying at a task for 1–1½ minutes to remain involved for 4–5 minutes. Visual skills such as sorting, matching, and sequencing improved tremendously. Peter still had great difficulty with many of the fine and large motor tasks. His drawings were similar to those of a two year old. He could not balance on one foot or accurately toss a bean bag at a large target. Verbal memory improved from being able to repeat two words to being able to repeat five or six words. His level of free play activity showed little change. Arriving for a session and leaving continued to be problems, with Peter frequently losing control, racing up and down the hall, shrieking, and so forth.

Peter was assigned to a new therapist, and another child was added to the sessions. Duo therapy was decided upon because of our concern about Peter's lack of social skills and because of our desire to increase distractions and see if Peter's control could be maintained. The second child was quieter and calmer than Peter, although he too had impulse control problems and lacked motivation to try and complete structured tasks. Verbally, he was as skilled as Peter; however, he played on a considerably higher level than Peter.

Twice-weekly sessions were held, always following the same routine: a 15-minute work time, snack, a 30-minute free play time. During the work time, a verbal mediation program was used. This involved having the therapist model a task while describing out loud the steps. The boys then did the same task, with the therapist describing the steps. Eventually, the boys were able to give themselves directions and to work silently and independently, giving whispered self-directions. During free play, the therapist helped the boys learn to play parallely and then began some work on cooperative play skills. She also reinforced imitation, using this as a way to teach Peter ways of using play materials.

Peter's impulse control deteriorated markedly during free play. He was very overbearing, shouting orders and getting angry when they were ignored. There was little improvement in his social skills. His level of play did improve, and both boys learned to respond to the verbal cues of "stop, look, and listen." Duo therapy continued for a summer, approximately two months.

For the first several months of Peter's treatment, his parents came for counseling weekly or biweekly. They canceled about half of their appointments because father was involved in looking for a new job and had frequent job interviews. While the focus of these sessions remained on child management issues, tension and hostility between the parents often surfaced, interfering with problem solving. Slowly and cautiously, the therapist pointed out the relationship between parents' relationship and the way they dealt with Peter. This was met with much denial, but slowly some changes started to occur.

In the fall, parents decided to enroll Peter in kindergarten. The first few weeks were very difficult for him. He was still far behind other five year olds in motor coordination, so many of the traditional kindergarten activities were extremely frustrating. His rule testing was responded to inconsistently. Verbal directions were not repeated frequently enough for him to use them as controls. His teacher was a nervous, fast-moving dramatic woman who filled her room with visual and auditory stimuli. After a month, Peter was transferred to a special education preschool class, set up using a behavior management approach. Peter is doing well with this structure. His teacher is emphasizing work on visual-motor skills. She reports that Peter whispers directions to himself over and over and gives himself both positive and negative feedback.

Peter continues to come to the mental health center, where he is a member of a socialization program and is also seen indivdually in traditional play therapy. Since his play has become more organized and sustained, he can use puppets and dolls to act out troubling experiences and express feelings. We now see the confusion and anger that Peter feels and appreciate the depression that has come as a result of so many past failures. He is able to relate experiences, tell stories, and carry on conversations with his therapist, so we are beginning to understand what happens with Peter at home that only adds to his sadness and anger.

COMMENT

Behavior modification techniques were initially needed to get Peter involved in the remedial program. Later, ideas borrowed from Santostefano (1978), Meichenbaum (1977), and Douglas (1975) were used. All the sophisticated training to get Peter to "stop, look, and listen" would not have been possible without the relationship that developed between Peter and his remedial assistant.

By the time Peter went to kindergarten, his ability to control impulses and sustain attention had improved considerably. The wish to please the remedial assistant had become a wish to do well at school. This was coupled by an increase in self-esteem based on many positive experiences in his remedial program. He was not ready for an overstimulating regular kindergarten program but is doing well in a smaller, well-structured special education classroom.

Peter still had unresolved conflicts which were expressed

in excessive anxiety. In our judgment, he had developed adequate self-regulation to make it possible for him to resolve these issues in traditional play therapy.

Children like Peter cannot initially profit from traditional play therapy techniques. Sometimes increased ability to regulate motility, attention, and impulses increases self-esteem and helps to resolve tasks of emotional development so that no further intervention is needed. In other situations children will need play therapy to resolve remaining emotional conflicts.

We have no controlled studies at this point to document the effectiveness of our therapeutic techniques. Our clinical impression is that we have been reasonably successful. We hope in the future to be able to present evidence of long-term effectiveness of our treatment approach.

SUMMARY

Our remedial plans vary considerably, but they are all based on the same general principles. These can be summarized in the following statements:

1. Remedial goals are stated in terms of behavior change.
2. The behaviors to be changed are selected on the basis of cognitive-interactive and psychoanalytic-developmental theories.
3. The change of behavior is not the goal by itself, but it is the only way we know that certain psychological structures have changed within the child, that is, that development has occurred.
4. Behavior change is achieved through offering the child new tasks and experiences via the remedial assistants who follow step-by-step directions. New tasks are carefully matched to the child's developmental level.
5. The child's need for encouragement and emotional support is recognized; the importance of a therapeutic

relationship between the child and the remedial assistant is stressed.

6. The success in learning new skills is used to increase the child's self-esteem, autonomy, and assertiveness.

7. The remedial plan is explained to the child's mother. When requested by the parent, the remedial assistant helps her to plan similar activities and suggests changes in child-rearing practices. The importance of a relationship between the remedial assistant and the child's family is stressed.

8. The child's teacher is kept informed and given suggestions about integrating aspects of the remedial plan into the regular classroom.

REFERENCES

Douglas, V. I. Stop, look and listen: The problem of sustained attention and impulse control in hyperactive and normal children. *Canadian Journal of Behavioral Sciences,* 1972, *4,* 259–282.

Douglas, V. I. Are drugs enough? To treat or train the hyperactive child. in R. Gittelman-Klein (Ed.), *Recent advances in child psychopharmacology.* New York; Human Sciences Press, 1975.

Laufer, N. W., Denhoff, E., & Solomons, G. Hyperkinetic impulse disorder in children's behavior problems. *Psychosomatic Medicine,* 1957, *19.*

Lebovici, S., & Diatkine, R. Normality as a concept of limited usefulness in the assessment of psychiatric risk. In B. J. Anthony & C. Koupernik (Eds.), *The child and his family* (Vol. 3). New York: John Wiley and Sons, 1974.

Meichenbaum, D. *Cognitive-behavior modification: An integrative approach.* New York: Plenum Press, 1977.

Milner, P. *Physiological psychology.* New York: Holt, Rinehart and Winston, Inc., 1970.

Pakes, H., Stewart, M., & Kahana, B. Porteus maze performance after training in self-directed verbal commands. *Child Development,* 1968, *39,* 817–826.

Piaget, J. The stages of the intellectual development of the child. *Bulletin of the Menninger Clinic,* 1962, *26,* 120–228.

Ross, D. M., & Ross, S. A. *Hyperactivity: Research, theory and action.* New York: John Wiley, 1976.

Santostefano, S. Beyond nosology: Diagnosis from the viewpoint of development. In H. E. Rie (Ed.), *Perspectives in child psychopathology.* New York, Aldine-Atherton Company, 1971.

Santostefano, S. *A biodevelopmental approach to clinical child psychology: Cognitive controls and cognitive control therapy.* New York: John Wiley, 1978.

Weiss, G. The natural history of hyperactivity in childhood and treatment with stimulant medication at different ages. In R. Gittelman-Klein (Ed.), *Recent advances in child psychopharmacology.* New York: Human Sciences Press, 1976.

Wolff, P., & Hurwitz, I. Functional implications of the minimal brain dysfunction damage syndrome. In S. Walzer & P. H. Wolff (Eds.), *Minimal cerebral dysfunction in children.* New York: Grune and Stratton, 1973.

Chapter 17

PSYCHOTHERAPY OF THE ADOLESCENT WITH TRUE BRAIN DAMAGE

Adolph E. Christ

Several technical modifications are necessary in the psychotherapy of children with true brain damage. The material for this presentation comes from the treatment of the following patients: one with a birth APGAR of 1; one with internal hydrocephalus, secondary right-eyed blindness, and nystagmus plus 11 shunt operations; one with an undiagnosed coma at age eight resulting in total memory loss for 72 hours, subsequent partial memory loss, and bitemporal epilepsy; three with birth injury resulting in grand mal epilepsy and mild to moderate spasticity; and one with no discerned etiology but with severe dyscalculia and total inability to orient himself spatially and temporal lobe epilepsy. These children are significantly distinct from those diagnosed as learning disabled or minimal brain dysfunction (MBD) children (Christ, 1977c; Rutter and Yule, 1975).

Although all of these youngsters have IQ scores in the dull normal to superior range, the difference between those who are at or below the preoperational stage of cognitive organization

(Christ, 1977a, b; Flavell, 1963, Piaget, 1951, 1952, 1954, 1962; Piaget & Inhelder, 1969) and those who are at the concrete or formal operational stage is important. As described by Christ (1977c) some emotionally disturbed adolescents with nearly normal IQ scores may have a preoperational level of cognitive organization resembling that of a five to seven year old. A similar phenomenon occurs in the truly brain-damaged population—one 15 year old with IQ of 87 is clearly preoperational, whereas another 15 year old with IQ of 93 is clearly concrete operational.

PREOPERATIONAL BRAIN-DAMAGED CHILDREN

Insight-oriented psychotherapy is not possible with brain-damaged children whose cognitive organization is at the preoperational or sensorimotor stage.

A is 14 years old and has a mild spastic quadriplegia secondary to birth injury. His grand mal epilepsy is fairly well controlled on 300 mgm of Dilantin per day. He is described as having had a high-pitched "organic" cry at birth, following a face presentation delivery. His development was slow: he walked with great difficulty at age two and said his first words at age three. Beginning in his early childhood, his parents were extraordinarily helpful, obtaining appropriate remedial help of all sorts, which probably partly accounts for his IQ of 87 at age 14. This score has the usual scatter of the organic child. A can multiply, divide, and add or subtract fractions, yet he cannot count out 12 checker pieces.

A has none of the abilities of the concrete operational child normally present at about age seven. He cannot put himself in another's place, see things as others might, or make judgments that take into account that a situation may have more than one dimension or have mitigating circumstances. What follows is that he does not automatically see himself as others might in a given situation or have the type of turmoil of other organically impaired patients that comes with the self-awareness or self-consciousness that is part of the concrete operational cognitive organization.

Most commonly, children or adolescents like A come to the attention of a child psychiatrist at times of planning, assessment, or medication management, or at a crisis. Such crises can include shifting from one school to another, moving the place of residence, or illness or death of a parent. Crises can be particularly catastrophic for such patients, regardless of the cause of the crisis because of at least three factors: crises change routine and alter predictable sequences; crises require a modification in solutions and approaches; crises tend to change the reactions and the demands from the significant people in the environment. With the cortically damaged patients, the need for predictable sameness, the symptoms of perseveration, the obsessive-compulsive defenses, the rigid "neatness" described by Goldstein (1930) in brain-damaged veterans all seem different manifestations of the same thing—the obviation of change, the elimination of the unpredictable. All this is changed in a crisis. All too frequently, the result is a rapid deterioration which requires careful psychotherapeutic work to bring such patients back to previous levels of functioning.

A second example of such cognitively limited children is B.

B is in a special class for intellectually normal but brain-damaged children. A crisis arose when he developed drug toxicity to Dilantin and was erroneously placed on phenobarbital for the control of re-emerging grand mal epilepsy. In common with cortically damaged children as well as many hyperactive syndrome children, he had a paradoxical reaction to barbiturates. He became much more hyperactive and distractible; his attention span became very short. He could not do his homework; his behavior became erratic and difficult.

C, a six-foot-tall 15 year old, intellectually more limited (IQ of 68) than A or B, had a similar very rapidly deteriorating course following the death of his father. He refused to go to school. He clung to his mother when she tried to go to work; when she managed to go, he telephoned her every 10 minutes with an insistent, angry, frightened pressure.

The initial deterioration manifested by the child at a time of crisis often elicits reactions from significant others which may aggravate the deterioration. Parents panic. Teachers threaten expulsion from school. Physicians, teachers, or relatives may give recommendations for residential or state hospital custodial institutionalization, further contributing to the parents' panic. The sudden loss of environmental equilibrium produces a circular deterioration that includes child, family, and school.

Therapy in these situations is predominantly some form of crisis intervention, best done by a therapist who knows that reintegration can be almost as rapid and dramatic as the deterioration. Certainly, any long-range planning must not be done until the reintegration of the patient is as complete as it can be. A rapid total assessment of the dysequilibrium is needed. Counseling of parents, teachers, pediatric neurologists, or pediatricians, as well as any significant others is called for. In C's situation, in addition to individual psychotherapy with him, several meetings of the therapist with his family were necessary to initiate his participation in a mourning process which could be meaningful to him. Exclusion of such a retarded child from painful family discussions, such as often follow the death of a parent, leaves the child to cope alone with the dynamics of such a situation (his or her own ambivalence, fear, anger, sense of loss, confusion, etc.) and does not provide the child with the new guidelines and new predictability that emerge from such discussions. Given that the brain-damaged child requires clarity and predictability, not only to understand the new situation but as basic coping methods and defense mechanisms, one can see how unhelpful such an exclusion can be. When children like A, B, or C participate in these family discussions, the crisis is often greatly mitigated for them.

Let us now concentrate on the psychotherapeutic work with these cognitively limited children. Psychoanalytically oriented insight-enhancing psychotherapy relies most heavily on concrete or formal operational cognitive strategies, strategies not available to these more primitive adolescents. Concrete operational strategies include the ability to conserve, that is, to see that things and situations have more than one dimension, and to decenter, that is, the ability to put oneself in another's place or to see that a sequence of events can be seen from more than one perspective. Formal operational cognitive strategies include the ability to engage in hypothetico-deductive thinking, that is, the ability to start with all hypothetical possibilities and deduct concrete examples from the possible, as well as the ability to think about the relationship of ideas to ideas. With the sensorimotor and preoperational child, a psychoanalytically oriented, developmentally sophisticated, metapsychologically aware psychotherapist is needed, who can, on the basis of this perspective, use instructional, supportive, direct interpretive, even operant techniques. For example, at times straightforward, unidimensional interpretation of the changed environment is helpful. "Your teacher got scared when you had your spell. She is afraid you will have another one." "You are much jumpier (B's word for hyperactive) than you were before—the change in medicine will help that." "You are not as clumsy as you were last week—that's great! In a few more days you will be like you were before." "You can't concentrate on homework like you did—try doing homework for 10 minutes, then walk around, then do homework for another 10 minutes. In a couple of weeks you will concentrate like you used to." "Your father died—is buried." (C): "No, don't talk about it!" "Oh—so you are sad. Cry, like your mother and sister. Your mother is sad, she goes to her room to cry. That is okay. She will come back."

For therapeutic intents, these preoperational adolescents are "retarded," even if their excellent training has kept their IQ out of the retarded range. For them, what has proven most beneficial has been a clearly crisis-oriented, supportive, reality interpretive approach. Equally important is the therapeutic intervention with the significant others in the child's milieu, be they parents, siblings, teachers, physicians, or relatives. Once predictable order and stability are reintroduced in the child's environment, the recovery to previous levels of functioning can be almost as rapid as the deterioration.

CONCRETE AND FORMAL OPERATIONAL BRAIN-DAMAGED CHILDREN

Brain-damaged children who have achieved concrete or formal operational levels of cognitive organization are amenable to traditional psychoanalytically oriented insight-enhancing psychotherapeutic approaches. The technical modifications required are more changes in emphasis than in basic techniques. Although such children's IQs may not be higher than those of the children described above and although their basic fund of information may not necessarily be greater, they are distinguished from the preoperational group by their ability to reverse, to see that a situation may have mitigating circumstances (i.e., be multidimensional), and to see things *and themselves* from more than one perspective (i.e., they decenter). If children have formal operational capacities, they would additionally engage in hypothetical deductive thinking and in abstract thinking, that is, think about the relation of ideas to ideas. A modified insight-oriented psychotherapy is possible with youngsters at these stages of cognitive development.

Brain-damaged youngsters, however, regardless of which of the two higher levels of cognitive organization they have attained, have special problems that require modification of the basic treatment technique. It is helpful to divide the treatment into roughly four "stages," each of which emphasizes a different treatment modification:

1. Development of a therapeutic alliance.
2. Development of workable mechanisms of defense.
3. Exploration and clarification of unalterable cognitive defects.
4. Interminable termination.

It is important to keep in mind that these stages are only loose guiding principles and that the course of a particular patient's therapy requires customized ebb and flow.

Development of a Therapeutic Alliance

In work with brain-damaged concrete or formal operational youngsters, the development of a therapeutic alliance requires particular care and some modification of standard therapeutic techniques. While doing a preliminary diagnostic evaluation, there is usually some relaxation of the youngster if there is an enumeration of the cognitive defects and behavioral problems for which he has been referred. Statements from parents or teachers as well as conventional psychological evaluations are paraphrased (Townes, Wagner & Christ, 1967), so the youngster knows what the therapist knows. At this point, he is most usually a passive but interested participant. Only much later does he actively participate in an elaboration of these problems and a working through of the ways they have affected him.

Following the definition of the problem, it is imperative to spend most of the initial hours exploring the child's strengths. Many have developed compensatory skills. One child might routinely beat the therapist at checkers; another might teach the therapist the mysteries of computer programming; another might show the therapist a "book" he is writing. Subsequent progress depends greatly upon the therapist's developing a genuine interest and respect for each youngster's specific cognitive skills, which must be clearly communicated. Typically, these children have a history of horrendous failure experiences. Defensively, they often act disdainfully toward anyone who loses a game to them or does not know as much as they do. Whereas such grandiosity must be challenged in the schizophrenic patient, in the brain-damaged child early challenge can lose the patient. Nor is the therapist's restraint always easily maintained. The child's grandiosity and disdain can arouse countertransference reactions in the therapist. After all, what therapist has not felt the mortification of stupidity or incompetence as a latency-age child? As the youngster feels the therapist's genuine respect and admiration for his competence, the disdain and grandiosity usually give way to a more relaxed dependent relationship. One cannot yet speak of trust, however; the defensive guarding occurs too quickly when anxiety emerges in the course of talking of painful subjects.

Development of Workable Mechanisms of Defense

Psychotherapy with non-brain-damaged patients in late latency and early and midadolescence is predominantly work in the present. The developmental thrust in adolescence, which includes the eruption of previously repressed affects, or the concentration in latency on cognitive development is as strong in these brain-damaged youngsters as in others with different diagnoses. In this stage of treatment, rather than emphasizing the intrapsychic determinants of distortions of current situations, it is essential first to help the youngster develop workable defenses. Although most of these nonretarded brain-damaged adolescents have some rudimentary defenses, such as displacement, rationalization, and intellectualization, they are very brittle and too easily shattered. In the routine treatment of nonorganically impaired children, the slow, gradual use of associations—dream associations, play associations, and so on—allows the therapist to simultaneously interpret the defense and what is being defended against. With the cognitively advanced but organically impaired children, even though they have a wider, more normal range of defense mechanisms than the "retarded" adolescents described earlier, the mechanisms easily become dysfunctional under minimal stress. Thus, providing and strengthening defenses is essential at this stage of treatment.

Before treatment, even with the wider range of available

defenses, the predominant one used by these youngsters is denial. This defense mechanism is totally unamenable to constructive use in therapy. When this defense fails, there are momentary painful symptoms. In the youngsters who have been treated, the symptoms commonly consist of suspiciousness, paranoidlike states, acute cognitive disorganization with confusion, mild disorientation, and even panic. It does not take many such experiences in the early weeks or months of treatment to lose a patient.

In this stage of treatment, the explorations of situations, of interpersonal conflicts, and so on are greatly weighed in the direction of building more appropriate defense mechanisms. Thus, while with the non-brain damaged adolescent, one clarifies the defense being used to make it more conscious, with the brain-damaged youngster one must do the opposite. For example, a situation the child is describing may be rephrased so it includes a defense. Rather than exploring the adolescent's participation in an episode, defenses may be built such as displacement: "Everyone I know feels angry when blamed," "A couple of other guys I know felt angry just like you do"; rationalization: "Maybe your teacher blew up because she had a bad day—got up out of the wrong side of the bed," "When you didn't do your homework, you probably just forgot—you were too busy with other things"; or intellectualization: "Getting jumpy is called hyperactivity. The medicine you are taking is Ritalin; its purpose is to stop that jumpy feeling," "That shunt operation is scary. Let's figure out exactly what they did . . ." It is hard to overemphasize just how gradual the process is, how long the frequent repetition is needed before defenses gradually develop.

At this stage, little effort is made to bring out the adolescent's contribution to a situation, how and why he provokes it. Whatever the unconscious determinants, the central issue is that the therapist focuses on building defenses that are more negotiable than denial or projection, so that he can subsequently increase the range and depth of the child's exploration of psychological realities. So long as denial and projection remain the child's predominant defenses, attempts to explore psychodynamic problem areas will commonly be interpreted as blaming, as siding with the others, as being against the patient.

After weeks or months of defense building, the brain-damaged adolescent increasingly discusses his life situations more freely. His own participation in the difficulties can be introduced on a reality level. "Teachers seem to lose their cool more on days you forget to take your Ritalin. Do you think *your* being more jumpy (hyperactive) makes them mad?" Now, rather than feeling attacked by the introduction of such discussions, the adolescent is able to feel in control during the therapy situation because he can begin to rely on an automatic *control of his own reactions.* The emphasis of the therapy is still on ego building, now however, with more emphasis on assessing reality than on building defenses. This "psychologizing," this analytic understanding of people and situations, the discussions of "what makes people tick" and "how come the situation shaped up this particular way"—all these devices develop the observing ego, whose growth in turn gradually allows the youngster to look at his own participation in troublesome situations. Thus, the youngster is now ready for another therapeutic stage —the understanding of his own intrapsychic distortions and the clarification of his cognitive defects that are secondary to the brain damage.

Exploration and Clarification of Unalterable Cognitive Defects

Once negotiable defenses are available to the brain-damaged concrete or formal operational youngster, the distortions, misunderstandings, and other difficulties that disrupt his life can gradually be related to idiosyncratic earlier life experiences, transference reactions, and other phenomena. These youngsters have all the "normal" problems—castration anxiety, unresolved oedipal wishes and guilts, sibling rivalry, and so forth. Working through these psychological problems in this phase of treatment is not unlike a similar stage in the treatment of the non-brain-damaged psychiatric patient. What is different is that the brain-damaged youngsters must also cope with irremediable cognitive and physical defects and the related ubiquitous traumatic experiences that occurred during their earlier school years.

Gradual clarification of their "feared" impairments usually best starts with rather specific areas. These fears are often much worse than the actual impairment warrants. The impairments include not only such disabilities as letter reversals, memory defects, and the like, but also such behaviors as short attention span, distractibility, and emotional lability. "My problem is I am sadder than anyone else and I am happier than anyone else," said a 14 year old with multiple shunt operations, as he described his emotional lability. The exaggerated importance of these symptoms is only gradually worked through and the secondary gain given up. As this happens, the patient is finally ready for the next step: an examination of the manifestations of true brain damage and a clarification of the emotional importance of this.

The true irremediable damage, such as one-eyed blindness, nystagmus, ataxia, dyscalculia, memory defect, emotional lability, and discrepancy between specific intellectual abilities to the point of retardation in one area and normal or superior abilities in others, now begins to preoccupy more of the treatment hours. What makes this process particularly painful is that the basic identity as brain damaged is closely tied to the defects. The pervasive identity as brain damaged, as retarded, as a creep, as odd, begins to unfold. Shyness, fear of contacting other youngsters in school, and unwillingness to be assertive in social activities are gradually reexamined, *but now in the new light of their connection with the symptoms of brain damage.* The most traumatic years in this context are the kindergarten and first few grades. It is then that the secondary brain-damage symptoms of hyperactivity, distractibility, short attention span, labile affectivity, and explosiveness are usually much less controlled and hence produce much greater difficulties with the teacher as well as with peers. In the psychotherapy of most non-brain-damaged patients, the reactions of peers during their earlier latency years is rarely a major issue. This is in marked contrast to the brain-damaged patients, where the reaction of peers during latency takes on major importance—usually much more than parental or sibling interactions. The feelings about such specific learning problems as reversal of letters and numbers, dyslexia, and dyscalculia are enmeshed with feelings of being bad, of being a behavior problem, as being the reason for being rejected by most students and teachers. This self-perception, this self-image as defective and rejected-by-peers, usually lasts until partly alleviated by psychotherapy. For example, one youngster described being panicked when two boys came up to him to say hello in a junior high school to which he had recently transferred. He felt they would laugh at him because he was too tall and because his feet were too big. As this was explored, he recognized his fear they would think him too old for this new school and would surmise he was retarded and had been in a special school. He then remembered how in first grade he was laughed at and picked on by classmates for being dumb because he could not find his way to various rooms. His classroom even had a special corner, known by all as his corner, to which he was sent when he was bad. He had eventually been completely ostracized by his peers. He now realized he feared the same reaction from the two new boys who came up to him.

Many months are spent working through the misperceptions of current situations by finding the links to specific earlier experiences. Gradually, more and more of the pervasive distortions of current life experiences are linked to the self-perception as impaired, as different, as a creep, as odd. Even if the parental acceptance of the youngster had been unambivalent, this destructive self-perception is present. Indeed, it is in this stage that the pervasive feeling of self as impaired, as damaged, as peculiar becomes apparent.

Treatment of these children highlights the enormous importance of peer relations in kindergarten and the first few grades, as well as the importance of the reaction of the first parent-surrogate, the teacher. The brain-damaged adolescent misinterprets current peer reactions, projects, and unwittingly provokes the very reactions most feared by defensive, grandiose, sarcastic, or shy, inhibited, even withdrawn, behavior. It must be underscored that this emotional reaction, this self-perception as bad, as crazy, as retarded, along with the memory of having been perceived by teachers and peers as such, is the most painful, the most pervasively defended against constellation of memories.

Up to now, treatment concentrated on the patient's reactions and feelings about the real and not so real sequelae of brain damage. These sequelae emphasized the more concrete manifestations. It is the older adolescent or young adult patient who has been brain damaged from earliest life who must explore and question his basic judgment. With help from the therapist, he now examines many life experiences that force a recognition of this more subtle consequence of brain damage. For example, by now the patient has seen the effects of his previous impulsively made decisions or of his inability to get information because not knowing means being defective or bad or retarded, a "fact" he must hide at all costs even if the consequence is destructive to him. He has remembered the effects of his bad memory—his needing to be reminded by parents yet resenting it at the same time. He is also remembering the subtle and not so subtle ways his parents questioned his judgment—wishing yet fearing his independence.

This stage of treatment is not easy on patient or therapist. Most brain-damaged patients have some residual problems with judgment: either the patient makes decisions impulsively, cannot automatically keep a number of possibilities in mind at the same time and make comparisons across them in a stepwise fashion, tends to perseverate and not change his course when it may be to his best advantage, and so on. One must be uncompromising in clarifying the residual judgment problems with the patient. This is in no way license for sadistic acting out by the therapist. Yet, the end result of such a clarification allows the patient a chance to explore and find alternative solutions.

Interminable Termination

One of the alternative solutions available to the brain-damaged patient is not to terminate treatment but to use the therapist as someone whom he can see at varying intervals, for varying numbers of interviews, to discuss issues requiring judgment. With these bright, cognitively more advanced patients, rarely does one need to give advice. Rather, the process of exploration, asking about alternatives, and so on, sufficiently structures the alternatives so that the patient can follow through and arrive at a workable conclusion.

A second reason termination may be interminable is that as each new developmental task arises, a short period of treatment may be necessary to lend the patient the observing and integrating ego of the therapist in order to reclarify that the anxiety experienced is *not* due to a process like the resurgence of early ostracism but that, for example, all adolescent boys are anxious when they first experiment with dating, with petting, with sex, with intimacy.

The basic cognitive defects remain. The emotional lability remains. The fragility of defenses remains. When there is sufficient intelligence and concrete or formal operational cognitive organization has developed, intellectualization, thinking through, and other time-comsuming, often tortuous, efforts to understand and reunderstand may be repeatedly needed in place of the much more efficient "automatic" defense mechanisms and thinking abilities of the non-brain-damaged individual.

CONCLUSION

The definition of the population of patients "with brain damage" is unclear. Bender (1953), Birch (1964), Chess (1971), Eisenberg (1972), Goldfarb (1972), Laufer and Shetty (1975), Pasamanick and Knobloch (1960), and others persuasively speak of possible central nervous system dysmaturation or possible subtle damage in large numbers of the childhood schizophrenic population. Kawi and Pasamanick (1959) point to developmental casualities among reading impaired children. Children diagnosed as MBD or learning disabled (Christ, 1977c; Rappaport, 1975; Rutter & Yule, 1975) raise further questions about many more patients with varying degrees of possible unintactness of the central nervous system.

Are there differences in the psychotherapy of children and adolescents with true brain damage from psychotherapy of other disturbed patients, particularly those with minimal brain damage, with "organic" childhood schizophrenia, or with other syndromes where central nervous damage is only suspected? Around 1970, the author began treating with intensive psychotherapy a few patients with unquestionable central nervous system damage, as manifested by clear-cut hard neurological signs, to see whether there were any differences between these and the large number of other patients with "soft" neurological signs. On the basis of the small number of patients treated so far, and the large number assessed, a more definitive study to answer this question is definitely warranted. Among the patients with true central nervous system lesions treated, there are two groups that require quite different therapeutic approaches.

The first group consists of youngsters who are at the sensorimotor or preoperational stage of cognitive development. Even though their IQ may place these children in the normal range of intelligence, their cognitive level is sufficiently primitive that they cannot use insight-oriented psychotherapeutic techniques. Active crisis intervention to restore the child to his previous level of functioning is imperative to abort a deteriorating course that can even end in permanent hospitalization. In general, except for the added problems that result from physical manifestations of the brain damage, such as partial blindness, motor, and coordination problems, the treatment of these children is not significantly different from the treatment of the more typically mentally retarded child.

The "bright" brain-damaged youngster who has attained a level of cognitive organization at the concrete or formal operational level can engage in intensive psychoanalytically oriented insight-oriented psychotherapy. There are, however, important modifications, if not in type, certainly in emphasis of therapeutic techniques. These differences include the following. (1) A much longer period where the cognitive strengths of the child are explored and where he is given a great deal of opportunity to show these strengths in the therapeutic hours. Only in this way can a therapeutic alliance be developed. (2) The mechanisms of defense that these children have available are more primitive and much more fragile than the defenses of other patients. Under minimal cognitive stress, the defenses crumble and the catastrophic-like reactions can ensue. A long period of defense building is necessary, so that such defenses as rationalization and intellectualization are added to and in part replace the more primitive and difficult defenses, such as denial and projection. (3) Only after more adequate defense mechanisms are available is the child ready to explore intrapsychically determined distortions, a process that therapeutically is now identical to the treatment of other psychiatric patients. What is unique to this patient population, is the need to clarify those unalterable physical and cognitive defects that are the consequence of the brain damage. Unlike such physical defects as asthma, traumatic amputations, and severe burns, the physical defects of brain-damaged children imply such eponyms as retarded or spastic to these children and are hence sources of great shame. The clarification of unalterable cognitive defects is essential for any realistic planning for the future. In areas like very slow reading and horrendous handwriting and spelling, the obvious nature of the manifestation allows for easier recognition and clarification. Much more difficult but equally important is the recognition of such problems as impaired judgment. (4) Unlike other groups of patients, brain-damaged patients may be unable to achieve true termination from psychotherapy. Each patient seems to return either as the next developmental task adds new pressures with which the child or adolescent is not able to deal because of the unalterable cognitive defects such as the need for sameness and perseveration, or when particularly important decisions demand outside help because of the unalterable but now recognized problems with judgment.

REFERENCES

Bender, L., Childhood schizophrenia. *Psychiatry Quarterly,* 1953, *27,* 663.

Birch, H. The problem of brain damage in children. In H. Birch (Ed.), *Brain damage in children: The biological and social aspects.* Baltimore; Williams and Wilkins, 1964.

Chess, S. Autism in children with congenital rubella. *Journal of Autism and Childhood Schizophrenia,* 1971, *1,* 33–47.

Christ, A. Basic systems and cognition: The role of cognitive development in the total world of the child. In R. C. Simon, & H. Pardes (Eds.), *Understanding human behavior in health and illness.* Baltimore; Williams and Wilkins, 1977a.

Christ, A. Cognitive assessment of the psychotic child—A Piagetian framework. *Journal of the American Academy of Child Psychiatry,* 1977b, *16,* (2), 227–238.

Christ, A. "MBD" and the learning disabilities of childhood. In R. C. Simon & H. Pardes (Eds.), *Understanding human behavior in health and illness.* Baltimore: Williams and Wilkins, 1977c.

Eisenberg, L. Psychiatric implications of brain damage in children. In S. I. Harrison & J. F. McDermott (Eds.), *Childhood psychopathology.* New York: International Universities Press, 1972.

Flavell, J. H. *The developmental psychology of Jean Piaget.* Princeton: D. Van Nostrand, 1963.

Goldfarb, W. An investigation of childhood schizophrenia: A retrospective view. In S. I. Harrison & J. F. McDermott (Eds.), *Childhood psychopathology.* New York: International Universities Press, 1972.

Goldstein, K. *The organism.* New York: American Book Company, 1930.

Kawi, A. A., & Pasamanick, B. Prenatal and paranatal factors in the development of childhood reading disorders. *Monograph of Social Research and Child Development,* 1959, *24* (4).

Laufer, M. W., & Shetty, T. Organic brain syndromes (in children). In A. M. Freedman, H. T. Kaplan, & B. J. Sadock (Eds.), *Comprehensive textbook of psychiatry* (2nd ed. Vol. 12). Baltimore: Williams and Wilkins, 1975, p. 2200.

Pasamanick, B., & Knobloch, H. Brain injury and reproductive casualty. *American Journal of Orthopsychiatry,* 1960, *30,* 298.

Piaget, J. *Play, dreams and imitation in childhood.* New York: Norton, 1951.

Piaget, J. *The construction of reality in the child.* New York: Basic Books, 1954.

Piaget, J. *The origins of intelligence in children.* New York: Norton, 1952.

Piaget, J. The stages of the intellectual development of the child. *Bulletin of the Mennenger Clinic,* 1962, *26,* 120.

Piaget, J. & Inhelder, B. *The psychology of the child.* New York: Basic Books, 1969.

Rappaport, S. F. Ego development in learning disabled children. In W. M. Cruickshank & D. P. Hallahan (Eds.), *Perceptual and learning disabilities in children* (Vol. 1). Syracuse: Syracuse University Press, 1975.

Rutter, M. & Yule, W. The conception of specific reading retardation. *Journal of Child Psychology and Psychiatry,* 1975, *16,* 181.

Townes, B., Wagner, N., & Christ, A. Therapeutic use of psychological reports. *Journal of the American Academy of Child Psychiatry,* 1967, *6* (4), 691–699.

Chapter 18

GROUP TREATMENT OF HYPERACTIVE CHILDREN WITH MINIMAL BRAIN DYSFUNCTION

Beverly Zbuska

Hyperactive children feel terrible about themselves. Their egos are impaired, and their self-images are poor. They have virtually no observing ego or self-reflective process. They are, and have always been, alone children, and have alienated others all their lives. Each child has been a self-stimulating system, behaviorally and emotionally, in his or her fantasies and unconscious life. Others have not been experienced in a real, interactive way. Yet, these children desperately need the contact and affection of others as everyone does.

A group gives them the first chance they have had to intensely experience other children and to gain a deeper awareness and acceptance of themselves. Providing this experience is not always easy for the group therapist.

Where does one start? It depends on how severe the child's problem is. This determines the kind of group the child needs. It can be (1) an inpatient group in a hospital or residential treatment center; (2) a homogeneous group in a school or outpatient hospital clinic in which all the children have minimal brain dysfunction (MBD); or (3) a heterogeneous group in an outpatient hospital clinic or in private practice which ranges from supportive to analytic.

INPATIENT GROUPS

The most challenging group situation is one with children in hospitals or residential treatment centers. These children are usually so impulse ridden that they cannot sit for more than a few minutes. The first goal then is just to engage their attention and to provide the structure to contain them. This is done by:

1. Providing at least three adults in a group of six to eight children. This may seem high, but it is essential in providing the control and relative calm that is needed. Only one of these adults need be the active group leader. The other two are necessary to act as resources to provide alternatives to the hyperactive behavior of the children. These adults may be social workers, teachers, art therapists, nurses, child care workers, or other people involved in working with children. Children often need these adults to control aggressive behavior. If the adults are interspersed between the children, they can physically interrupt impulsive behavior before it spreads. The children can also whisper to or touch the therapist, thus gaining the attention they previously sought by being disruptive.

2. Shortening sessions to 30 or 45 minutes, two or three times a week, rather than using longer, less frequent sessions. These children cannot sit still for longer than this. When a topic comes up that they get involved in and which is not resolved by the end of the session, the children themselves will ask for the session to be extended.

3. Providing a few basic ground rules, no matter what age children.

a. "You have to stay in your chair or *ask* to leave." Hyperactive children need to get up every so often during a session. Going to the bathroom, getting a drink of water or just changing seats can provide the necessary outlet. Having them ask for the change helps them to begin to consciously recognize their need.

b. "You cannot hit other children or therapists"; each person's physical space must be respected.

c. "One person speaks at a time." This is often difficult when the group grows larger than five members, particularly when everyone is caught up in the same topic.

The content of the sessions initially needs to be structured by the therapist. This depends on the age of the group members. Younger groups, with children from five through seven or eight, can be paired off for short games and activities. These include games like: Chutes 'n' Ladders, Headache, Trouble; coloring books and playing "radio announcer-interviewer" with a tape recorder. The purpose of this is to have the children begin to share and interact with one other person at a time and to gradually accustom them to being with others in a calmer, less hyperactive way. During these sessions, the therapist can comment on what the children seem to be experiencing. For example, "Ralph, it's hard for you to sit and wait your turn while Joseph is jumping your man. Your turn will come right away." It is far better to comment on the positive. Oftentimes a negative comment like "I know you want to knock his men off the table," will precipitate exactly that!

After eight months of the above structure, one group of seven to eight year olds told their therapist that they did not want games any more, just talk. The physically active stimulation, provided by the therapist, was slowly broadened to include verbal stimulation in which the children then found pleasure.

As the groups advance in age and verbal skills, the following questions arise: "How much content should the therapist provide by raising specific issues for discussion, or does the therapist let members do this?" Usually, in the beginning phase of a group, the therapist provides the input via questions: "Why do you think it would be good to have a group?" and "What are some important things to talk about?" Themes that emerge are: "Why are we in a hospital?" "Do our families love us?" "Nobody here really cares about us." "What is 'hyperactive'?" "Drugs are to punish us for bad behavior?" "Why did X and Y have that fight?" Arrivals and departures of staff and other children in the hospital often trigger the above themes, and even though groups want to ignore the topic, it is crucial that it be discussed.

In very new groups, where anxiety is high and cohesiveness low, specific topics in the beginning of each session can be used to help bring members together cooperatively, for example, "What does everyone want to eat at the Halloween party?" or "Where should we go on our outing this week?" Sometimes this very concrete format needs to be maintained from a few weeks to a few months, until the group feels ready to venture into new territory.

One question most frequently asked by the therapist is: "How do you control aggression?" Again, one of the most important things is to have a good ratio of adults and children. The adults should be interspersed among the members, and they can then act quickly to interrupt any aggressive behavior. Often this is done by moving in front of the child; sitting next to him; taking him to another part of the room, away from the group; or if the aggression is too overwhelming, by taking him out of the room altogether. This is not punishment but rather an aid in controlling the overwhelming impulse. The child himself will often tell the therapist sitting outside with him when he feels ready to go back in. Therapists should also agree beforehand who will take any disruptive child outside, so that the main focus of the group is not lost during the session.

The physical arrangement of the room is also important. A sturdy table in the middle of the circle provides a good obstacle, so that the added time it takes for a child to jump around or over it gives the adults a chance to reach him before he reaches another child. It is sometimes enough time, too, for the aggressive impulse to subside. Providing "cubbyhole corners," where a child can go for a few minutes is important. Posters, paintings, and windows in the room allow the child to wander off for a few moments to another "place" and can offer a substitute for the activity that often results in aggression.

There are two things that should *not* be changed in these groups unless absolutely necessary: the room and the therapists. The constancy of these provides the basic security that these children need to help them venture into the new world of group - and of others. If any changes do occur, they should be thoroughly discussed before and after. One new group of six year olds decided to keep meeting in a room that was too small rather than move to a new room. It was "their room."

OUTPATIENT HOMOGENEOUS GROUPS

The next type of group is an outpatient homogeneous group. All the members in this group will be MBD, with hyperactive behavior. The most usual setting is in schools or outpatient pediatric, neurology, or child psychology clinics in hospitals.

The advantages of this type of group are that it provides a safe, protected place where the members will not be made fun of or be scapegoated by other children for their particular problems. It helps circumvent attempts at denial, that is, they face that they are there *because* of their shared problems.

The format of these groups follows that of inpatient hospital groups. However, unlike inpatient groups, they often cannot meet more than once a week, so that longer sessions are necessary. They can also be run as crisis-intervention groups on a short-term basis, from eight weeks to eight months or a normal school year. These groups do not change basic character structure but provide for successful contact and interaction with other people, which in turn lays the groundwork for further ego development.

Outpatient Heterogeneous Groups

The third type of group is the outpatient heterogeneous group. The setting can be a hospital, school, or private practice. Hyperactive children or adolescents are mixed in with others having different presenting problems and diagnoses. No more than two to three hyperactive children should be placed in a group of six to eight members.

In this type of group, the advantages are that the child comes across a cross-section of the world in a different way, and he has to face how his problems are dissimilar from other children's as well as how some of the struggles are similar (such as relating to parents, siblings, and peers).

Before hyperactive children are placed in this group, they need to have some individual work with the therapist, to establish a relationship and to help them begin to verbalize their special difficulties. They have often never talked about this problem with peers or are defensive if they do. The first question that group members ask him is "Why are you here?" and they need to be able to answer this as best they can. What usually comes out is "I've always had trouble learning in school" or "I have trouble sitting still." The therapist then needs to add a concise explanation of "hyperactivity." This does not happen until the third or fourth session, when the child feels a little more relaxed and can even bring it up himself.

In this type of group, especially with adolescents, the therapist does not have to provide as much structure or content. Other members of the group provide it, by sharing and discussing their problems. It is as though the hyperactive child's favorite television program or comic book series has been translated to real life - and the child becomes involved and fascinated by it.

Gradually, they begin to participate by taking sides in another member's problem - the side of the parent or sibling or girlfriend, often as a superego figure ("How could you yell at your mother like that?") or as an impulsive id figure ("You could have bashed him one"). At times they borrow the therapist's ego and try being "cotherapist." When this happens, they are ready to begin to reflect on themselves via question like "What would you feel in that situation?" They begin to make statements about themselves. These comments are usually about concrete things, and for a long time their participation on this level can be expected because denial still operates to such a degree as to preclude real exploration and insight.

At times when a subject that is hard for any adolescent to express in words comes up, like self-image, the author will bring in clay and everyone sculpts. One hyperactive child, Jack, made an armored car and placed it on the table next to the therapist's piece. Another child, Don, made a flat pancake with a hole at one end and a penis like protrusion at the other. He placed it over another member's flower. The desperate need for contact and closeness, as well as the shaky and highly defended self-image, is evident in both of these examples.

THE THERAPIST

How does the therapist feel about working with hyperactive children? It is exhausting and challenging. Expectations for a neat verbal group have to be relinquished. The therapist has to be active, verbally as well as sometimes physically. He/she has to temporarily leave his own ego gestalt and enter into the child's and experience what the child feels.

In the training of therapists who work with hyperactive children, the author has used some specific exercises to help therapists with this experience. The therapists role play an adolescent group. People take turns as the hyperactive, aggressive members. Once the therapist gets into this, it is hard to leave it. The impulse-gratifying behavior is a high and it is difficult to return to the observing ego.

The therapist also needs to let him/herself be used as a substitute ego for identification by the child. This is a basic dynamic process that occurs once the hyperactive behavior is reduced. It is a step that was missed in the development of object relations when the child was three or four. In a group, this is when the child or adolescent goes through an advice-giving phase. As they do this, they really begin to form close attachments and affections for others. They begin to get positive feedback, which is an incentive to reach out even more.

Then finally, one day, the therapist may hear, as the author did recently from a patient, "Bev, I think I'll make it."

BIBLIOGRAPHY

Berkovitz, Irving H. (Ed.). *Adolescents grow in groups.* New York: Brunner/-Mazel, 1972.

Leventhal, Donald S. The significance of ego psychology for the concept of minimal brain dysfunction in children. *Journal of the American Academy of Child Psychiatry,* 1968, *7,* 242–251.

MacLennan, B. W., & Felsenfield, N. *Group psychotherapy and counselling with adolescents.* New York: Columbia University Press, 1968.

Rachman, Arnold W. Group psychotherapy in the treating of the adolescent identity crisis. *International Journal of Child Psychotherapy,* 1972, *1*, pp. 97–118.

Renshaw, D. C. *The hyperactive child.* Chicago: Nelson-Hall, 1974.

Slavson, S. R., & Schiffer, M. *Group psychotherapies for children.* New York: International University Press, 1975.

Strunk, C. S., & Witkin, L. J. The transformation of latency age girls groups from unstructured play to problem focused discussion. *International Journal of Group Psychotherapy,* 1974, *24,* 460–470.

Chapter 19

FAMILY INTERACTION AND TREATMENT OF THE HYPERACTIVE/MBD CHILD

Mollie S. Schildkrout

This chapter will focus on the interaction within the family of the hyperactive child: why, how, and when parent-child and sibling relationships become disturbed; how they evolve as the child grows older, and what may be done about these broader aspects of the problem. Issues will be viewed from a pediatric as well as a psychiatric point of view.

In the case of an organic diagnosis, there is a widespread cliche that the professional alleviates the pain and guilt of the parents by indicating that the cause of their children's difficulties is inborn and was never under their control. This has not been found to be true—it is too simplistic. Complex problems must be faced to be solved or just to be lived with. Questions of blame and guilt have more to do with fantasies of lost parental omnipotence than they have to do with reality. Parental responsibility for child care has to be aroused if absent and balanced when excessive. Parental grief and disappointment must be empathically understood and dealt with.

Evaluation of the Child and Family

It seems quite impossible that a child suffering from an organic brain syndrome could conceivably be free of emotional complications. True, there are questions of degree and disturbance as in any disorder or illness. To quote E. James Anthony (1973): "Experience has shown that organic patients, once so diagnosed, are frequently separated from the content and process of their minds; even sympathetic, dynamic observers are inclined to approach them from the outside as if the internal sphere was solidified into predictable and stereotyped, concrete slabs of expression." (p. 53)

Children with minimal brain dysfunction (MBD) are not just clusters of symptoms. They are developing organisms, living in time and space with others. They have their own construct of reality and have lived through multiple experiences to which they have reacted in their own idiosyncratic fashions. They feel, they suffer, they search for gratifications, and they gradually build mechanisms of defense, healthy and unhealthy, to protect themselves from the blows of anxiety and frustrations emanating from inner and outer sources. They are constantly burdened by feelings of shame, anger, and guilt when they feel different, deficient, unable to control impulses and movement, slow to learn, and so forth. How can they then *not* have emotional complications? They would have to be less than human?

However one conceptualizes the problems of these children, one is confronted at all times by the forceful impact and modifying influence of the environment on the inborn errors which cause their atypical development. Parental and societal responses to their inherent difficulties help to shape the complications and alter the course of the child's life. Longitudinal studies have demonstrated that hyperkinesis gradually diminishes in puberty and perhaps disappears in about 50 percent of cases by the age of 15 but that problems of learning and coping and social adjustment persist into adult life. Morrison and Stewart (1973) offer data supporting the hypothesis that the proband who has a similarly afflicted parent or sibling is more likely to have a cousin, aunt, or uncle also suffering from the syndrome. Significantly, more siblings than half-siblings show signs of the disorder. Natural parents have a higher incidence than foster parents. The further implication of these findings is that these children live in an environment where there are apt to be more impulse-ridden, restless, and awkward individuals with lower frustration tolerance, when in fact, they require the very opposite. The more stable persons in the environment may be taxed at times beyond their stress capacity in having to deal with more than one hyperactive relative.

There are difficulties that may be encountered by parents and infant from the moment of birth. The newborn with this syndrome may have a high-pitched cry, irritability, hyper-motility, or lethargy. The vegetative nervous system functions discordantly, causing disturbed feeding patterns, vomiting, colic, and jitteriness. Mothers respond to these manifestations with deep concern, anxiety, and inconsistency, even the most stable among them. Above all, they experience intense fatigue due to lack of sleep and the need for constant mothering. As a result, resentment, feelings of inadequacy, guilt, and ambivalence may grow to alarming proportions. Unconscious infanti-cidal wishes may have to be repressed at great cost to psychic energy.

Fathers and siblings share in this drama, leading to extended conflicts and superimposed tensions. Father's loss of sleep may interfere with his job efficiency, and often enough he scapegoats his wife, considering her an inept mother. The couple's sex life, about to be renewed, is instead victimized. To top it all off, the turmoil in the home tends to reinforce the baby's aberrant behavior.

As the child enters the toddler stage, the family is confronted with new problems. In addition to the child's flitting motor activity, his barging into objects, and lack of staying power, he is often late in developing speech. Not only is there a lag in this important area of development, but there may be a subtle deviance from the norm in his language. It is important to emphasize that the development of concepts and language go hand in hand.

More attention has been paid in educational research to the correction of perceptual-motor deficits than to language. Katrina de Hirsch (1973) makes the significant point that, as children progress in school, the demands for perceptual performance decrease while those for linguistic and conceptual abilities increase. Without the latter, the child experiences reading failure. Without them, there are serious breaks in family communication.

Anna Freud (1959) stressed the importance of verbalization in the development of the ego. Language is needed for impulse control and the understanding of the need to postpone gratifications in the process of socialization. If young children cannot express their fears, and those of hyperactive children are particularly acute, they become flooded with primitive anxiety which may remain as a lifetime neurosis. There are other neurotic manifestations commonly seen in hyperactive children. Living in a state of chronic anxiety, low self-esteem, and shame, aggravated daily by their inadequate coping skills and the criticism and sneers of adults and peers, they tend to become chronically depressed as well. Their depression is often masked by acting-out behavior. Paul Adams (1973) states that a higher percentage of brain-damaged children than of the general population become obsessional neurotics.

In the latency years, families and index children resort more and more to projective mechanisms, blaming the schools, doctors, playmates, neighbors, and so forth for their manifold difficulties. In adolescence and adult life, projection may evolve into paranoia of greater or lesser degree.

In narcissistic families, one or both parents are unable to accept the reality of their child's deviation from the norm. They experience the child as so much an extension of themselves that they are compelled to resort to defensive maneuvers which include unconscious denial, rationalization, and displacement. In such families, diagnostic consultation may not be sought until the child enters school, when teachers' observations and peer reactions force parental confrontation with the child's multiple disabilities. It is these parents who shop high and wide for a diagnosis compatible with their unrealistic wishes, who compound the child's confusion, and defer the professional help which works optimally when given early.

It is not a simple matter for the diagnostician to tease out and separate the purely emotional from the organic signs, and in any case, it is usually an exercise in futility, since treatment must be directed toward the *whole* child, his family, and the daily environment. Nor can one ignore the fact that these children will grow up to be parents and may transmit the disorder genetically.

A study by Dennis P. Cantwell (1974) underscores another problem. He found that one-half of the parents of a group of 50 hyperactive boys, aged 6–11, suffered from alcoholism, sociopathy, and hysteria—a much higher incidence than among normal controls and nonbiologic parents of hyperactive children. Current data indicate that these children may indeed supply a large part of the pool of juvenile delinquency which plagues all of society.

In evaluating each child, one must ask what this child would be like if he did not have central nervous system dysfunction—that is, one must evaluate the child's strengths and assets. Intelligence, ego strengths, an attractive physical appearance, and large muscle aptitudes certainly help him to compensate. But perhaps most important of all is a supportive, warm, tolerant family. It is a fact that the children of higher socioeconomic groups fare better with this disorder, which may afflict anyone and exists in all countries from which there are reports.

THERAPY

Hyperkinetic children are brought for psychotherapy only when their parents are able to recognize that the child, as well as they, is suffering and that medication and special education are only partial responses to his problems. When they reach this stage, the family has perceived in some way that the time has come for their excessively dependent child to individuate and that, to achieve this, the family homeostasis must be altered to try to meet everyone's changing needs. The psychotherapist must consider a multiplicity of factors in deciding what form of therapy is best for any given patient, but the key to success remains a holistic approach within the framework of the family and the total environment.

The therapist must first overcome the not unusual resistance of the family to accepting the diagnosis and understanding its meaning. This is a difficult task because it is still not possible to give the family as clear and concrete a picture of the syndrome as they would like and because it takes a certain amount of sophistication to have even a vague concept of the complex workings of the nervous system. Any mention of deviation in the functioning of the brain deeply alarms people from all walks of life.

The doctor must help the family to accept the need for medication, when it is found to be helpful, over a relatively long period of time. Parents who obstruct the administration of medication by direct refusal or forgetting to give it, and this happens often enough, instill distrust and fear of outer controls in their children. These negative feelings extend to the physician, therapist, teachers, and eventually society, and sometimes result in a paranoid stance. The family may have irrational reasons for resistance, and these have to be ferreted out and understood.

Assuming that the medication does quiet the child, improve his concentration, and make life more tolerable for all concerned, the problem is still far from resolved. It has been the general experience that treatment which stops more or less at this point, except for the renewal and adjustment of medication, is not sustained. Visits are sporadic and with the first reversal of the child's behavior or disappointment in his grades, the parents may become discouraged and either abandon treatment or seek magical solutions from unreliable sources. Fras and Normile (1974) of the Broome County Mental Health Clinic of Binghampton, New York, report a drop in the attendance attrition rate from 30 percent to 10 percent over a two-year period when they combined parental counseling, behavioral techniques, and medication. If progress was not made or sustained, they then referred the children for more intensive psychiatric treatment.

In evaluating the family dynamics, the parents must be seen together, individually, and with the child and siblings in a series of diagnostic visits. These contacts provide the therapist with a history, an awareness of which parent is the dominant talker, if not figure, an introduction to their defense mechanisms, and an approximate appraisal of the prognosis. Failure to see the father is one of the most prevalent reasons for subsequent sabotage of treatment.

In the case of an adolescent, it is preferable to see the designated patient first, since the decision regarding family treatment is more delicate at this stage for such classical reasons as confidentiality, excessive hostility, and trust. In either case, the patient is seen alone at least once in the evaluative stage. In this visit, the primary goal is to make interpersonal contact in order to pave the way for an eventual therapeutic alliance.

All of this is not much different than the course of action one might take in a nonorganic case, which is the point, since the organic component of the problem is a single important facet which has overdetermined other aspects of the case. By the time the evaluation is completed, therapy is actually well under way—that is, a relationship has been established between family and therapist.

If the decision is for family therapy, the therapist should still retain the prerogative of seeing individual family members when it may help forward movement. One cannot promise them full confidentiality from one another, since such a promise is impossible to fulfill. Even if one does not opt for family treatment, close contact with the families of hyperactive children should be maintained. This is important because of the need to restructure the management of the child's daily life through behavioral techniques, to meet crises, to increase family tolerance toward the patient, and to buoy their flagging spirits at times. Nor should treatment be terminated in any definitive fashion—the door must always be left open for an ongoing relationship.

The situations for focusing primarily on the family, with the expectation that the child will benefit maximally at this particular time in his life are:

1. Families where there is a "conspiracy of silence" either because of unconscious denial and/or conscious shame. In these families, attitudes toward the hyperactive child tend to fluctuate wildly from overprotection to severe criticism. The child's ego development is constantly undermined, treatment is postponed, and everyone suffers. Such families are notoriously poor observers, follow instructions inconsistently, and project their troubles onto others. Although confrontation techniques are often required, these must be used cautiously, gradually, and only after the family's alliance has been won through support and empathy.
2. Families who unite in scapegoating the hyperactive child, blaming him for *all* their troubles.
3. Families who are so overwhelmed by the hyperactive child that they opt for neglect except under social pressure. This is more common among poor, large families.
4. Families where the hyperactive child tyrannizes parents and siblings and no one has the capacity to set limits or act as an accessory ego.
5. Families where there are multiple hyperactive members, adult or child.
6. Families who are in a crisis situation—either through

a behavioral catastrophe precipitated by the child or the impending breakdown of a parent, usually the mother, for whom the stress has been too great.

7. Families of some index children, usually of latency age, who cannot be reached through individual therapy, either because of difficulties in communication or in the child's capacity to relate to others. Such children are usually markedly ego restricted and/or depressed.

8. Families in whom the adolescent is in crisis, which most often takes the form of an acute depressive or paranoid psychosis, precipitated by work, study, social, and sexual frustrations.

SUMMARY

This chapter has attempted to demonstrate that the hyperactive child must be regarded holistically. The multiple problems within a family and life setting must be studied. Treatment by manipulations of drugs, vitamins, or diet alone is not likely to perform an adequate service. For centuries, it has been said, but perhaps not totally understood, that the concept of mind and body, or put in another way, functional and organic, must not be viewed dichotomously. Minuchin (1974) goes so far as to point out, quite aptly, that a family's irritability and anxiety in stress situations may indeed induce further biophysiological changes in a child and vice versa and that one cannot escape from our purely cellular origin.

This chapter has outlined the types of families where a flexible approach to both individual and family therapy is tried. In all cases, the goal is to change the system, to modify the present, to increase mutual tolerance, and to pave the way for future optimal performance, independence, and maturation on the part of the child.

REFERENCES

Adams, P. *Obsessive Children.* New York: Brunner/Mazel, 1973.

Anthony, E. J. A psychodynamic model of minimal brain damage. *Annals of the New York Academy of Sciences,* 28, February 1973. 205, 52–60.

Cantwell, D. P. A model for the investigation of psychiatric disorders of childhood: Its application in genetic studies in the hyperkinetic syndrome. Read before the annual meeting of the American Academy of Child Psychiatry, San Francisco, California, October 1974.

de Hirsch, K. Early language development and minimal brain dysfunction. *Annals of the New York Academy of Sciences,* 28 February 1973. 205, 158–163.

Denhoff, E. The natural life history of children with minimal brain dysfunction. *Annals of the New York Academy of Sciences,* 28 February, 1973. 205, 188–205.

Fras, I. & Normile, R. The treatment of the hyperactive child: an effective approach. *Sandoz Psychiatric Spectator* 1974. 9(7), 1–3.

Freud, A. *The psychoanalytical treatment of children.* New York: International University Press, 1959

Huessy, H. & Cohen, A. Hyperkinetic behaviors and learning disabilities followed over seven years. *Pediatrics,* 1976. 57(1) 4–9.

Minuchin, S. *Families and family therapy.* Cambridge, Mass.: Harvard University Press, 1974.

Morrison, J. R. & Stewart, M. A. Evidence for polygenetic inheritance in the hyperactive child syndrome. *American Journal of Psychiatry,* 1973. 130(7) 791–792.

Part V

EPILOGUE

Chapter 20

THE STATE OF THE ART
Iris Spano

We have come a long way in the past 10–12 years in recognizing
learning disabilities, but we still have a long way to go. We have
moved from a position of complete denial of the existence of
learning disabilities to the enactment of federal and state laws
which mandate that public education serve every child's unique
learning style. Our present status was summed up in 1977 by
William Cruikshank, who wrote:

> In my considered opinion, the status of learning disabilities in the
> public schools of this nation is one of educational catastrophe.
> We have too many instant specialists in positions of leadership,
> positions which, because of their lack of preparation or knowl-
> edge, they must defend with the pretense of expertise. This can
> be rectified if a hard line is assumed. There is sufficient knowl-
> edge available to put together overnight a splendid program of
> university professor preparation. Within two years, a corps of
> well-qualified professors could be ready which, with some na-
> tional support to universities, could result in the beginning of a
> steady stream of qualified teachers being released to function in
> the public schools (Cruikshank, 1977, p. 58).

It is sad that more than two years have passed and this quote is still apropos. Because of the failure of our higher education system to educate our teachers and specialists properly, we in the parent/professional organizations dealing with children with learning disabilities often find ourselves adversaries, when in reality we are all on the same side—that is, to help the child.

It is generally agreed that early diagnosis and proper intervention would reduce school failure and the resultant social problems. The diagnostician—whether a school psychologist, psychiatrist, nursery school team, learning disabilities specialist —should be able to pinpoint the child's specific areas of weakness and strength and then prescribe the proper remedial educational treatment. Unfortunately, many diagnosticians are not yet doing this because of inadequate university training and lack of in-service or continuing professional education to upgrade their skills. But I feel optimistic that increasing awareness and better training for diagnosticians are heading us toward better diagnosis.

In my opinion, the greatest tragedy that is occurring today is that too many teachers, when confronted with a proper diagnosis and the child, have absolutely no idea how to effectively follow the prescription. Instead, throughout our schools, remedial programs have been instituted that fragment services for the learning disabled child. In a given day this child may be seen by the learning disability teacher, remedial reading teacher, remedial math teacher, school psychologist, physical therapist for motor development and, of course, the classroom teacher. This fragmentation serves to feed the child's disorder rather than to remediate the child's problems.

Educational intervention should be done as a total program. The teacher should be trained to implement the diagnosis and evaluate progress. Ideally, the classroom teacher should be able to teach reading, writing, spelling, and math to every child placed in that classroom, no matter what that child's learning style. I realize we are far from this ideal. More realistically, then, I would like *one* skilled specialist to work with the child, in developing basic skills.

As a result of poor teacher training at the higher level, we do not have this single specialist who is skilled in the language, reading, writing, and arithmetic areas. Therefore, I believe that one of the most important steps to be taken is to mandate that elementary education teacher training include these skills and that the existing level of that training be sharply improved.

Most parents are shocked when they discover that their child has a learning disability. Much too often the problem is not detected until the child exhibits failure in school. At the early stage in the child's development, the pediatrician should be able to recognize the developmental problems and deficits and make the parent aware of the possible consequences. Too often, what happens is that the pediatrician, because of the lack of education, assures the parent by saying "Don't worry, your child will outgrow it."

Education for parents to be able to deal with their child's learning problems is sadly lacking. Parents must learn how to recognize very early on that the child has a problem, what should be done about it, and how to deal with their own feelings and expectations. This should be done by increased public education programs in the media, in nursery schools, by clinics, and in other such institutions.

Throughout the child's development, the parents should be able to count on such professionals as teachers, educational specialists, mental health hospital and clinic workers, psychologists, psychiatrists, neurologists, and pediatricians to help them and their child realize the child's potential. Education for all these professional services must also be upgraded.

It is essential that our children learn how to read, write, and spell in order that they be able to function successfully in our society. If we continue to fail them, the cost to them and to the rest of society will be enormous. Studies have shown that a large majority of nonreaders exhibit delinquent behavior, emotional disorders, and suicidal tendencies; are often drug abusers and are generally unable to cope with the pressures of day-to-day living. They become the submarginal members of the society, who have difficulty in earning a living, who strain our communities' resources, and who lead bitter, frustrated lives.

In summary, now that we have official recognition of learning disabilities and legislation to ensure that public education meets these children's needs, we still have a long way to go. One major problem is the lack of training and skill for early and appropriate diagnosis and for effective interventions on the part of the teachers and specialists in the public schools and on the outside. Also, parents need education to recognize possible difficulties in their child's development. The role of the elementary grades classroom teacher is especially crucial, and marked upgrading of teacher training should be required. We need to take the position that, no matter what their problems are, learning disabled children can all learn if properly diagnosed and if the education interventions are appropriate.

REFERENCE

Cruikshank, W. M. Myths and realities in learning disabilities. *Journal of Learning Disabilities,* January 1977, *10,* 51–58.

INDEX